ARABELLA

ARABELLA

THE DARK MONEY NETWORK OF LEFTIST BILLIONAIRES SECRETLY TRANSFORMING AMERICA

SCOTT WALTER

ENCOUNTER BOOKS   NEW YORK · LONDON

First American edition published in 2024 by Encounter Books,
an activity of Encounter for Culture and Education, Inc.,
a nonprofit, tax-exempt corporation.
Encounter Books website address: www.encounterbooks.com

Manufactured in the United States and printed on
acid-free paper. The paper used in this publication meets
the minimum requirements of ANSI/NISO Z39.48-1992
(R 1997) (*Permanence of Paper*).

FIRST AMERICAN EDITION

LIBRARY OF CONGRESS CATALOGING-IN-PUBLICATION DATA IS AVAILABLE

Information for this title can be found at the Library of Congress
website under the following ISBN 978-1-64177-381-2 and LCCN 2024002926.

CONTENTS

ACKNOWLEDGMENTS

T HIS IS NOT MY BOOK. It is much more a book by my colleagues, especially Kristen Eastlick and Hayden Ludwig, who have worked alongside me at the Capital Research Center, the institution that deserves the byline for this tome. But books must have a person for an author, so I enjoy here, as so often, the privilege of bragging about the work of the Capital Research Center, America's investigative think tank.

Kristen did more than anyone to assemble and improve the existing research that went into this book, as well as supplying new research that filled in gaps. Hayden was the original investigator who produced more of that research than anyone else, though many other colleagues also produced original investigations into and analysis of the Arabella empire, including Parker Thayer, Ken Braun, Robert Stilson, Michael Watson, Michael Hartmann, and Jonathan Harsh. Sarah Lee and Katie Cook are our excellent communications staffers who so effectively publicized this work, and CRC editor Jon Rodeback improved much of the original material as it was published. Indeed, all of my Capital Research Center colleagues have made important contributions without which the book could not appear, such as Dan Thompson, Beth Bottcher, and Madeline Matney, who raised money to fuel Capital Research Center; and Chris Krukewitt and Catherine Heravi, who watched over and channeled that fuel in the finance department; and especially our chief of staff, Laura Elliott, who holds us all together and keeps me out of many troubles. An old friend, outside editor

Ellen Wilson Fielding, once again helped me edit a book for publication.

A special word of thanks is due to the sharp local journalist who, first in the world, discovered Arabella's meddling in Americans' lives: Dave Skinner of Montana. He kindly contacted us when we began following in his footsteps, and we commissioned him to write the original version of chapter 1. Many of the other chapters also began life in somewhat different form, written by others. The most I can say for myself is that I often shaped these essays' commissioning and joined in their original editing before first Kristen and then I reworked them for this book.

I also owe major debts to Roger Kimball and all his colleagues at Encounter Books, including Sam Schneider, Julie Ponzi, and Elizabeth Bachmann. As someone who's been involved in the gestation of many books, I recognize how far above average they are in the midwifery required to put pages between covers. Roger's own intellectual jousting against the hydra-headed Left has been an inspiration for decades, and Julie's editorial judgment shaped what you're reading into something much stronger and sharper than would otherwise have appeared.

Older debts are owed to the men and women who strengthened and sharpened what passes for my thinking over the years: professors like Fr. James Schall, S.J.; Walter Berns; Hadley Arkes; Richard Stevens; Diane Yeager; and George Carey; and colleagues at AEI like Karl Zinsmeister, Karlyn Bowman, Chris DeMuth, Bill Schambra, Robert Bork, Leon Kass, Bill Kauffman, and Gayle Yiotis, as well as Adam Meyerson, late of the Philanthropy Roundtable.

I should perhaps thank Arabella and its founder, Eric Kessler, for providing such a target-rich environment for critique. But my deepest debts are owed to my wife, Erica—the true intellectual in the family—and our four children, though I must steal a line from Walter Berns and say I owe them "more than I am willing to express here." To steal a closing line from George Carey, let me add that everyone mentioned "must bear some part of the responsibility" for any errors and inadequacies in the book, but the lion's share of the responsibility lies with me.

How Demand Justice Revealed the Left's 'Dark Money' ATM

T HE ORIGINS of this Arabella exposé began with a simple question from an old friend on Capitol Hill who was already in the midst of another fierce fight over a Supreme Court nominee. It was the summer of 2018, and my friend worked on the Senate Judiciary Committee. Justice Anthony Kennedy had just announced his impending retirement.

"We don't even have a nominee yet," my distraught friend said over the phone, "and already Chairman Grassley, the committee, and the president are being trashed online and on TV and radio—by something called 'Demand Justice'? Nobody's ever heard of it, and we can't find anything out about it. What is Demand Justice, and what can we do?"

"Well," I replied, "I've never heard of it either, but Capital Research Center"—where I work—"*can* do something. I'll be back in touch soon." I clicked off the call and immediately rang one of our top investigators, Hayden Ludwig, and told him to start digging. Two hours later, he emailed me a dossier that explained a lot.

No one had ever heard of the group because it had only sprung into existence a few months before, after Brian Fallon, a Democratic operative, spoke to a left-wing donor cabal co-founded by George Soros (see chapter 9 for more on the Democracy Alliance). Fallon pitched the donors on helping him launch Demand Justice, which was to be a new group focused on attacking and blocking, if possible, every Trump judicial nominee, from the Supreme Court down to the humblest district court in the boondocks. Ludwig's dossier showed that Soros had written a seven-figure check to the cause, and it also showed the backgrounds of all the staff involved, where the headquarters was located, what strategies they'd announced, and more.

I forwarded this to my Capitol Hill friend, saying I hoped it was helpful and apologizing that I couldn't talk because I was sitting down with a donor. She wrote back one line: "Tell them you're invaluable."

But the story doesn't end there. By that afternoon, still before Brett Kavanaugh was nominated to fill Kennedy's seat on the high court, Ludwig had turned his dossier into an entry on our website InfluenceWatch.org. For the rest of that grim Kavanaugh summer, as the Left waged the ugliest Supreme Court brawl of all time, Ludwig's InfluenceWatch write-up on Demand Justice was the top entry for Google searches of the group, ahead of their own website. (These days we typically come in third or fourth.)

Yet that's not the end of the story either, as we'll see.

The Birth of Demand Justice

Born in early 2018, Demand Justice was originally nothing more than a website and a glowing *New York Times* article.[1] It was led, as noted, by Brian Fallon, former press secretary for Hillary Clinton's failed 2016 presidential campaign, former aide to Senator Chuck Schumer (D-NY), and a partisan to his marrow.

After Fallon launched the group with millions from the shadowy Democracy Alliance, Demand Justice led the Left's unsuccessful campaign to smear Brett Kavanaugh as a gang rapist during his Supreme Court confirmation. Demand Justice protested against the nominee's "extremism" outside the Supreme Court *before Kavanaugh's name was even announced*, wielding pre-printed signs opposing all possible picks from Trump's shortlist ("Stop Kethledge," "Stop Hardiman," "Stop Barrett," "Stop Kavanaugh").[2]

Signs prepared shortly before Brett Kavanaugh was nominated to fill the Supreme Court seat vacated by Justice Anthony Kennedy.
Credit: Hayden Ludwig. License: Capital Research Center.

Demand Justice even purchased the website StopBarrett.com in 2018 (two years before Amy Coney Barrett was nominated) and spent $317,000 in electioneering communications to block Kavanaugh's confirmation.

At a glance, Demand Justice appeared to be an activist group like any other. But closer inspection of its website by my Capital Research colleague Ludwig showed the group was really a front for the Sixteen Thirty Fund, a 501(c)(4) nonprofit, the kind that is typically referred to as "dark money." Only a few news outlets that summer began to realize that Demand Justice didn't exist as a normal nonprofit. It differed dramatically, for example, from the 501(c)(4) nonprofit that was the main group *supporting* Brett Kavanaugh's nomination, which had long been an independent nonprofit that publicly disclosed its expenditures, lobbying, vendors, and more. No news outlet reached all the way to the bottom of the Demand Justice story, as Ludwig and Capital Research Center would do, uncovering its life inside the Arabella empire.

One outlet that at least began to comprehend the story was the left-leaning OpenSecrets. It reported that the Sixteen Thirty Fund was Demand Justice's "fiscal sponsor." That is to say, Sixteen Thirty is a nonprofit that allows start-up groups like Demand Justice to come into existence and take advantage of their sponsor's nonprofit status and administrative expertise. (Lobbying filings posted by the Federal Election Commission later confirmed the relationship.) OpenSecrets went on to explain how this arrangement helps a group like Demand Justice remain much more hidden from public view than most Washington nonprofits.

I will quote OpenSecrets' report at length to assure readers on the left that I am truthfully describing exactly how this major left-wing effort operates.[3] No right-wing conspiracy theories here.

Following the practice of nearly all such nonprofits, neither Demand Justice nor its comparable group on the right, observed OpenSecrets, discloses its donors. But unlike its counterpart, which

> follows the well-established "dark money" model of incorporating as a tax-exempt nonprofit organized under section 501(c) of the Internal Revenue Code that is required to file annual 990 tax returns, Demand Justice is a non-tax-exempt entity organized by a fiscal sponsor—making their finances even more opaque.

OpenSecrets confirmed that the Sixteen Thirty Fund had recently added Demand Justice to its long list of trade names (also known as "doing business as" names) that it fiscally sponsored. As fiscal sponsor of Demand Justice, the Sixteen Thirty Fund was lending the group its legal status as a 501(c)(4) nonprofit, which in turn means that "Donors who steer money to Demand Justice would report donations to the fiscal sponsor rather than Demand Justice itself, adding an extra layer of secrecy that further obscures the source of funds." In other words, no donor need ever disclose donations to Demand Justice.

Under this secretive arrangement, "Demand Justice is not required to file annual 990 tax returns with the IRS," which gives Demand Justice advantages over its opponents: "Although tax-exempt nonprofits are required to disclose spending on lobbying and grassroots operations, Sixteen Thirty Fund merely discloses lobbying spending totals for all of the sponsored initiatives collectively," which number in the dozens, "without parsing out which portions of that money were directed through each initiative. This arrangement makes it virtually impossible to determine who funds the group and how that money is being spent."

Having explained how Demand Justice was much more "dark" than its "dark money" opponents, OpenSecrets went on to reveal more about its parent, the Sixteen Thirty Fund, which in 2018 was sending dozens of these super-dark groups into political battle on all sorts of controversial issues. "Sixteen Thirty Fund acts as a fiscal sponsor for over 45 initiatives that lack tax-exempt status or do not exist as separately incorporated entities," OpenSecrets explained, so Sixteen Thirty Fund "consolidates all of its fiscally sponsored projects into a single tax return." In this way, if the public seeks information about a particular project like Demand Justice, it will find "the project's activities, funding, and spending remain largely hidden among all of [Sixteen Thirty's] other projects."

This OpenSecrets report was the most informative of the non–Capital Research Center sources, although the Associated Press around the same time at least reported that Demand Justice was a fiscally sponsored project of the Sixteen Thirty Fund and that Sixteen Thirty had "nearly 40" other such projects.[4] *Politico*, a publication for the inside-the-Beltway crowd, was much less scrupulous. It mentioned Demand Justice's birth and its haste to buy ads that attacked various Trump judicial nominees, but it failed to mention the group's sponsorship by the Sixteen Thirty Fund. During the Kavanaugh controversy all of these outlets failed to recognize that just as Sixteen Thirty had dozens of secretive "projects" like Demand Justice, Sixteen Thirty itself was only one of (then) four umbrella nonprofits that were created by one "Beltway bandit" firm, Arabella Advisors LLC, a for-profit consulting firm.

Just as Sixteen Thirty spun into existence dozens of groups like Demand

Justice to wage political war, simultaneously lending its nonprofit status to those pop-up groups and cloaking their donors more darkly than any normal nonprofit group could hope to do, the three "sister" umbrella nonprofits to Sixteen Thirty—the New Venture Fund, Hopewell Fund, and Windward Fund—likewise launched dozens, nay *hundreds*, of not-quite-real groups into the fray.

In reality, each of these groups was little more than an accounting code at one of the sister nonprofits and (usually) a website on the same server. But in the unreality of our current politics, policed by media that are sympathetic to the goals pursued by the Arabella empire and ignorant of the means it employs, these groups could pretend to be grassroots Americans demanding "justice" on all kinds of issues, from climate change to abortion to Obamacare to the election process. Whatever the issue, Arabella Advisors used these in-house nonprofits to pop groups like Demand Justice into and out of existence as political situations—and fat-cat donors—demanded.

Unlike the mainstream media, Capital Research Center refused to stop digging into all this amazing political architecture.

Arabella Comes to Light

Founded in 1984, Capital Research Center originated as a "philanthropic watchdog," created to investigate and expose the activities and financing of public policy groups, foundations, and other special interests. Since then, we've investigated tens of thousands of think tanks, advocacy groups, unions, trade associations, political action committees, activists, and more to help the public understand which special interests are being protected by what means. That explains why we kept digging into the Demand Justice question, especially as the Kavanaugh hearings intensified.

Searches of the IRS nonprofit database showed Demand Justice wasn't listed. What *did* turn up in an online search was a downtown address on Connecticut Avenue shared by *dozens* of other groups, including Sixteen Thirty Fund. Other organizations based at that address included Arabella

Advisors, the New Venture Fund, Hopewell Fund, and Windward Fund. Since we made this discovery, we've continued researching the complexities of the Arabella network, a puppet-master-like group that likes to describe itself as providing "support services to changemakers who are dedicated to achieving social and environmental impact."

At its helm is Arabella Advisors, an influential philanthropic consulting firm in Washington, D.C., catering to donors like the Rockefeller Family Fund, the Ford Foundation, and George Soros's Open Society Foundations. The firm belongs to Eric Kessler—Arabella's founder and chief string-puller—a child of wealth turned environmental activist and Clinton administration staffer who now operates in the highest echelon of Democratic Party politics.

More Supreme Court Battles

The latest chapter in Arabella's battles to assist the Democratic Party in its Supreme Court fights is far less epic than the brutal Kavanaugh contest, but it offers more insights into how this nonprofit operates and how Capital Research Center helps to slow it down.

Obviously, Demand Justice failed in its efforts to stop the confirmation of Justice Kavanaugh, despite all the bitter controversy, and also failed to block Justice Amy Coney Barrett. But the Left never gives up, so now that the Court has a non-left majority, the aim is to weaken it in various ways, whether that be by adding justices to pack the court, or in forcing term limits on existing members, or harassing the Court with new "ethics" rules, or simply delegitimizing it in the eyes of citizens in hopes of weakening the wills of sitting justices to do their duty and strike down unconstitutional power grabs by the president and Congress.

Demand Justice continues to bray about such matters, but as often happens in the Arabella empire, this 501(c)(4) political nonprofit, fiscally sponsored by Arabella's Sixteen Thirty Fund, was joined at the barricades by a 501(c)(3) "charity," fiscally sponsored by Sixteen Thirty's "sister" the

New Venture Fund. This charitable front group is named Fix the Court, and while it can't legally take out multimillion-dollar ad buys explicitly attacking a judicial nominee, it comes in handy for the Left in the current battle to smear conservative justices for alleged ethics violations.

To appreciate Fix the Court, you must recall the scene at the end of *The Wizard of Oz*, when Dorothy and friends have returned to the grand hall in which the huge and terrifying wizard booms orders and threats at them, only to be exposed as a single unimpressive gent hiding behind a curtain and using illusions to project his spurious authority. This kind of fraud is rampant in so much of Arabella's work, but perhaps nowhere is it more apparent than in Fix the Court.

Fix the Court has long been lauded by the mainstream media and other enemies of the conservative court majority like Senators Dick Durbin (D-IL) and Sheldon Whitehouse (D-RI), who treat Fix the Court as a source of "nonpartisan" deep thoughts on court reforms. Sen. Whitehouse's official website, for instance, has cited Fix the Court half a dozen times in just the last couple of years, and the *New York Times* has repeatedly cited Fix the Court and invited its executive director, Gabe Roth, on to its exclusive editorial pages. In the first half of 2023, as Durbin, Whitehouse, and others furiously campaigned against the Court, the *Times* had Roth on speed-dial, citing his group eight times in six months.

And what did Fix the Court have to say to the *Times*? Well of course Roth accused the justices of "hypocrisy" and demanded much greater legal disclosure regarding anything justices receive of value.[5] But if you thought that means Roth and Fix the Court are keen to disclose what they receive of value, you'd be wrong.

Fix the Court, like Demand Justice, left its Arabella-managed fiscal sponsorship in 2021—perhaps because Capital Research's relentless exposure of the two groups' relationship with Arabella's "dark money" kingdom was becoming too harmful to their PR campaigns. But when Roth submitted the group's 2021 IRS filing, signed under penalty of perjury, he filed a postcard version of the standard 990 form, which is only permitted if a group receives no more than $50,000 in revenues. Parker Thayer, an intrepid colleague of mine at Capital Research Center, found that Arabella's New Venture Fund gave Fix the Court $111,677 that year.[6] (Notice how officially "leaving" Arabella's domain and becoming "independent" often means a group's money still comes mostly via Arabella's in-house nonprofits.)

Thayer passed this disturbing fact on to Gabe Kaminsky, a reporter for the *Washington Examiner*, who called Roth to ask for an explanation. The supposed ethics expert and champion of disclosure melted down. He scrambled to file a revised Form 990 with an honest accounting of his 2021 revenues, which consisted almost entirely of the New Venture grant of $112,000 and a grant from the Hewlett Foundation for $175,000, and then he sent the *Examiner* his schedule of contributors without redacting the donors' names (redacting donor names, but not amounts, is permitted by law). Then he really panicked about this inadvertent disclosure, telling the reporter, "S***, I'm not legally allowed to send you those. I really messed up."

Actually, there's nothing illegal about revealing donor names, yet Roth told the reporter he "wanted to fix the mistake as soon as possible" because his "donors don't want their names out there." Digging himself further into a hole, Roth raved,

> "I'm not a good CPA. I'm a klutz. Schedule B [i.e., the donor list] is not something that is sent out, right? It's not made public. Like, if you're donating to a 501(c)(3), the IRS gets to see who donates to you, but the general public doesn't."
>
> "I mean, basically, I've tried to donate money; I have failed," Roth added. "I tried to raise money; I have failed. I have only two foundations that give me money, and if their names become public, they're never going to talk to me again, and Fix the Court is over. My screwup this morning probably cost me my job."

Did I mention that the first thing Fix the Court ever did with its Arabella money was to launch a six-figure ad campaign that attacked Supreme

Court justices for their "disdain for openness and transparency," as *USA Today* quoted the ad's complaint?[7]

So Fix the Court, treated as a nonpartisan actor possessed of wide support and unimpeachable authority by prestigious newspapers and senators—the grand Oz who wows Dorothy—is in fact one rather unimpressive fellow sitting in his Brooklyn apartment who either can't keep the simplest books or doesn't want to risk disclosing his donors by filing honest tax returns. And who do those donors turn out to be? In 2021, they consisted of one Arabella nonprofit and one billionaire foundation; in 2022, the Rockefeller Brothers Fund and two other foundations (speaking of ethics, the Rockefeller Brothers Fund has received criticism for giving millions of dollars to Hamas-associated groups).[8] Yet despite receiving such few megadonors' support, Roth told a C-Span audience in April 2022 that Fix the Court is "funded by average Americans just giving us funds, who think that we're doing a good job."[9]

To be fair, Roth is clearly a man with the highest qualifications to judge hypocrisy. And thanks to Capital Research Center's removing the curtain Roth hid behind for years, Sen. Mike Lee (R-UT) was able to tweet, "The 'dark money' group unfairly attacking Justice Thomas just got caught with its pants down."[10] But as this book will show, there are many more such Arabella scams to be revealed.

Even Mainstream Media Have Begun Exposing the Arabella Network

While the powerful effects of left-wing political giving by billionaires like George Soros, Mark Zuckerberg, Bill Gates, and Warren Buffett are well known, few Americans know about the amazing "dark money" operation run by Arabella that receives much of this money and channels it into particular causes. Americans across the political spectrum will likely be shocked to learn how this empire secretly operates, using arrangements that produce the darkest of "dark money."

After Capital Research Center's intense coverage, even the mainstream press has begun to notice the scandalous story, which reveals Arabella as a major player in political battles like

- Supreme Court nominations,
- radical environmentalism,
- abortion,
- Medicare for All,
- fake "local news" websites,
- so-called "Zuck Bucks" used to manipulate of government election offices,
- lawsuits brought by Democratic superlawyer (and Steele dossier booster) Marc Elias,
- and much more.

The money involved is staggering: In the 2018 election cycle, Arabella-controlled nonprofits took in $1.2 billion, more than double the fundraising of the Democratic National Committee and the Republican National Committee combined. In the 2020 election cycle, Arabella's fundraising spiked 100 percent to $2.4 billion, outraising the national party committees by $1 billion. This mountain of money explains why even left-leaning major media, which normally would be sympathetic to Arabella, have begun to sound alarms. Arabella is:

…"the massive progressive dark-money group you've never heard of…the indisputable heavyweight of Democratic dark money."

—*Atlantic*[11]

…a "dark-money behemoth" —*Politico*

…"an opaque network managed by a Washington consulting firm, Arabella Advisors, that has funneled hundreds of millions of dollars through a daisy chain of groups supporting Democrats and progressive causes. The system of political financing, which often obscures the identities of donors, is known as dark money, and Arabella's network is a leading vehicle for it on the left." 　　　—*New York Times*

The *Atlantic* article just quoted is particularly revealing. The words come from an interview with Arabella's then-president in which the *Atlantic* repeated questions Capital Research Center raised in a *Wall Street Journal* op-ed criticizing Arabella.[12] The *Atlantic*'s liberal interviewer finally demanded, "Do you feel good that you're the left's equivalent of the Koch brothers?" Arabella's president could only croak out a hesitant, "Yeah." Similarly, the *New York Times* used Capital Research Center's research in its highly controversial news story, "Democrats Decried Dark Money. Then They Won With It in 2020."[13]

Actually, Arabella *isn't* equivalent to the Koch brothers for several reasons. True, those two libertarian billionaires—one of whom died in 2019—have been major donors and have organized other major donors to give to various causes, but their network of groups hasn't reached Arabella's nonprofit revenues of billions a year. Nor has the Koch network in recent years been as partisan and focused as Arabella. That is, Arabella is a powerful force-multiplier for the Democratic Party, while the Koch network famously pulled back from Republican Party politics during the Trump administration and now is overtly hostile to the leading GOP standard-bearer Donald Trump. As the *Washington Post* puts it, "The Koch network has stayed on the sidelines since 2015, when it identified five approved presidential candidates, all of whom fell to Trump," but in 2023 it is reentering presidential primaries to oppose Trump.[14] Whether one applauds or condemns the Koch position, it differs greatly from the relationship between Arabella and the Democratic standard-bearer Joe Biden, who has nothing to fear from Arabella.

In addition, the Koch network is not aligned with large swaths of the GOP on issues like trade and criminal justice policies. Agree or disagree with the network's position, no similar disparities can be found between Arabella and the Democratic Party faithful. And while Arabella's loyalty to the Democratic Party helps explains the empire's enormous growth in recent years, the Koch network's nonalignment with the Republican Party has weakened its strength. The *Post* story just quoted explains that, "In the years since the Koch network stepped back from presidential primaries, many of its top donors drifted away toward other outfits or their own causes, and many of its most prominent strategists and operatives…moved on to other jobs."

In another difference with Arabella, the Koch network includes a major project, the Quincy Institute for Responsible Statecraft, which it helped to launch with major funding from left-wing billionaire George Soros.[15] No equivalent across-the-aisle project exists in the Arabella world.

In short, while there are non-leftist billionaires in America, nothing they have created is nearly so well-aligned and coordinated with a political party, so strategic in its operations, such that it could equal, and counter, Arabella Advisors' network. The Koch brothers have never built anything as effective—and wealthy—for their causes as the empire Arabella has achieved. Instead, the Kochs have functioned as bogeymen, used to drive left-of-center voters to the polls and to scare left-wing donors into writing big checks.

What This Book Will Reveal

This book strives to illuminate the darkest reaches of America's political battles, where billionaires and their minions fight to achieve a fundamental transformation of the nation championed by some, vigorously resisted by others. It describes how one trust fund kid's dream of manipulating philanthropy grew into a multibillion-dollar political empire that shapes political races and public policy on abortion, environmentalism, federal regulation, healthcare, election laws, and much more.

I hope to demystify the complex structure of Arabella Advisors and the hundreds of projects that operate under its umbrella. Chapter 1 lays out the obscure origins of the empire—an environmental campaign in Montana in the mid-2000s that annoyed local citizens, especially when they discovered that their backwoods recreations were being disrupted by rich folks who lived far away. The chapter shows how Arabella's founder product-tested his first pop-up groups and launched the New Venture Fund, cornerstone of today's "dark money" ATM that is Arabella Advisors.

Chapter 2 maps out the various entities in the Arabella constellation—the five different tax-exempt entities that sponsor its front groups. This chapter exposes the structure, finances, pop-up groups, and issue collaboration that happens between groups. It also reveals the billionaire megadonors who supply so much of the empire's cash, including Bill Gates, Warren Buffett, George Soros, Pierre Omidyar, Hansjörg Wyss, and more.

Chapters 3 through 10 provide case studies documenting the wide-ranging left-wing battles in which Arabella entities engage. Each case study exposes different components of how the "dark money" empire operates, highlighting the aggressive and deceptive tactics used as it serves Warren Buffett's abortion agenda, Mark Zuckerberg's election meddling, a foreign billionaire's political interventions, and the collaboration among billionaires and centimillionaires in George Soros's Democracy Alliance.

Shamefully, the mainstream media never exposed the Arabella empire even as its finances broke into the billion-dollar range. Yet starting in 2019, largely because of Capital Research Center's efforts, Arabella Advisors' ability to engage in anonymous issue advocacy has been compromised. Not only have various news outlets—including even the *New York Times*—begun to track their political activity and the involvement of foreign actors in their campaigns, but more watchdog organizations now zero in on suspicious activity and help expose who's behind the pop-up organizations. And so chapter 11 explores how the increased scrutiny has affected the leadership of Arabella, caused some groups in its empire to spin off into supposedly independent organizations, triggered embarrassing employee lawsuits, altered some financial disclosures, and leveled the issue advocacy playing field. As Arabella Advisors increasingly draws attention and criticism, its projects are no longer able to operate in the shadows and avoid charges of hypocrisy.

Even so, the Arabella empire remains the 800-pound gorilla of American politics. Nor is it easy to think of legal reforms that could defang the beast without harming nonprofits that don't deserve to be hobbled with false "fixes" like government-coerced disclosure of donors.

The book's concluding chapter tackles possible solutions to America's Arabella problem. But no one can figure out how to counter this beast without first understanding how its tentacles grew and now operate. No better ammunition for countering Arabella exists than a knowledge of what it has done to America as it serves, not the public, but a handful of billionaires, many of them with the same last name: Foundation.

I promise readers will be shocked to discover just how many different ways Arabella affects our country, and how powerfully and ingeniously it manipulates public policy on issue after issue at all levels. Arabella achieves all this while blissfully ignoring the Left's usual whining for campaign finance "reform" as it piles up a war chest that, in conservative hands, would be called "dark money." The beginning of any effective response to what Arabella has wrought is to expose it to the public, who will have reason to reject it once they understand how this stalking horse for billionaires tries to manipulate us.

Indeed, I'm often asked why left-wing donors and operatives relentlessly insert themselves into Americans' lives. While I can't read minds, I think the answer must lie in a lust to control others, especially to keep people from doing things their "betters" feel are wrong: to use an old vocabulary, these elites want to keep people from *sinning*. This longing to control others was summed up by the wit H. L. Mencken, who said that such puritanism is "the haunting fear that someone, somewhere may be happy." We discover a similar hankering for control when we investigate today's megadonors, like Bill Gates or the Hewlett Foundation, as they push "population control,"[16] or when we study their progenitors in the early 20th century—foundations like Carnegie and Rockefeller—who enthusiastically advocated eugenics in America and Germany to control the population. As one Rockefeller report put it in the 1920s, that foundation aimed to "increase the body of knowledge which in the hands of competent technicians may be expected in time to result in substantial social control."[17]

We'll begin by looking at Arabella's birth in just this controlling context. Innocent, ordinary people in Montana who loved to ride off-road on that beautiful state's trails had their happiness threatened by some group they'd never heard of. Who wanted to control them, to thwart their way of life? None other than Arabella, serving rich donors who'd never spoken a word to the Montanans and who were hiding behind a noble-sounding fake group that Arabella popped into existence to do their bidding.

1

Excavating Arabella's Origins

'WHO THE HELL is Responsible Trails America?" asked Idaho motorcycle-riding enthusiast Brian Hawthorne in 2008. Hawthorne had worked in the Western "multiple use" arena since the early 1990s. Raised in a resource town, he loved cross-country motorcycle trail riding and worked for BlueRibbon Coalition, an advocacy group for motorcycle trail riders. A grassroots organization funded by living, breathing members scattered across multiple states, the coalition found money tight to nonexistent. But members showed up in droves when they were asked.

Hawthorne was used to knowing all the players in the thinly populated world of motorcycle trail riders and the Western multiple use arena, but Responsible Trails America rang no bells. He turned to David Skinner, an investigative journalist and fellow Montanan, to dig into it, and a quick Google search came up with an even stranger name: Arabella Legacy Fund.

It appeared that Arabella was controlled by Eric Kessler, a left-wing campus radical and automotive-trust-fund millionaire baby, who happened to be a close relative of another trust-fund millionaire, Dan Weinberg, then a left-wing Montana state senator. Weinberg, a Democrat, had just withdrawn from his reelection campaign after a Whitefish, Montana, hometown hero, retired Navy SEAL Ryan Zinke, filed to run as a Republican against him. (Zinke later became first a U.S. congressman and then secretary of the interior in Trump's administration; he was hounded into resigning by environmental groups but won a bid for another House of Representatives seat in November 2022. For more on this story, see chapter 6.)

Skinner penned a report on Arabella's backing of Responsible Trails America for *BlueRibbon Magazine*, which still can be found (archived) on the Internet.[1] It included this prescient sentence: "as a 'strategic advisor' to some major foundations, [Eric] Kessler is in a position to 'advise' the plowing of major money into a major campaign of deception to close your roads and trails."

Arabella Trails

At this time point in our story—the first decade of the new millennium—Kessler was still just testing the waters. But today, Eric Kessler's Arabella Advisors controls a multifaceted and opaque empire generally regarded as the largest "dark money" network in America. In brief, here's how his present operation works.

At the top of the Arabella pyramid is Kessler's consulting firm, Arabella Advisors LLC, which provides boutique services to well-heeled donors and advice to left-leaning foundations about ways to give away their money—primarily to political causes. In the middle of the pyramid, Kessler & Co. have now built five in-house nonprofits, all with vague names and all but one (North Fund, the last to be created) listing the same address in Washington, D.C. Three are 501(c)(3) charities: New Venture Fund, Hopewell Fund, and Windward Fund. The fourth, Sixteen Thirty Fund, is a 501(c)(4) social welfare nonprofit, as is the most recent addition, North Fund.

These in-house nonprofits provide a powerful advantage to big-dollar donors: Those nonprofits can create "pop-up" groups designed to do the donors' bidding, but those groups can only be traced back to one of the in-house nonprofits Arabella runs. Because each of the in-house nonprofits runs *many* pop-up front groups, no one will ever know which big donor was paying for a particular group when he or she wrote a check to, say, New Venture Fund. These hundreds of front groups form the base of the Arabella pyramid, and the pyramid, as a whole, enables donors to fund the "progressive" political causes they want without being seen wading into grubby activism.

And fund them they do. Between Arabella's founding in 2005 and 2021, Kessler's nonprofit empire pulled in an amazing $6.5 billion, nearly all of it flowing to countless D.C. policy and litigation nonprofits, exclusively on the left. Much of that money also sponsored hundreds of pop-up groups, so called because they are little more than websites designed to look like standalone nonprofits, when in fact they are just fronts for a (usually unmentioned) Arabella nonprofit.

More than a decade and a half ago Arabella's clumsy, even inept initial efforts in Montana, enabled Kessler's company to cheaply prove its conceptual framework. With proof of concept and lessons learned, the Arabella network grew rather quickly into a nationwide political Godzilla, gobbling up $1.7 billion of often partisan, yet largely tax-sheltered "charity" in *a single year* (2020). (Revenues dropped by $148 million in 2021, the most recently available data.[2])

And it all began in the middle of nowhere, with Responsible Trails America.

So Who Is Eric J. Kessler?

Kessler comes from a wealthy Chicago family whose fortune originated with the 1998 sale of auto-parts manufacturer Fel-Pro, their "fifth-generation family-owned business," for a reported $750 million. He's a board member of the Family Alliance Foundation, his family's grant-making nonprofit, which largely funds medical causes. The foundation also funds the World Resources Institute. An environmentalist nonprofit created with start-up capital from the MacArthur Foundation, the World Resources Institute has hailed an extreme carbon-tax proposal as a "good starting point" for "cut[ting] emissions in line with the goals of the Paris agreement."[3]

Kessler co-owns three ritzy restaurants in the District of Columbia, one of which, Graffiato, closed in July 2018 following a sexual harassment settlement against co-owner and chef Mike Isabella. Kessler is also active on many boards, including the Chef Action Network, the Washington Regional Association of Grantmakers, and the James Beard Foundation, which promotes leftish education and healthcare policies under the guise of "good food for good."

An environmental conservation graduate of the University of Colorado (Boulder), Kessler connected with radical environmentalist David Brower while Brower was in Boulder for a guest lecture. (Brower's support for eugenics may be his most radical characteristic.[4]) Kessler then "hitchhiked" to California to "volunteer" with Brower's Earth Island Institute, according to an Earth Island website biography. Brower then sent Kessler to newly post-Soviet Russia to pioneer a Brower operation in the Baikal region.

Kessler returned to America as "national field director" in 1992 for the League of Conservation Voters, founded by Brower. Shortly after, he followed Bruce Babbitt—former Democratic governor of Arizona (1978–1987) and an aggressive environmentalist who then headed the League of Conservation Voters—into the Clinton administration as Babbitt became Interior secretary (1993–2001). At Interior, Kessler would encounter the future Wyss Foundation president Molly McUsic, who was also working for Babbitt in the Interior Department. (See chapter 7 for more information on the Wyss Foundation's Swiss billionaire founder and his nonprofit empire's activities.)

How closely McUsic and Kessler worked together is unclear, but both were political appointees from the broader activist world. Kessler came from the League of Conservation Voters, while McUsic, who served on Babbitt's legal counsel team, had clerked for the liberal U.S. Supreme Court justice Harry A. Blackmun (author of the Court's opinion in *Roe v. Wade*) and for U.S. Ninth Circuit Court of Appeals judge Dorothy W. Nelson, a Carter appointee.[5] McUsic now sits on the League of Conservation Voters' board.[6]

Although Kessler didn't start Arabella Advisors until 2005, it appears his ties to McUsic connected him to Swiss-born billionaire and funder of left-wing political causes Hansjörg Wyss, as the Wyss Foundation began making six-figure annual grants to the New Venture Fund (then the "Arabella Legacy Fund") in 2007, just one year after the fund's creation. In fact, Wyss could be described as the progenitor of the Arabella network. His foundation's 2007 grant accounted for 55 percent of New Venture Fund's revenues for that year.

At least one Wyss Foundation staffer, Kyle Herrig, jumped ship to Arabella.[7] Herrig has served on the advisory boards of at least five New Venture Fund projects and was a Wyss Foundation staffer from 2012 to 2013.[8] He now runs the left-of-center activist group Accountable.US, a former New Venture Fund project that controls a number of anti-Trump groups that also began life as New Venture Fund projects: Restore Public Trust, American Oversight, and Western Values Project, which ran an attack site on Trump's Interior secretaries, Ryan Zinke and David Bernhardt.[9] (Chapter 6 goes into greater detail on the Arabella network's more recent environmental activism.)

After the end of the Clinton administration's eight-year run, Kessler spent six years with the National Democratic Institute (NDI), co-founded by former secretary of state Madeleine Albright; then he created Arabella. Today, he sits on NDI's board of directors, itself a "Who's Who" of prominent Democrats.

Kessler's association with federal cabinet departments has apparently revived in the Biden years. As *Fox News* reported on May 16, 2023, communications obtained by Americans for Public Trust reveal that beginning in July 2021, and continuing through early 2022, top Department of Agriculture staff—including Agriculture secretary Tom Vilsack—were soliciting Kessler's input and welcoming his continued involvement in an internal initiative to force meat prices lower through a "transformed food system." Kessler appears on high-level group emails as the only non-administration member, proposing and commenting on the department's plans.

Starting Small

Politics often comes down to money—specifically diverting other people's money to your cause or your cronies. The money at issue for Responsible Trails America back in 2008 originally consisted of a tiny federal fund, the Recreational Trails Program (RTP). From federal fuel taxes of 50 cents per gallon, as the motorcyclist Brian Hawthorne described it, "Off-highway-vehicle and snowmobile enthusiasts 'taxed' themselves." Grassroots lobbying in Congress led to passage of RTP, earmarking the return of some gas taxes paid (to all 50 states) by recreationists who burnt their highway-taxed gas on dirt, not pavement.

Hawthorne explained:

> Most states leverage [RTP funds in combination with] OHV/snowmobile registration fees. In most states there exists a board that will review and recommend which grant gets funding [for] everything from trail maintenance to snowmobile trail equipment and even law enforcement.

> Keep in mind that RTP is a tiny federal program. In my huge home state of Montana, the state RTP program administered about $1.5 million for 2021. But that little money is critical for keeping primitive public trails safe and environmentally benign. Diversion of that funding would do great harm to the rider experience over time.

Enter Responsible Trails America. In early 2008, Hawthorne recalls, "I believe I saw a news story about this new OHV [Off-Highway Vehicle] trail group in New Mexico" that wanted to shift trails money from motorized to nonmotorized, divert construction and maintenance funds into closing trails, and massively increase off-highway law enforcement. "I was befuddled," Hawthorne continues, "having worked among that OHV community for about 5 years and never heard of [Responsible Trails America]. Almost immediately I received a call from supporters in New Mexico asking if I knew who they were."

He adds,

> That same week came another news story about a Montana-based hunting group [Backcountry Hunters and Anglers]. And it was the same crowd, saying the same things! After confirming from Russ Ehnes [a Montana rider and activist who today is chairman of the American Motorcyclist Association] and others that they'd never heard of them, I called [Dave Skinner, a freelance investigative reporter in Montana].

Following the Money

Because Responsible Trails America was so new, there was minimal search clutter to wade through. A brief computer search confirmed that at least two foundations among the usual suspects, both "environmental grant-makers" with billions in assets, had bankrolled RTA, at least in 2007.

Wilburforce Foundation gave $25,000 to support "Responsible Trails America" through the "Arabella Legacy Fund." Hewlett Foundation gave $500,000 for "General Support of the Responsible Trails America Program," again through Arabella. So that was $525,000 poured into an unproven, unknown "Arabella."

Why? Compartmentalization and deniability, of course. While Wilburforce and Hewlett are obligated under law to identify their grant recipients, Arabella (and later its first offshoot, New Venture) as well as other nonprofit recipients have no such duty, and they almost never voluntarily reveal their funders. If funders are named, the amounts given are never publicly disclosed.

In short, Arabella was a fiscal cutout because RTA's real funders realized exposure of a direct fiscal link would, if discovered, wreck RTA's narrative. RTA's "responsible riders" (none of whom actually seemed to own or ride any off-highway vehicles of any kind) would have about as much political credibility as equally Astroturf "responsible gun owner" groups have had. Standing up a new group via this kind of "fiscal sponsorship" would at least prevent the funding trail from being discovered, thanks to the lack of disclosure requirements.

This may be the place to explain briefly how fiscal sponsorship works, although we delve deeper into the topic in the next chapter, which sets out the relationships among Arabella, its nonprofits, and the huge number of pop-up groups they service.

When Arabella describes the connection between its (now) five umbrella nonprofits and their 500-plus pop-up groups as "fiscal sponsorship," what exactly does that mean? Sponsorship is not a concept Arabella invented, but a relationship between an established nonprofit and a fledgling project it incubates—tracking and accepting donations to the project, helping manage the project's activities and the like—during the time period (generally a year or longer) when a new nonprofit is awaiting approval from the IRS for its own independent nonprofit status.

Again, there is nothing nefarious about fiscal sponsorship in and of itself, and Arabella certainly did not invent the arrangement. As the National Network of Fiscal Sponsors puts it, the process "has evolved as an effective and efficient mode of starting new nonprofits, seeding social movements, and delivering public services." Conservative charities have made use of fiscal sponsorship to help launch some liberty-minded nonprofits. And other left-wing nonprofits like the Tides Foundation (founded in 1976) have used it extensively—Tides has incubated dozens of new activist groups, including Norman Lear's People for the American Way.

As we will see throughout the course of this book, however, Arabella has fully exploited the financial and political advantages of fiscal sponsorship to an astonishing extent, and in ways that seem less than transparent.

The Responsible Trails Campaign

In the short run, Brian Hawthorne and his BlueRibbon Coalition group for motorcycle trail riders alerted Western off-roaders to Responsible Trails America. In 2007 and 2008 successful funding diversions left RTA appearing especially "innovative and effective" in New Mexico. Brian Hawthorne pointed out:

> New Mexico has a unique OHV/Snowmobile registration program. If I remember correctly, at the time board members were chosen from recommendations made by state agencies with little, if any, input from active user groups. Kessler chose his first target well.

Arabella funders were clearly delighted. In 2008, funds funneled through Arabella Legacy Fund nearly quadrupled, to $6.1 million in gross receipts, $732,000 of which was for "responsible trails." Tellingly, the Arabella Legacy Fund's biggest line item was $1 million for "voter registration fund." Regrants and pass-throughs were also becoming significant: seventeen grants totaling $2.1 million went out, with $600,000 roughly split between the groups Progressive Futures and Project Vote.

Clearly, the last two ideas signaled Arabella's future focus.

Another signal came from Arabella Legacy Fund's biggest "non-program" 2008 expense: $555,931 to Arabella Philanthropic Investment Advisors (of which Kessler owns 35 percent) for management and operations services, a vigorish of about 9.1 percent.

But by 2009, RTA ran up against informed opposition. In Colorado, as OHV user Glenn Graham explained on a chat post, "normally, about 85 percent [of state gas tax funds] would go to maintenance and new trail construction." RTA's representative proposed to divert funds and split them one-third for law enforcement and one-third for trail closures (not maintenance), leaving the last third for education and trail maintenance. But as Graham later reported, RTA's "coalition" submitted only 77 letters to the trails committee in support, while off-road users submitted 1,572. The funds were not diverted.

RTA generally stalled afterward, fizzling out completely by 2014.

Following the People

The first person affiliated with Responsible Trails America was executive director Harrison Schmitt. Despite the identical name, RTA's Schmitt is emphatically not astronaut and conservative Republican U.S. senator Harrison Schmitt (R-NM). Instead, this Schmitt was a veteran of Ralph Nader's U.S. Public Interest Research Group, the Democratic Congressional Campaign Committee, and the League of Conservation Voters, just before he was hired to run RTA.

Also tellingly, Schmitt's RTA business address was a post office box in Arlington, Virginia, similar to current New Venture projects "domiciled" in UPS Store box "suites."

On the Ifish.net chat board was an email string in which Schmitt wrote on a Blackberry that "We [RTA] are funded directly by Arabella. We are not affiliated with industry or environmental organizations." Apparently a half million bestowed in a single check from the Hewlett Foundation, an environmentalist megadonor, doesn't count as "affiliation."

We, Myself, and I

As for the rest of RTA's "we," there were perhaps a total of eight people identified with it during its existence. One example illustrates: Carrie Sandstedt, who testified on behalf of "Nevada Responsible Trails Alliance" before a state legislative committee. Although her testimony is irrelevant, her résumé is revealing. Prior to her "responsible" gig, which lasted just eight months, she had been an organizer for the Sierra Club, worked with the Wilderness Society in Washington, D.C., and been the Northern Nevada director for the Service Employees International Union (SEIU).

Most recently, her LinkedIn page shows she's a senior manager with Pew Charitable Trusts, after managing Pew's subsidiary Campaign for America's Wilderness.

In Colorado, RTA was fronted by Politicalworks lobbyist Scott Chase. Next door in Arizona, Responsible Trails Arizona was fronted by lobbyist Genevra Richardson of Ziemba Waid Public Affairs. In fact, all confirmed RTA associates were either lobbyists, environmental staffers, or both.

The Parasite

Obviously, RTA was the parasite while Arabella was its host. Guidestar posted Arabella's 2006 and 2007 IRS Form 990s, which revealed $545,000 in "program service revenue" for 2006, with $499,402 in cash at year end. No rent, no fundraisers.

Arabella's mission? "To support innovative and effective public interest projects," with RTA as its very first.

Despite doing nothing but deposit cash its first year, Arabella revenue tripled to $1.66 million in 2007. Arabella did start spending, listing RTA as a $722,061 expense (including $114,623 paid to contractor Ziemba Waid, Genevra Richardson's firm), suggesting that Hewlett and Wilburforce were not RTA's sole funders.

Lessons Learned

Far from bicoastal, big-city spotlights, and operating on what would seem a laughably small scale compared to its future enterprises, Arabella could test-drive its obfuscatory pattern of multiplied, seemingly independent advocacy organizations legitimized by websites and press releases referring to unidentified and unnumbered supporters. The gas-tax stakes were small, so learning-curve mistakes would not be too costly. But looking back after some fifteen years of much higher stakes and bigger-bankrolled campaigns, the pattern becomes clear.

RTA's narrative shamelessly copycatted other progressive efforts. It existed as an "organization" or "coalition" mostly through numerous professionally written press releases. Those in turn directed journalist inquiries to an anonymously registered website and the cell phones of various expensive lobbyists contracted to Arabella, with RTA's only "asset" being a rented post office box in Virginia. Relative anonymity, limited traceability, turn-on-a-dime flexibility, website-cloning capability—all were already hallmarks of Arabella's pop-up group operations.

But as far as immediate success in attaining RTA's ends goes, the group wasn't "innovative and effective," it was laughably unsophisticated, even crude. What little news copy RTA gathered simply regurgitated RTA messaging, and there would be no "investigative journalism" into RTA (or, until recent years, dangerously little into Arabella, New Venture, and Eric Kessler's other "ventures"). Did Arabella eventually understand that RTA, perhaps even Arabella Legacy Fund, had been "found out" even if no credentialed journalists (other than Skinner) had written any news stories? Absolutely—and it reacted rather quickly. In the late fall of 2010, when Form 990 nonprofit returns for the year prior normally become publicly accessible, Skinner discovered that Guidestar had not posted Arabella Legacy Fund's return, nor were there any new Arabella Legacy Fund listings in Google. But he noted that Arabella Advisors still had a website, listing "high net worth" clients such as Bill and Melinda Gates.

Searching by its old EIN (the employer identification number businesses use with the IRS, similar to a Social Security number for individual taxpayers), Skinner located Arabella in action again, but this time under the name "New Venture Fund." This was a brilliant name for Arabella to use, because googling "New Venture Fund" unearths large numbers of extraneous items reporting on random "new venture funds," making it more difficult to dig down to the less sought after New Venture Fund.

Obviously, somebody had realized that Arabella Legacy Fund was too unusual a name.

Even though RTA eventually failed, it functioned as a relatively inexpensive real-world proof of concept for Arabella's core model, an experiment conducted in the lab-like political isolation of the inland American West. Thereafter, through its more nondescript name, New Venture Fund, Arabella Advisers could begin applying that model much more broadly on the national level.

Brian Hawthorne recalls:

> Public lands was a huge part of the radical Left's agenda, but then the focus shifted. I can't remember exactly when, or why, but it seemed to me that money and staff seemed to move from Public Lands to energy/climate. And then soon after went (as Arabella rose in prominence) overtly political, meaning direct efforts to influence elections, support candidates, wage war on Republicans, etc.

Over time, Arabella Advisors would eventually come to oversee multiple "charitable" groups with tax-sheltered revenues that approach $2 billion annually in recent years, dedicated to multiple major campaigns of major deception. Now you know how, and where, it all began.

Postscript

Recall that the Montana state senator representing Whitefish, Montana, from 2004 to 2008 was Daniel C. Weinberg. Weinberg had burst onto the local scene after using his Angora Ridge Foundation to make large contributions toward the construction of a swimming pool at the nonprofit Whitefish Wave fitness club. Soon after, he ran for state senate and beat the Republican incumbent.

But as we noted, Senator Weinberg's career as an extremely progressive Democrat ended when Whitefish hometown hero Ryan Zinke (a Republican) came back from the Navy SEALs. Weinberg chose not to run again in 2008.

Zinke was elected to the U.S. House in 2016 and then, after winning reelection in 2018, was nominated and confirmed as U.S. secretary of the interior in the Trump administration. In chapter 6 we'll hear more about his travails at the hands of the Left, and his eventual forcing out. But for now we'll note that throughout Zinke's federal service, he was plagued by negative ads and endless "scandal" allegations generated by entities like the "Western Values Project," headquartered in a Whitefish UPS Store mailbox. The project's very first press release (in 2013) declared it "receives financial support from New Venture Fund."

Clearly, we need to understand more thoroughly how these tentacles of Arabella operate across America, though they are tightly focused in a Washington, D.C., headquarters that caters to donors seeking to control Montanans and others in "flyover" states.

2

———

The $1.6-Billion-Pound Gorilla

Today's Arabella Advisors

Today the Arabella Advisors firm comprises five different tax-exempt entities—three charities and two "social welfare"
groups—operated by the for-profit Arabella Advisors consulting firm
through its Washington, D.C., headquarters. In 2021, the nonprofit side
of this empire pulled in $1.6 billion in funding across all five nonprofits—
most of which could be considered "marketing" dollars to change the way
people think about public policy issues. Some funding goes directly to support or oppose candidates for public office, and every year $100 million
or more is transferred between and among the five nonprofits and their
for-profit manager, Arabella Advisors.

Over the years since Capital Research Center's Hayden Ludwig first
uncovered the Arabella network, CRC staff have been tracking Arabella,
its money trails into and out of its nonprofits, its modus operandi, and its
work on behalf of hundreds of left-wing causes and campaigns. The process
of unearthing all this information was anything but straightforward, but
here, thanks to CRC research, we can present a straightforward account

of what Arabella and its enterprises are; how money passes in, out, and among these entities; and how temporary "pop-up" groups mimic grassroots organizations to funnel "dark money" into hundreds of issue-driven left-wing ad hoc campaigns.

Introducing Arabella

Operating under the aegis of "philanthropy," this network is housed in and staffed by a for-profit, privately held consultancy called Arabella Advisors, LLC. Arabella manages five nonprofit entities—the New Venture Fund (which began operations in 2006), Sixteen Thirty Fund (2009), Windward Fund (2015), Hopewell Fund (2015), and the North Fund (2019)—all of which share interlocking officers and almost all of which (except the North Fund) have shared an address.

As we saw in chapter 1, at the helm of the whole operation is Arabella Advisors, an influential philanthropy consulting firm in Washington, D.C., catering to groups like the Rockefeller Family Fund, the Ford Foundation, and George Soros's Open Society Foundations. The firm belongs to Eric Kessler, whom we met in chapter 1.[1] Kessler is Arabella's founder and string-puller-in-chief—a high-powered Democratic operative who served in the Clinton administration's Department of the Interior.

Kessler is a veteran not only of the Clinton administration, but also of the League of Conservation Voters (which received $19 million from Sixteen Thirty Fund in 2021—making it Sixteen Thirty's top grant recipient that year). And his connections with Biden administration officials in recent years run quite deep. As we saw in chapter 1, Kessler operates as almost an unofficial deputy secretary of Agriculture,[2] which is another indication of the extent of Kessler's reach throughout the Democratic Party. It also demonstrates a cavalier disregard—on both Kessler's part and the part of key Biden administration staff—for respecting institutional boundaries.

Uncovering More of Arabella's Layers

Documents uncovered by my Capital Research Center colleagues in early 2022 reveal additional peculiarities in Arabella's structure.[3] Arabella Advisors, LLC, which was founded in Virginia but headquartered in the District of Columbia, reports one beneficial owner: Jennifer Steans. She is president and CEO of Financial Investments Corporation and a partner at Concentric Equity Partners. Both entities are Chicago-based private asset management firms, and Concentric Equity Partners is owned by Steans's Financial Investments Corporation.

Steans herself has no apparent connection to Arabella Advisors or its founder, Eric Kessler, but she is a substantial Democratic donor, giving at least $226,000 to Democratic candidates since the mid-1990s.[4]

According to reports from the Illinois secretary of state, Arabella Advisors, LLC, is controlled by Arabella Acquisition, LLC, which is either a Virginia or Illinois corporation—online reports vary, and neither state lists it in their databases.[5] So who owns Arabella Acquisition, LLC?

Add another mysterious entity found in the District of Columbia's business records: Arabella Advisors Holdings, LLC, formed in June 2021. Unlike Arabella Advisors itself, this holding company (assuming that's what it is) lists a number of beneficial owners, including:

- Founder, senior managing director, and principal Eric Kessler;[6]
- Senior managing director and principal Bruce Boyd;[7]
- Former Arabella CEO Sampriti Ganguli;[8]
- Chief Operating Officer Chris Hobbs;[9]
- Senior Managing Director Gwen Walden;
- Chief Strategy and Impact Officer Hilary Cherner;
- Chief Financial Officer Wilbur Priester;
- Bruce W. Boyd 2017 Gift Trust; and
- Concentric Equity Partners II, LP – Arabella Series.

There's no publicly available information on the Boyd Trust, though it's named for longtime senior Arabella leader Bruce Boyd. Steans's Concentric Equity Partners is also a black hole, but likely a fund managed by the private investment firm for Kessler's benefit. (Where the "II" comes into play is still unclear.)

Arabella's Shell Game

So what's the true structure of Arabella Advisors—a set of nonprofits interlocked with a consulting firm that, to borrow a verb from the company, "manages" a fleet of politically active groups? Very little of this arrangement is clear, and we are not finished unveiling Arabella's secrets. But what's certain is that there's far more to Arabella Advisors than meets the eye.

Arabella Advisors—and Eric Kessler

At the heart of all this is Arabella Advisors, a for-profit consultancy whose nonprofit nexus raked in $1.6 billion in 2021 alone, and a stunning $6.5 billion from 2006 to 2021.

As we saw in chapter 1, Arabella rather quickly spawned the New Venture

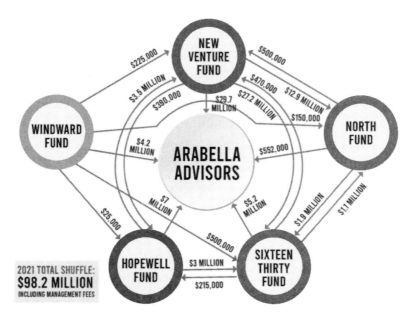

Fund and over the years has added four additional nonprofits, each of which plays a slightly different role in the network. But all share the same basic functions—sponsoring pop-up groups (also called "projects") and paying out grants to other left-wing nonprofits. Arabella's Sixteen Thirty Fund is the largest and oldest 501(c)(4) group in the network.[10] This kind of nonprofit is permitted by tax laws to engage in considerable politicking. Two famous 501(c)(4) groups are the Democratic Socialists of America on the left and the National Rifle Association on the right. In 2021, Sixteen Thirty reported $191 million in revenues and paid Arabella Advisors $5.2 million in consulting fees.

Like so many puppets dancing to the puppet master's tune, all five nonprofit entities feature management contracts with their "management" company (Arabella) and share overlapping boards of directors (including senior officers at Arabella itself). That includes Arabella founder Eric Kessler, who at one point or another sat on the board of each nonprofit save for the North Fund. He was the chairman for New Venture Fund's board of directors in 2017; in 2018, he was no longer on the board. Kessler also resigned from the Sixteen Thirty board in June 2021.

Kessler's primary job is as senior managing director of Arabella Advisors. Arabella's Andrew Schulz served as general counsel from 2014 through 2021 (according to his LinkedIn account) and Wilbur Priester served as Arabella's chief financial officer from August 2013 through May 2023.

New Venture Fund president Lee Bodner is a former managing director for Arabella Advisors. As of 2021, Bodner was also president of the Hopewell and Windward Funds.

Other board members are drawn from the ranks of the left-wing elite in Washington, D.C., and are either prominent activists, influential political consultants, or members of the boards of other major policy organizations and foundations.

THE NEW VENTURE FUND is the network's flagship and the largest and oldest of the "five sisters." It was founded as the Arabella Legacy Fund in 2006 by Eric Kessler, one year after he founded Arabella Advisors itself.

Interestingly, New Venture was originally conceived as hosting two niche projects: one aimed at "preserving the environment from the detrimental effects of off-road vehicle use" (as we saw in chapter 1), and the other directed toward seeding an "evangelical environmental message" in pastors' sermons. New Venture is a financial powerhouse. Since its birth, NVF has spent $3.1 billion on its activities. Starting in 2018, the organization has spent an average of roughly a half billion dollars each year (with a low of $373 million in 2018 to a high of nearly $659 million in 2020).

Among its notable board members as of 2021 is the treasurer, Katherine Miller, who is senior director of food policy for the James Beard Foundation, a restaurant and culinary arts group (Eric Kessler is a James Beard board member). Before that she was senior managing director for the high-profile consultancy Hattaway Communications, whose founder, Douglas Hattaway, is a Sixteen Thirty Fund board member. Adam Eichberg is on the boards of both the New Venture and Windward Funds. An environmental consultant, Eichberg runs the Denver-based firm Headwater Strategies, which advises on environmental policy.

THE SIXTEEN THIRTY FUND was the sole 501(c)(4) advocacy group amid its 501(c)(3) "charity" siblings until the latest of the siblings, North Fund, appeared in 2018. And as that tax status suggests, Sixteen Thirty has functioned as the lobbying shop for the Arabella network. It was created in 2009 and typically sponsors the "action" arm of another sibling's project. For example, Allied Progress Action (a Sixteen Thirty Fund project) is the action arm of Allied Progress (a New Venture Fund project).

Using these project pairs, Arabella maximizes the most useful characteristics of a 501(c)(3) nonprofit, whose donors may write off their donations as tax-deductible, and a 501(c)(4) group, which may spend significantly more on lobbying. (In addition, tax laws make the former type of nonprofit easier for private foundations to fund than the latter.)

For a few years, there was another benefit: The Sixteen Thirty Fund paid $4 million in salaries and employee benefits in 2018 but didn't originally disclose its highest-paid employees, since its payroll is paid by the New Venture Fund—effectively masking its staffers' identities and salaries. (The organization changed its practices when it filed its 2019 Form 990 in November 2020 and began disclosing the salaries of highly paid project directors and campaign directors. Perhaps coincidentally, CRC's first report on Arabella Advisors appeared in April 2019, and both *Politico* and the *Washington Post* editorial boards criticized the "dark money" practices of these groups in November 2019.)

Among Sixteen Thirty's board members have been Michael Madnick (who left Sixteen Thirty's board in mid-2018), a senior advisor to the Albright Stonebridge Group, the strategic diplomacy consultancy co-founded by former Clinton secretary of state Madeleine Albright. Another is Douglas Hattaway, founder of the high-profile firm Hattaway Communications, who in 2008 was an advisor and spokesman for Hillary Clinton's presidential campaign.

THE HOPEWELL FUND was launched in 2015 with $8.4 million in start-up capital from the left-leaning Susan Thompson Buffett Foundation, endowed by her husband, Warren Buffett of Berkshire Hathaway. It hosts groups like the pro-abortion Equity Forward, which attacked the Trump administration for revoking Obamacare rules that had compelled religious groups to pay for birth control.[11] Hopewell also sponsors projects related to income inequality. (We will see Hopewell in action in chapter 5.) Hopewell grew quickly, spending $50 million *more* in 2018 ($78 million) than in 2017 ($28 million). Starting in 2018, the organization has spent $120 million a year, on average. Michael Slaby, a Democratic Party operative and former chief technology officer for both of Barack Obama's presidential campaigns, is a board member.

THE WINDWARD FUND is the network's environmental and conservation wing, also formed in 2015, thanks in part to huge grants from the Rockefeller, Kellogg, and Walton (of Walmart fame) Foundations. Windward will play a prominent role in chapter 6, which recounts Arabella's

What's in a Name?

The names of Arabella founder Eric Kessler's nonprofits and company have a distinctly maritime theme. "Windward," for instance, is a reference to the side of a ship facing the wind (as opposed to the "leeward" side).

As strange as it sounds, the reason for this theme is perhaps hidden in the New Venture Fund's 2006 application to the IRS for tax-exempt status. At that time, the nonprofit was known as the Arabella Legacy Fund, a name almost certainly taken from Kessler's for-profit consultancy (Kessler himself served as founding president of the Fund). It adopted its current name in 2009. According to its organizational documents filed with the IRS, the New Venture Fund was created to turn evangelical Christians into environmentalist activists, going so far as to provide an "Environmental Toolkit . . . designed to enable Pastors to integrate creation care teaching into their ministry":

> The Pastor's toolkit will include materials . . . to educate Pastors regarding creation care's basis in Scripture, as well as fact sheets for Pastors and their congregations on various environmental topics and suggestions for how congregations can take action to care for God's creation.

While neither Arabella Advisors nor Eric Kessler have disclosed the origins of their groups' names, this early effort to embed environmentalism into evangelical Protestant churches may have informed the names Kessler gave to three of Arabella Advisors' original four in-house nonprofits (and the company itself): the Arabella Legacy Fund (now New Venture Fund), Hopewell Fund, and the Sixteen Thirty Fund.

The names appear to be linked to early American history and specifically to the Puritans of the seventeenth century. John Winthrop, founder of Boston and leader of the second wave of Reformed Protestant émigrés who fled Anglican England, is perhaps best-known for his celebrated sermon "A Model of Christian Charity," in which he exhorted his flock "that we shall be as a city upon a hill."

The sermon completed, Winthrop and his followers then set forth for the New World aboard 11 ships. Their flagship was named the *Arbella* or *Arabella* and was closely followed by the ship *Hopewell*. They departed in the year 1630.

long war against the Trump administration's environmental policies, particularly as championed by his Interior secretaries. Windward doesn't typically engage in full-throated climate change activism, but instead usually sponsors projects that advocate against genetically modified food (GMOs) or focus on ocean conservation and taxpayer funding of renewable energy.

Harry Drucker, a trustee for the massive conservationist group Nature Conservancy, is a board member for both the New Venture and Windward Funds. Another board member is Charles "Chuck" Savitt, founder of Island Press, a major publisher of environmental books. For example, Island Press has published books by population control advocate Paul Ehrlich, author of the alarmist tract, *The Population Bomb* and arguably the father of overpopulation extremism. Yet another board member is Kristen Grimm, political consultant and founder of Spitfire Strategies, a left-wing firm that has performed paid work for the New Venture Fund.

THE NORTH FUND, set up in 2018, is the newest member of Arabella Advisors' $1.6 billion "dark money" network to appear.[12] Like Sixteen Thirty, the North Fund is a 501(c)(4) group. Unlike the network's other nonprofits, however, North Fund doesn't share Arabella's L Street address in Washington, D.C., but lists the address of a virtual office space provider on Connecticut Avenue, Carr Workplaces.[13]

But North Fund's books and records are in the care of Arabella Advisors, with which the nonprofit "contracts" to provide "admin[istrative], operations, and management services," according to its annual tax forms. North Fund paid Arabella Advisors $551,809 for its services in 2021. This mirrors the close relationship between Arabella Advisors and the other members of its nonprofit network, which are legally distinct entities that contract with the company for compliance, grant-making guidance, and staffing support and use Arabella's office space. While this arrangement isn't uncommon, what *is* unusual is the role Arabella senior leadership played in founding each of these nonprofits—in effect creating the company's own "clients."

North Fund is no exception. Arabella general counsel Saurabh Gupta, whose background includes extensive work with teachers' unions and "state-wide ballot initiatives," is listed among North Fund's beneficial owners in its filings with the District of Columbia.

Gupta is not listed as a member of North Fund's board of directors, which is led by Jim Gerstein, founding partner of the Democratic polling firm GBAO Research and Strategy.[14] Gerstein is a former campaign advisor to multiple Democratic politicians and the 1996 Democratic National Convention, and he led James Carville's Democracy Corps, a nonprofit polling group that services the Left.[15]

Notably, GBAO's clients include eBay co-founder Pierre Omidyar's Omidyar Network, the Rockefeller Foundation, Center for American Progress, Sierra Club, Service Employees International Union (SEIU), Planned Parenthood, and Arabella's Hub Project—among dozens of other Democratic committees, politicians, ballot measures, and "progressive" advocacy groups.

Other North Fund board members include Christina Uribe, a union organizer with the National Education Association, and Melanie Beller, a Texas consultant who works on "voter enfranchisement" and "health care reform," among other issues.[16] Beller is a former vice president of government affairs for the environmentalist Wilderness Society.[17]

The Big Shuffle

Almost nothing is known about the purpose of the tens of millions of dollars in Arabella's inside-the-network grants, much less about the original donors of this money. The most likely explanation is that the grants between these funds both further obscure the Arabella network's donors and fuel its complex pop-up campaigns, using 501(c)(3) dollars to free up (c)(4) funds for advocacy purposes, since money is fungible.

Pop-Ups

Regardless, North Fund's involvement in this intricate money flow further highlights its place in the network. That includes funding *former* Arabella pop-up groups, such as States Newsroom, a national set of left-leaning online news outlets incubated as the Newsroom Network by Arabella's Hopewell Fund. In 2020, North Fund funneled $85,000 to States Newsroom for "capacity building."

Capital Research Center has also identified North Fund's involvement in at least one (c)(3)-(c)(4) pop-up pair: Voting Rights Lab Action, the (c)(4) advocacy arm of the New Venture Fund (c)(3) front group Voting Rights Lab, a self-described "campaign hub" designed to "supercharge the fight against voter suppression" and "transform our voting systems."[18] (Voting Rights Lab has since been spun out of Arabella and is now a doing-business-as name of the Secure Democracy Foundation. For more on the tangled web of Voting Rights Lab and Secure Democracy, see chapter 11.)

Arabella's Original Funders

One of our most important discoveries about the Arabella network is the identity of Sixteen Thirty's original funders, discovered in documents obtained via a public records request. In its incorporating documents filed with the IRS in February 2009, Sixteen Thirty was seeded with over

$350,000 from five major left-wing groups: Association of Community Organizations for Reform Now (ACORN), Americans United for Change, the Sierra Club, USAction, and Working America.

These founding groups have some unsavory history. The corrupt ACORN declared bankruptcy in 2010 after Congress ended federal funding to the group upon revelations that ACORN employees had offered advice on running a prostitution ring when prompted by undercover conservative activists. ACORN was infamous as a machine for churning out likely Democratic Party votes in large part by paying employees bonuses for every voter registration they made. In 2008, the group claimed to register 1.3 million new voters—of which some 900,000 were thrown out as invalid by election officials. As the *New York Times* put it, the tally was "vastly overstated."

The *Times*' understatement aside, by 2010 at least 18 ACORN employees were convicted or had confessed to voter registration fraud, and the group was under investigation in eleven states. Stripped of federal funding, ACORN declared bankruptcy in November 2010. (Sadly, numerous ACORN affiliates simply restarted themselves with identical boards and addresses, many of which live on today.)

Then there's Americans United For Change, a group so furtive even the left-leaning Sunlight Foundation has called it a "dark money group" for its quiet support of Democrats and left-wing causes. Americans United is as secretive as they come; the multimillion-dollar group doesn't even have a website. It was born in 2005 during the Left's fight against President George W. Bush's efforts to reform Social Security. It later expanded to broader efforts to aid Democrats on illegal immigration and minimum wage hikes, among other political fights.

Like ACORN, Americans United is wreathed in scandal. During the 2016 election, Project Veritas—then headed by the activists who exposed ACORN in 2009—covertly recorded Americans United field director Scott Foval revealing that the group had hired homeless people and the mentally ill to provoke violence at Trump rallies. Foval organized his anti-Trump deception with felon and veteran Democratic strategist Bob Creamer, who was indicted in 2005 on sixteen charges of tax violations and $2.3 million in bank fraud. Project Veritas claimed that Creamer's firm, Democracy Partners, may have helped Americans United to skirt laws against campaign collusion with the Clinton campaign.

Creamer and Foval's efforts coalesced into a nationwide campaign of fake anti-Trump protests designed to make the Republican nominee's supporters appear violent. For example, Shirley Teter, a sixty-nine-year-old lifelong protester, was hired by the group to infiltrate a Trump rally in North Carolina. When Teter was punched by a Trump supporter, the media relished the opportunity to expose Trump's backers as violent savages. "She was one of our activists," according to Foval. After the videos were posted online exposing the operation, Foval was immediately fired by AUFC, Creamer resigned from his contract with the Democratic National Committee, and Teter soon sued Project Veritas for defamation; that case was dismissed by the federal district court.

You may be familiar with Sixteen Thirty's other seed funders. Working America is the get-out-the-vote arm of the AFL-CIO and is heavily funded by that union federation. The Sierra Club, a Green New Deal supporter, is the oldest environmentalist group in America. And USAction (now People's Action) is a spin-off created by activist Ralph Nader that was a key founder of Health Care for America Now, the campaign formed to pass Obamacare (which has since been reinstated as an Arabella project; see chapter 3).

Who Are the Big Donors?

Arabella's top donors over the years run the gamut of major left-leaning foundations. They pour rivers of money into Arabella and its group of funds, and (except for those monies swallowed in management fees or mysteriously punted from one nonprofit to another) these rivers of liquidity are then used to irrigate a dizzying number of left-wing campaigns in areas like healthcare, abortion, voter registration, environmentalism, and opposition to conservative Supreme Court justices. Think of almost any left-wing position and Arabella money—usually a lot of it—can be found promoting it.

These were the top nonprofit donors to Arabella's empire in 2020 (the last year for which fairly complete data are available):

The Bill and Melinda Gates Foundation was the single largest donor to Arabella groups yet identified, weighing in at close to $456 million since 2008, including $127 million in 2020 alone.[19]

The Ford Foundation gave Arabella's nonprofits $25 million in 2020. Many of its grants specify public health and education as their targets, yet even these philanthropic-sounding purposes are focused on political advocacy, "social justice," and "narrative change."[20]

For instance, one Ford Foundation grant funds the "Ohio Transformation Fund to promote criminal justice reform and civic engagement." That last term is code for voter registration and turnout that helps the Left and the Democratic Party gain power. Another Ford grant funds "state policy advocacy, civic engagement, and strategic communications" for the All Above All Reproductive Justice Coalition, an Arabella front group that lobbies to overturn the Hyde Amendment, which bars the federal government from using tax dollars to pay for abortions in most circumstances.[21] The group also wants to legalize mail-order abortifacients for at-home abortions up to ten weeks, particularly among African Americans and minorities.[22]

Another $700,000 from Ford Foundation paid for "education and training for grassroots organizations to increase engagement . . . in state redistricting." The redistricting process is inherently political because it involves lawmakers vying for legislative maps that favor *their* political party. What business does the tax-exempt Ford Foundation—legally barred from intervening in elections—have meddling in 2022's biggest political fight? History supplies the answer: In 1967 Ford massively boosted a mayoral candidate's election by funding targeted voter registration. Though Ford's candidate was a Democrat, its meddling so outraged a Democratic-controlled Congress that they passed the Tax Reform Act of 1969, whose restrictions on electoral interference by the philanthropic sector remain law today.[23]

The Rockefeller Foundation, another pillar of the Left, gave Arabella's empire $15 million, though specifics are unclear because of very limited disclosure.[24]

The Susan Thompson Buffett Foundation gave roughly $28 million to Arabella's nonprofits in 2020.[25] Because that foundation is Warren Buffett's chosen vehicle for moving billions of dollars into the pro-abortion camp, this money likely supported pro-abortion groups.

Few have heard of the Gordon and Betty Moore Foundation, founded by a Big Tech pioneer, but it's one of the biggest funders of environmental activism in America.[26] It's also a top Arabella donor, giving $22 million to the network in 2021 alone. Most of this money funded climate- and conservation-related causes, including $12.8 million for the creation of a "finance hub" to push awareness of "natural resource risk among financial institutions." The goal is to push global warming as a key component of lenders' risk assessments, in order to forcibly move Western economies to a zero-carbon future—the eco-Left's plan for reshaping the world in its own misanthropic image.

The William and Flora Hewlett Foundation—created by the co-founder of Hewlett-Packard—moved $12 million to the Arabella empire in 2020.[27] A $1 million grant went to fund the Trusted Election Fund, which Capital Research Center has documented was created by Big Philanthropy to help Democrats oust President Donald Trump and silence criticism of the 2020 election's integrity issues.[28]

Similarly, we've traced $11.5 million in 2020 and 2021 combined from the David and Lucile Packard Foundation, the philanthropy of Hewlett-Packard's *other* co-founder.[29]

Staying with retail brands, the W. K. Kellogg Foundation (of breakfast cereal fame) gave roughly $9.5 million to Arabella's groups in 2020 and 2021 combined, while the Robert Wood Johnson Foundation—named for the son of a Johnson & Johnson co-founder—provided another $18.6 million in the same period.[30]

Then there is the Swiss-born Hansjörg Wyss, neither a citizen nor a permanent resident of the United States, who established the Hub Project at the Arabella-run New Venture Fund with funding from the Wyss Foundation.[31] Essentially, the Hub Project was created to allow the Wyss Foundation to bypass IRS election intervention laws and elect Democrats (see chapter 7). Although most donors to Arabella are not foreign nationals, Arabella exists in large part to help left-wing donors like Wyss funnel huge sums into political groups or even establish Arabella-run front groups like the Hub Project that don't file IRS disclosures. From 2010 through 2020, the Wyss Foundation gave nearly $52 million to Arabella entities.

Relations between personnel at the Wyss Foundation and Arabella Advisors long predated the existence of Arabella, as we noted in chapter 1. Wyss Foundation president Molly McUsic and Arabella Advisors founder Eric Kessler both worked for Clinton administration interior secretary Bruce Babbitt, and Kessler's ties to McUsic may explain the Wyss Foundation's large annual grants to Kessler's network, which began soon after the network's birth and makes Wyss appear as the godfather of Arabella.[32] And as noted, at least one Wyss Foundation staffer, Kyle Herrig, left the foundation to work at Arabella.[33]

Finally, we've uncovered $119 million flowing to the Arabella network from the Silicon Valley Community Foundation in 2021 alone, and almost $106 million from the Fidelity Charitable Gift Fund that same year.[34] Both of these nonprofits are donor-advised fund providers, which means their grant dollars originally came from unnamed donors who use these providers as pass-throughs.[35] New Venture Fund, Arabella's flagship 501(c)(3) charity, received each of these donor-advised fund providers' third largest grant in 2021.

Omidyar Shares His Wealth with Arabella

The co-founder of eBay, Pierre Omidyar, maintains an extremely low profile, despite the large amount of his politically flavored giving. He has a set of his own funds, which we call the Omidyar Nexus, our name for the roughly half dozen or so groups Omidyar funds and leads in the San Francisco Bay Area.[36] We've traced over $32 million from the Omidyar Nexus to Arabella's nonprofits between 2015 and 2021 (most of it since 2018): $12.8 million from Omidyar's Democracy Fund, $7.6 million from the Omidyar Network Fund, and $14.6 million from his (c)(4) Democracy Fund Voice. Many of these grants were tagged for specific Arabella projects—all of them political.

For instance, in 2017 the Democracy Fund granted $280,000 to the Arabella-run Hopewell Fund as "program support" for the Center for Election Innovation and Research (CEIR), which was one of two "charities" that distributed hundreds of millions of "Zuck Bucks" from Mark Zuckerberg and his wife in 2020.[37] In its own disclosure for 2017, Hopewell shuffled $281,952 to CEIR—almost certainly a case of a foundation using a pass-through to fund 501(c)(4)-style political work its lawyers would likely insist it not fund directly. In addition, Democracy Fund Voice gave Sixteen Thirty Fund several grants in 2020:

- $500,000 for the Center for Secure and Modern Elections Action Fund, which works with the Zuckerberg-funded Center for Tech and Civic Life (CTCL), the other "charity" that distributed the partisan "Zuck Bucks" grants in the 2020 election;[38]
- $1,680,000 for the Trusted Elections Action Fund, set up to stop "viral misinformation" and "post–Election Day violence" by angry Trump supporters (a Democracy Fund representative also sits on the group's steering committee);[39] and
- $132,000 for Co-Equal, an Arabella-run campaign to privately fund lawyers to help House Democratic climate campaigns, an arrangement that breaks congressional ethics rules.[40]

It's the same story with grants from the Omidyar Network Fund and Democracy Fund to Arabella-run nonprofits in recent years:

- $3,000,000 to the Tipping Point Fund, which repackages grants and funnels them to public policy advocacy groups focused on "social justice";[41]
- $1,500,000 for Democracy Docket Legal Fund, founded by partisan superlawyer Marc Elias to help Democrats by such efforts as challenging Republican-drawn redistricting maps and locking in Democrats' own favorable congressional maps;[42]

- $700,000 for the Trusted Elections Fund, the (c)(3) "charitable" arm of Trusted Elections Action Fund;[43] and
- $1,250,000 for the 2020 Census Project, a mysterious pooled fund to influence Census turnout in Democratic-controlled states, in hopes of boosting their electoral college votes and the federal spending sent there.[44]

Readers will learn more about Omidyar's collaboration with Arabella leading up to and including the 2020 election in chapters 4 and 7.

Arabella's Progeny: How Much Do They Spend?

Since they were launched, Arabella's nonprofits have paid out close to $5 billion in issue education and advocacy—the network is nothing if not a gigantic money-laundering machine for left-wing megadonors. Let's fill in some numbers for spending by Arabella's progeny over time.

THE NEW VENTURE FUND (the largest of the groups) has been the biggest spender, with a total of $3.1 billion since 2006. Growth was steady; it took just three years for the group to spend over $10 million in one year, then just another five years before it spent well over $100 million. Starting in 2018, New Venture has spent roughly $500 million per year in its education and issue advocacy efforts, reaching nearly $659 million in spending in 2020 before declining—for the first time in its history—to $552.5 million in 2021. Of course, this just shows how political the Arabella network actually is. Note that there was significantly more activity during the 2020 presidential and congressional election year than there was in 2021, when there were fewer big races. The odds are good that Arabella again spent more in 2022, but as usual the Arabella in-house nonprofits are waiting until the last legally possible minute to disclose their 2022 data.

THE SIXTEEN THIRTY FUND, which spends cash on a combination of education, lobbying, and campaign ads, has spent just under $1 billion since

Total Arabella Entity Revenues Over Time

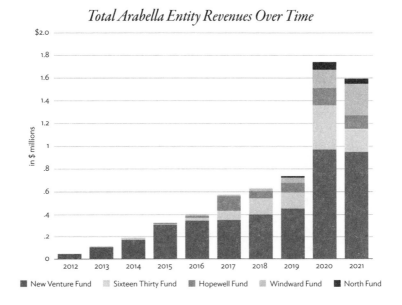

its 2009 inception. Spending fluctuates more dramatically for Sixteen Thirty than for New Venture, with higher spending levels coinciding with election years. For example, Sixteen Thirty spent nearly $47 million in 2017 and almost $99 million in 2019, compared to $141 million in 2018 and $410 million in 2020. In addition to unlimited lobbying, 501(c)(4) organizations may spend a limited amount on influencing the outcome of elections (usually by running ads supporting or opposing candidates for public office). While that type of election intervention was always allowed to some degree by IRS regulations, in the last few years the IRS clarified that at least 51 percent of a 501(c)(4) "social welfare" group's expenses should go toward lobbying and education, while no more than 49 percent should go toward campaign spending.

THE HOPEWELL FUND has spent just under $473 million since it launched in 2015. Starting in 2019, the organization has averaged expenses of around $120 million annually.

THE WINDWARD FUND, the smallest of the (c)(3) charity sisters, has logged just $231 million in expenses since its founding in 2015, although nearly half its spending (46 percent, or $107 million) occurred in 2021 alone, so more growth is likely.

THE NORTH FUND only came into existence in 2019 with all its funding coming from Arabella's other (c)(4) group, Sixteen Thirty Fund. But it maximized its donor engagement quickly: In just three years (2019–2021) North Fund spent over $84 million. It took the Sixteen Thirty Fund over eight years to hit that spending threshold. In 2020 alone, North Fund gave $500,000 to the network's biggest 501(c)(3), New Venture Fund, which gave $11 million back to North Fund. Similarly, in 2021, Sixteen Thirty Fund donated $1.9 million to North Fund; North Fund then gave $1.4 million back to Sixteen Thirty.

Indeed, the five funds regularly shuffle tens of millions of dollars around the network. For example, New Venture granted $2.3 million to Hopewell and almost $27 million to Sixteen Thirty in 2018. The reasons behind this funding merry-go-round are inscrutable, but the vague grant descriptions suggest political activism and issue advocacy. The 2018 New Venture grant to

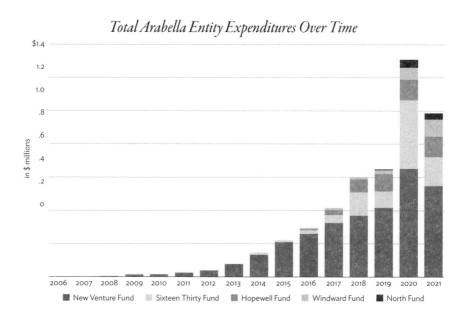

Total Arabella Entity Expenditures Over Time

Hopewell was for "civil rights, social action, advocacy," while New Venture's grant to Sixteen Thirty simply says it's for "capacity building." (Significantly, the latter grant made New Venture the second-largest donor to Sixteen Thirty in 2018. The fact that Sixteen Thirty didn't disclose the grant's source—New Venture—spurred the *Washington Post* editorial board to express angst over left-wing "dark money.")[45] Grants were made to the same organizations in 2021 ($390,000 to Hopewell; $27.3 million to Sixteen Thirty), both were for "civil rights, social action, advocacy."[46]

One likely explanation for some of the tens of millions of dollars flowing from New Venture to Sixteen Thirty: As a 501(c)(3), New Venture can provide individuals with a tax deduction that the same donors could not receive if they wrote checks directly to Sixteen Thirty, a 501(c)(4) nonprofit. Foundations also much prefer to give to a (c)(3) rather than a (c)(4), because giving to a (c)(3) is less likely to draw ire from both IRS auditors and nonprofit watchdogs. Too bad the mainstream media—usually keen to criticize 501(c)(4) "dark money groups"—have failed to ask Sixteen Thirty whether the massive "donations" it receives from New Venture are

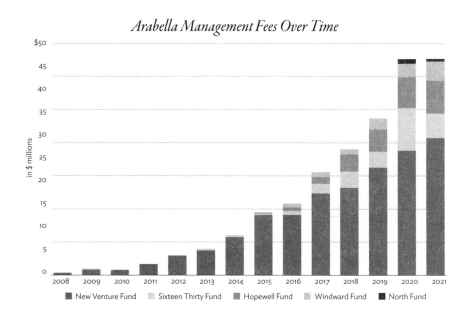

Arabella Management Fees Over Time

designed to grant donors both anonymity ("darkness") *and* tax advantages for their political giving.

Philanthropy or Politics?

To be fair, not all of the Arabella network's grants go to explicitly left-wing or even political organizations. And Arabella stresses its clients' "ideological diversity," to quote a recent glowing profile it received from the left-leaning *Inside Philanthropy*. "Because its work is so varied," the publication reports, "Arabella doesn't position itself in the ideologically pointed terms of some of its peers." Of course, Arabella's "positioning" may stem from a lack of harsh ideology, or it may just reflect the savvy of a Beltway bandit operation hiding its true colors.

The company itself has tried to deflect scrutiny by claiming the activism it sponsors is philanthropic, not political, yet its definition of "charity" nearly always involves changing public policy. In this way the Arabella empire provides a model of how to push every edge of the legal envelope in order to score political victories by blending nonprofits and for-profits. Arabella tweeted on January 7, 2020: "by establishing [for-profit] LLCs as their philanthropies' primary home and partnering with 501(c)(3) and (c)(4) intermediaries, philanthropists can support more political activities and better achieve meaningful policy change."

That tweet linked to an Arabella blog post entitled, "Four Promising Practices for Philanthropies to Advance Advocacy and Policy Change."[47] There Arabella reported on a phenomenon it no doubt hoped to encourage, both to enrich its own coffers and to advance its political ideology: "Philanthropists are increasingly willing to spend on lobbying and elections and are creating institutional structures that allow them to do so." This is politics by another name.

The politics-without-shame approach to "charity" was pushed even harder in Arabella CEO Sampriti Ganguli's March 2020 interview with the *Chronicle of Philanthropy*, the premier philanthropy news outlet. Ganguli gushed over her clients' political spending—and how her company helps them bypass those pesky IRS funding restrictions:

> people are thinking about social enterprises and nonprofits inter-changeably, and on the nonprofit side, nonprofits are thinking about earned revenue models. So those traditional silos between grantee and grantor are really blurring, and you're seeing an explosion, a blossoming of a lot of these platforms. Now, from my perspective, what I would say is: *these platforms are really solving for an end—I don't want to say an end run—but they're a work-around to the tax regime.* Structurally, it might be worthwhile to think differently about the tax regime, but nonetheless, these platforms are an evolution of some of the constraints that have been put on these respective platforms, if you will, or respective charitable vehicles [emphasis added].[48]

One wonders what liberal critics of money in politics would say if Arabella were offering *conservative* donors a "work-around to the tax regime."

Again, sometimes its clients use the company's nonprofits to support genuinely charitable causes. In 2018, for example, New Venture donated to Akeela, a substance-abuse and mental health nonprofit in Alaska. But only a few charitable grants are at the business end of Arabella's "dark money" pipeline.

And that's not surprising given the number of New Venture Fund board members tied to major left-wing funders, including the Annie E. Casey Foundation, NARAL Pro-Choice America, Environmental Law and Policy Center, Hattaway Communications (a for-profit firm whose clients include numerous Sixteen Thirty Fund projects), and the left-leaning think tank Center for Global Development, co-founded by ex-Obama administration official Brian Deese (creator of the infamous Cash for Clunkers car buyback program). The board members of the other groups have similar interests and pedigrees.

So aside from a relatively few grants that the outside observer would deem charitable, the rest fund the Left's bread-and-butter political groups. Just consider the organizations receiving more than $15 million in grants starting in 2019.

New Venture Fund's Top Grantees Since 2019

	2019	2020	2021	Total
Sixteen Thirty Fund	$33,013,025	$86,234,295	$27,270,554	$146,517,874
America Votes	$2,192,266	$44,261,222	$7,092,436	$53,545,924
Center for Technology and Civic Life	$166,400	$24,829,000		$24,995,400
North Fund		$11,171,248	$12,870,870	$24,042,118
Bill and Melinda Gates Foundation		$15,802,170		$15,802,170

Ignoring the $170 million given to other Arabella entities, over $75 million went to both America Votes and the Center for Technology and Civic Life. America Votes is a thinly veiled get-out-the-vote operation for Democrats, created in the wake of President Bush's reelection in 2004 by Clinton official Harold Ickes, SEIU president Andy Stern, Sierra Club executive director Carl Pope, EMILY's List founder Ellen Malcolm, and Partnership for America's Families president Steve Rosenthal.[49] The Center for Technology and Civic Life, led by Democratic voter organizing expert and Obama Foundation Fellow Tiana Epps-Johnson, was the major group behind "Zuck Bucks."[50]

Sixteen Thirty Fund's Top Grantees Since 2019

	2019	2020	2021	Total
America Votes	$7,060,000	$128,976,147	$1,525,000	$137,561,147
North Fund	$9,300,500	$19,390,584	$1,136,250	$29,827,334
League of Conservation Voters	$166,400	$24,829,000		$24,995,400
Future Forward USA Action*		$15,232,000		$15,232,000
Advancing AZ	$3,950,000	$2,477,000	$8,750,000	$15,177,000
Defending Democracy Together		$10,050,000	$500,000	$10,550,000

* Sixteen Thirty Fund also provided $8.9 million to the Future Forward USA PAC (in a 2019 grant of $1.4 million and a 2020 grant of $7.5 million), so the total given to the Future Forward USA entities was $24,147,274.

America Votes, as noted when it was discussed under New Venture Fund grantees, works to turn out Democratic voters in elections. Its $129 million grant from Sixteen Thirty in 2020 more than doubled the group's entire 2019 budget, and its harsh tactics aimed at forcing Democrats to vote have drawn criticism from some allies on the Left.[51] Future Forward USA Action is the 501(c)(4) "dark money" group that funnels cash to the Joe Biden–supporting Future Forward PAC; this camouflaging of PAC money has been criticized by the left-leaning Center for Responsive Politics.[52] Advancing Arizona is, *Politico* reports, a "Democratic dark money organization."[53] Defending Democracy Together is a never-Trump political effort headed by former conservative activist Bill Kristol.[54]

Hopewell Fund's Top Grantees

	2019	2020	2021	Total
California Commission on the Status of Women and Girls	$10,290,000			$10,290,000
Sixteen Thirty Fund	$3,060,248	$3,827,001	$3,087,645	$9,974,894
Acronym		$8,078,980	$615,260	$8,694,240
Salk Institute for Biological Studies	$8,359,623			$8,359,623
The Nature Conservancy			$6,378,340	$6,378,340

The California Commission on the Status of Women and Girls was created by the state's legislature "to promote equality and justice for all women and girls by advocating on their behalf with the Governor, the Legislature and other public policymakers, and by educating the public."[55] Acronym mobilizes voters and churns out advocacy campaigns for various Democratic candidates and causes. It also "controls a number of for-profit companies that are major players in Democratic Party politics, including campaign consulting firm Lockwood Strategy, a peer-to-peer political technology company known as Shadow, and a media company that invests in local left-leaning news outlets called Fwiw Media."[56] The Salk Institute conducts research not just in medical areas but also climate change.[57]

Windward Fund's Top Grantees Since 2019

	2019	2020	2021	Total
Carbon Mapper, Inc.			$10,080,638	$10,080,638
Potential Energy Coalition, Inc.			$4,500,000	$4,500,000
Tides Center		$4,013,868	$440,311	$4,454,179
Water Foundation	$250,000	$2,176,000	$1,648,727	$4,074,727
Isaiah		$200,000	$3,050,000	$3,250,000

Except for the Environmental Defense Fund (a major climate change advocacy group), Windward's grants are the most unusual of the five sisters, because they show a less obvious inclination toward hot-button issues.[58] But nearly every one of its grants bears the tagline "environmental programs."

North Fund's Top Grantees Since 2019

	2019	2020	2021	Total
Future Forward USA Action		$6,736,650		$6,736,650
New Approach Montana		$4,727,500		$4,727,500
Colorado Families First		$4,400,000		$4,400,000
Sixteen Thirty Fund		$800,000	$1,900,000	$2,700,000
Missourians for Health Care	$500,000	$1,913,370		$2,413,370

Following the lead of the Sixteen Thirty Fund, the North Fund also helped Future Forward USA Action, the main "dark money" group that passed millions of dollars to Future Forward Action PAC to fund pro-Biden campaign ads in the last few weeks of the 2020 presidential election. But outside of its grants to the Sixteen Thirty Fund, the North Fund's other recent top grantees have been state ballot initiative groups. In fact, what triggered the unmasking of the North Fund as a fifth "sister" nonprofit in Arabella's arsenal was funding to New Approach Montana's work in support of a 2020 ballot initiative to legalize marijuana in the state. North Fund also donated to Colorado Families First, the group behind a ballot initiative campaign for statewide paid family leave during the 2020 election. Missourians for Health Care supported a Medicaid expansion ballot initiative in the August primary.

Taken together, Arabella's collective grant activity paints a clear picture: Far from a philanthropy, Arabella operates a political machine created to funnel money from ideologically motivated donors to campaigns designed to change public policy and, often, to elect Democrats. Few Americans outside professional liberal philanthropy would call that "charity."

New Venture Fund in the Trump Years

During Trump's administration there was an explosion of activity from the Left aiming to block every part of his agenda, and Arabella played a leading role. Together with its "sister" Sixteen Thirty Fund, New Venture Fund unleashed a menagerie of fake pop-up groups that did everything from targeting all of President Trump's judicial nominees to fighting for abortion-on-demand to harrying Interior Department political appointees.[59]

Because the New Venture Fund's projects can appear one day and disappear the next, they tend to be run as short-term, high-intensity media campaigns targeting the news cycle. This was perhaps most obvious during the Left's effort to derail the confirmation of Supreme Court justice Brett Kavanaugh in 2018 (refer back to the introduction for more about Arabella's role in the campaign against Kavanaugh). In that bitter summer, a crowd of activists led by a mysterious new group called Demand Justice waved preprinted signs that demanded, "Stop Kavanaugh."[60] At a glance, Demand Justice was an activist group like any other. But closer inspection of its website showed that the group was really a front for the Sixteen Thirty Fund. (Lobbying filings posted by the FEC later confirmed this.)

The New Venture Fund's projects are often created in support of these lobbying front groups. The ironically named Fix the Court, for instance, could be considered Demand Justice's unofficial research arm, though the two groups don't advertise their relationship to Arabella Advisors.[61] Yet when asked during a 2016 C-Span interview how much of his group's money comes from the New Venture Fund, executive director Gabe Roth admitted: "All of it."[62]

Both groups ran parallel campaigns attacking federal district court judge Thomas Farr, Justice Brett Kavanaugh, and Judge Naomi Rao. Perhaps nothing better illustrates the fake "grassroots" activism at play against the justices than when Demand Justice cited Fix the Court as "a nonpartisan watchdog group" to justify its Freedom of Information Act request demanding over one million pages of documents from Kavanaugh's days in the Department of Justice and Office of Independent Counsel Ken Starr.[63]

While the Sixteen Thirty Fund's projects are generally created to lobby, the New Venture Fund's projects often take a subtler approach to advocacy.[64] In December 2018, the *Wall Street Journal*'s Kimberley Strassel reported on the so-called ethics resistance then barraging President Trump with Freedom of Information Act requests and lawsuits intended to derail his administration—if not set him up for impeachment by House Democrats.[65]

Citing Capital Research Center's original discoveries, Strassel identified three innocuously named nonprofits targeting Trump: Democracy Forward, American Oversight (founded in 2017), and Restore Public Trust (founded in 2018). Of the three, two sport direct connections to the New Venture Fund—such as Restore Public Trust, a supposedly "non-partisan public interest group" created in November 2018.[66] The New Venture Fund is also represented on American Oversight's board of directors by Kyle Herrig, who also serves on New Venture's board and runs Accountable.US, which had previously been a project of New Venture.[67] (After being birthed at Arabella, Accountable.US later became a stand-alone 501(c)(3) "charity," and Restore Public Trust eventually became a project of Accountable.US.)

These groups—and consequently, the New Venture Fund—were enmeshed in top tiers of the professional Left and the Democratic Party. Democracy Forward's founding board of directors, for instance, included Hillary Clinton campaign chairman John Podesta; Ron Klain, who later became President Joe Biden's chief of staff; and Marc Elias, the prominent Democratic Party lawyer who, among many other things including being paymaster for the Hillary Clinton campaign's Russiagate hoax, spearheaded the Democrats' new national redistricting effort and only recently parted ways with the Democratic National Committee.[68] American Oversight's founding board includes Melanie Sloan, former executive director of the leftist attack group Citizens for Responsibility and Ethics in Washington (CREW), and Caroline Fredrickson, former legislative director for the abortion-on-demand group NARAL Pro-Choice America.[69]

The New Venture Fund claims it's supported almost 500 projects since its inception in 2006, and the same annual report claimed to be currently hosting more than 130.[70] Again, while the New Venture Fund and its sister nonprofits maintain these hundreds of campaigns, the money originates with paying, undisclosed clients. Arabella Advisors, in other words, provides customers with ready-made platforms for their advocacy campaign of choice—just cut the check and Arabella takes care of the rest, with no donor fingerprints.

Nothing Ventured, Nothing Gained

Some of New Venture Fund's projects are even projects within projects. Take the case of its Civic Engagement Fund.[71] The Fund is a "nonprofit civic incubator" housed within an incubator. In reality, it's no such thing—whatever projects the Fund "sponsors" are as much projects of the New Venture Fund as the Civic Engagement Fund is itself—but it stands as an example of the layers Arabella Advisors has built in order to distance itself and its donors from many of their creations.

ALL ABOVE ALL. This New Venture Fund project originally advocated for Congress to overturn the Hyde Amendment, a legislative provision that first passed in 1976 and continued with annual bipartisan support for decades. The amendment forbids the use of federal funds to pay for abortions except in extreme circumstances. In 2017, All Above All and its Sixteen Thirty Fund–sponsored lobbying arm backed the Equal Access to Abortion Coverage in Health Insurance ("EACH Woman") bill, which would have "ensur[ed] abortion coverage and care through the federal government" in Medicaid and Medicare while simultaneously barring state legislatures from restricting abortion coverage in private health plans. Since the 2022 Supreme Court decision *Dobbs v. Jackson Women's Health Organization* returned the authority to regulate abortion to the people and their elected representatives, All Above All now claims they are "a catalyst for abortion justice."

CAMPAIGN FOR ACCOUNTABILITY. This is one of the most hypocritical groups incubated by New Venture Fund. It was created in 2015 as a project of New Venture; in 2016, it was transferred to the Hopewell Fund, and later became an independent 501(c)(3) charity. Campaign for Accountability's noble mission is "expos[ing] misconduct and malfeasance in public life," and one of the group's broadest initiatives targeted tech giant Google for its entanglements with Washington, D.C., politicians.[72] The Campaign's so-called Google Transparency Project could have done laudable work if it had pulled back the curtains on a company that—in addition to its influence over the administrative state and ability to powerfully manipulate Internet search results—has viciously targeted employees who don't conform to the radical ideological "echo chamber" the company has created.[73]

But alas, the Campaign for Accountability isn't very accountable. For one thing, it has disproportionately targeted Republican Party politicians for supposed ethics violations, and it's been represented in lawsuits by none other than American Oversight—the anti-Trump "watchdog" whose board of directors includes a New Venture Fund board member, Kyle Herrig.[74] Campaign for Accountability co-founder and former executive director Anne Weismann was chief counsel for a decade for Citizens for Responsibility and Ethics in Washington (CREW), the David Brock–affiliated Democratic agitation group.[75] And current executive director Michelle Kuppersmith was previously director of special projects at Accountable. US, an Arabella-spawned group that specializes in smearing conservatives and Republicans.[76]

But most disturbing is the revelation that the tech firm Oracle financed Campaign for Accountability's Transparency Project while the company was locked in a $9 billion intellectual property lawsuit with Google (the amount donated to the Campaign is unknown).[77] As Oracle vice president Ken Glueck put it in 2016, "Oracle is absolutely a contributor (one of many) to the [Google] Transparency Project. This is important information for the public to know."[78]

It wouldn't be fair to lay Campaign for Accountability's hypocrisy concerning transparency at New Venture's door, of course, since the group is now independent of the Fund. It's one of the few New Venture Fund projects to come into its own as a fully-fledged, independent nonprofit. But this kind of mercenary behavior is part and parcel of many of New Venture Fund's projects, and perhaps it should be expected: the fund itself *exists* to foster such campaigns for clients, after all.

AMERICA VOTES. This group has enjoyed major grants from both New Venture Fund and Sixteen Thirty Fund, receiving over $314 million combined from 2017 to 2021. Despite its generic-sounding name, the only part of America that America Votes wants to see voting is the Left. Greg Speed, the head of America Votes, is a former staffer at the Democratic Congressional Campaign Committee, a group whose sole purpose is to elect Democrats to the House of Representatives. Its founding president was Anne Bartley, a former aide to First Lady Hillary Clinton and a wealthy Democratic donor involved in founding numerous prominent leftist organizations, including the Democracy Alliance, a political donor cabal that includes George Soros and similar billionaires.[79]

The board of America Votes is a who's who of the Left, including at one point or another Doug Phelps, head of the activist behemoth Public Interest Network; Gene Karpinski, president of the League of Conservation Voters; Cecile Richards, former president of Planned Parenthood; Deepak Bhargava, former president of the Center for Community Change; Karen Nussbaum, head of Working America; Page Gardner of the notorious Voter Participation Center; Michael Podhorzer, longtime political director of the AFL-CIO (later credited by *Time* with helping to "save" democracy in the 2020 election); and Rob McKay, longtime chairman of the Democracy Alliance.[80]

Speaking of the Democracy Alliance, it's no surprise that America Votes is an original member of that shadowy collective of mega-funders and influencers who meet annually to coordinate spending on left-wing infrastructure. In fact, the Democracy Alliance even praises America Votes as "the common link between many of the largest and most influential issue and membership organizations in the country."

Arabella's Take on Fiscal Sponsorship

As mentioned at the end of chapter 1, Arabella's relationship between its five nonprofits and their hundreds of pop-up projects falls under the legal category of "fiscal sponsorship," where an established nonprofit houses a fledgling project while the new group waits for the IRS to recognize it as a new tax-exempt group. The "incubated" group is run as a "project" or "program" of the fiscal sponsor until it is spun off as an independent nonprofit.

But Arabella Advisors offers a unique take on fiscal sponsorship: creating websites designed to fool the casual viewer into thinking these groups are stand-alone activist organizations with grassroots support. Many of these websites give the impression of depth when in fact they're more like masks: sophisticated websites made to create the illusion that they're more than just a small digital space owned by a much larger entity. Yet these misleading ghost soldiers are often powerful enough to win political battles.

Because websites can disappear as quickly as they go live, their ephemeral quality makes Arabella's pop-up groups difficult to track. That offers a huge advantage to Arabella's clients in today's politics, where the news cycle is driven at the speed of a tweet. Why wait for the wheels of bureaucracy to turn when you can quickly create a website for a "new" group to spread your message?

Arabella has tried to paint its hundreds of "pop-up" groups as independent from the company and its staff. In an interview with the *Chronicle of Philanthropy*, then Arabella CEO Sampriti Ganguli claimed these projects "have independent advisory boards [and] independent governance and budgetary structures," and merely "benefit" from sheltering beneath the umbrella of Arabella's nonprofits for financial and administrative reasons.[81] But is that true? Arabella's individual project budgets are a black hole, but a few years ago the Capital Research Center examined the 130-odd known Arabella pop-up groups to see how many actually had advisory boards. Just fifteen with a steering committee, advisors, or board of directors listed on their websites could be discovered.

A far more damning revelation occurred in 2022, when Rick Cruz, Arabella's then president, wrote to the *Wall Street Journal* to complain about an editorial that suggested Arabella dominates its in-house nonprofits.[82] Cruz insisted his for-profit firm just provides its "client" nonprofits with "operational support" for "human resources, compliance and accounting," but "we work for our clients, not the other way around." Unfortunately for him, one of my colleagues responded with his own letter, revealing "proof Arabella doesn't operate as it claims."[83] The letter cited

emails unearthed by Government Accountability and Oversight and analyzed by Capital Research Center.[84] Seeking business from Gov. Jay Inslee (D-WA), the head of an Arabella "client" copied "my colleagues Bruce Boyd and Ryan Strode from Arabella. They lead our collective work on climate policy and advocacy." Elsewhere, Arabella and "client" promise to "secure fundraising." A four-page memo has Arabella's logo before its client's and often describes Arabella as acting alone. For instance, "Arabella developed the program strategy, identifies grantees, makes funding recommendations, and executes all grant-making." It concludes, "We look forward to continuing our discussion about how Arabella can best support the US Climate Alliance going forward."

Why, my colleague asked, "won't Arabella proudly admit its success in building a multibillion-dollar empire that's a pillar of the Democratic Party?"

Networks and Penumbras

Thanks to its impressive reach and value to the institutional Left, Arabella plays a powerful role in expanding left-wing political infrastructure. Arabella prizes its image as "the only provider of a true end-to-end platform of philanthropic services" in the United States.[85] The company specializes in "philanthropy and impact investing" services, or what it calls "strategic philanthropy."

Arabella's version of "strategic philanthropy" usually takes the form of guiding grants to left-wing causes, a service that evidently pays well. It's taken in $230 million in fees from its in-house nonprofits from 2008 to 2021, and no one outside knows how many more millions it's received from clients it didn't create. But my colleagues did study databases of nonprofit filings, which revealed that from 2012 to 2018, Arabella Advisors received at least $6.1 million in payments from foundations and other nonprofits outside its network. Arabella even received foundation grants, as if it were a charity, such as $1.9 million from the Susan Thompson Buffett Foundation (a pro-abortion philanthropy funded by Warren Buffett) for a "reproductive health project" and $487,000 from the David and Lucile Packard Foundation for "local grant-making."

Arabella is the largest philanthropy consultancy in America, and until it began receiving serious scrutiny from my colleagues, Arabella used to brag it "has helped hundreds of clients representing more than $100 billion in assets increase their philanthropic impact" (this language has disappeared from its website).[86] Similarly, Arabella's New Venture Fund used to preen that "more than half of the 50 largest US grantmaking foundations have funded projects hosted at NVF, including 8 of the top 10."[87]

But Arabella's true value lies in what it calls its "deep partnerships" with the New Venture Fund and its sister nonprofits. "Deep partnerships" is a euphemism; the firm's relationship to these five nonprofits couldn't be more hierarchical.[88] As we mentioned at the beginning of this chapter, key Arabella officers control the boards of directors of this network of nonprofits.

While Arabella Advisors doesn't hide its connection to four of its five funds (North Fund, the most recently created, is something of an exception, as we'll see in chapter 8), the firm is curiously hesitant to explain just how "deep" its partnerships with the funds run. Littering the groups' websites are myriad descriptions of the supposedly "independent" funds managed under an "administrative agreement" with Arabella Advisors. The New Venture Fund awhile back admitted that it and Arabella "share a commitment to evaluation and measuring impact."[89] (It also shares something else with Arabella—an address.)

Altogether, the five Arabella-run funds represent a substantial force on the Left, raising just under $1.6 billion in 2021. According to 2022 figures from *Forbes*, that would make the funds the seventh largest public charity in America, were they a single nonprofit—ahead of Goodwill International Industries, the YMCA, and Habitat for Humanity.[90]

A Lobbying Giant

We've described Arabella's vast web of pop-up groups, but there's another key aspect of the system: lobbying. While the Sixteen Thirty Fund is Arabella's main in-house lobby shop and so conducts the most lobbying in the empire along with the North Fund, the Hopewell and New Venture Funds have also spent millions of dollars lobbying Congress.

Arabella's lobbying covers a range of issues. The groups have weighed in on multiple appropriations bills over the last decade, though it is not clear what in those bills was the locus of their concern. They've also lobbied for bills affecting charter schools (the details remain unclear) and for an increase in the earned income tax credit, which is applied to low-income taxpayers.

During the Trump administration, they were involved in short-lived efforts to institute term limits for the U.S. Supreme Court. In 2018 and 2019, Arabella's groups lobbied for "protecting the work and role of the Special Counsel," referring to Special Counsel Robert Mueller and his investigation into President Trump's alleged wrongdoing in the 2016 election.

Arabella's nonprofits lobbied for "full funding" of the U.S. Census Bureau ahead of the 2020 Census, which would affect congressional representation for the next decade. In 2017, they backed Rep. Barbara Lee's (D-CA) EACH Woman Act, which would have would have mandated that private health insurance providers cover abortions and that abortion coverage be guaranteed in public health insurance programs such as Medicaid, Medicare, and the Children's Health Insurance Program.

Arabella's groups have lobbied for more protections of the Western sage-grouse, a bird that's become a poster child to a campaign by left-leaning groups for more costly environmental regulation. Arabella groups also supported 2017 legislation that would have reversed the Federal Communications Commission (FCC) decision to repeal "net neutrality," a set of regulations written by the Obama-era FCC that largely handed control of the Internet to the federal government to be regulated like a 1930s public utility.

During the Biden administration, Arabella's nonprofits have registered to lobby for everything from D.C. statehood to expanding the number of justices on the U.S. Supreme Court. The groups supported the administration's Build Back Better proposals, advocated to "modernize" the Senate by eliminating the filibuster, and supported a variety of transparency and accountability provisions. In all, between the New Venture Fund and the Sixteen Thirty Fund, Arabella groups spent over $3.2 million in federal-level lobbying in 2021 alone.

Lobbying against "Dark Money"?

The strangest bill that the Sixteen Thirty Fund has yet lobbied for is the For the People Act (H.R. 1), the House Democrats' celebrated bill designed to fight "dark money." The bill passed the House in early 2019 and died in the U.S. Senate (as did the reintroduced bill in 2021). It would dramatically expand campaign finance regulations and create onerous new disclosure rules that severely burden free speech and open up the potential for harassment of donors giving sums as modest as $10,000 to groups engaged in vaguely defined "campaign-related disbursements." Leftists have championed the bill as a "slate of significant reforms to get money out of politics." The far-left website *Vox* wrote:

> The sweeping bill is aimed at getting money out of politics and increasing transparency around donors, cracking down on lobbying, and expanding voting rights for Americans by implementing provisions like automatic voter registration.... [House Democrats] hope the message they are sending is one the public buys—that money and corruption in politics should be eradicated.

One would think shadowy funders like Arabella Advisors would oppose a crackdown on anonymous political spending, given that they exist to carry it out and do so to the tune of hundreds of millions of dollars. In fact, their website insists, on a page devoted to their complaints about Capital Research Center's criticisms of Arabella, that "We respect donor and client privacy."[91] Nevertheless, *Politico* reported the Sixteen Thirty Fund had hired a former Democratic congressional chief of staff-turned-lobbyist to lobby for "the campaign finance and ethics reform bill." How many

Democrats, one wonders, considered Arabella's "dark money" monster when they passed the bill in March 2019 on a party-line vote?

To more deeply understand how Arabella and its Democratic friends work in tandem to manipulate public opinion, we now turn to a classic example of these efforts, the campaign to control every American's health care.

3

Health Care for America Now

*How the New Venture Fund and the
Sixteen Thirty Fund Collaborate on
Legislative Campaigns*

I N THE LEAD-UP to the 2018 midterm elections, if you listened to
ads from activist groups like Save My Care, Protect Our Care, and
Get America Covered, you might have had the impression an army of
concerned citizens was desperately trying to save Obamacare from the
ash heap. "Healthcare is the most important issue to Americans," wrote
Save My Care. "The results are in, [and 2018] was the healthcare election,"
chimed in Protect Our Care. The aptly named Health Care Voter bluntly
stated that the midterm election was "all about healthcare."

Whether voters had healthcare on the top of their minds when they
went to the polls in November 2018 is highly debatable, considering the
wealth of other issues then at stake, including immigration, impeachment,
and the confirmation of Supreme Court justice Kavanaugh. Even less convincing was the claim by these groups that a large number of single-issue
"healthcare voters" existed.

What explains all the healthcare noise? Save My Care, Protect Our

Care, Get America Covered, and Health Care Voter were all front groups for Arabella funds. In fact, at least thirteen pro-Obamacare organizations were never independent groups at all, just websites hosted by Arabella's Sixteen Thirty Fund, New Venture Fund, and Hopewell Fund.

Perhaps unsurprisingly, the campaign to save Obamacare with pop-up lobbying groups like Health Care Voter closely resembles the original campaign crafted by professional activists that passed the landmark healthcare bill in 2010. Brad Woodhouse, a co-chair for Health Care Voter, previously served on the steering committee for Health Care for America Now, or HCAN, the 501(c)(4) umbrella group that ran the "$60 million five-and-a-half year campaign to pass" Obamacare in 2010—something HCAN itself brags about.[1]

Like Health Care Voter, HCAN's own origins are shadowy. In its original incarnation, HCAN fueled its $60 million Obamacare campaign with $27 million from Atlantic Philanthropies, which was only able to give such support because it's chartered in Bermuda, where philanthropic foundations don't face restrictions on support for politicking.

Woodhouse also heads Protect Our Care, the self-described "war room for the ACA" (that's the Affordable Care Act, the official name of Obamacare). This group supported Democrats in the 2018 midterm elections, and it's another project of the Sixteen Thirty Fund.

As if to quietly admit just how fake these supposedly grassroots groups really are, Health Care Voter's coalition includes at least nine groups that are also projects of an Arabella-run fund: Tax March, Save My Care, Ohioans for Economic Opportunity, New Jersey for a Better Future, Michigan Families for Economic Prosperity, SoCal Health Care Coalition, Keep Iowa Healthy, Keep Birth Control Copay Free, and Floridians for a Fair Shake. Many of those groups—including other ostensibly state-based groups not on the coalition list—are so similar that they share carbon-copy websites.

If that's not convincing enough, consider Health Care Voter's recent list of co-chairs. In June 2023, the list included Protect Our Care's Brad Woodhouse; Anton Gunn, a former Obama-era Health and Human Services communications director; Laura Packard, a Democratic political consultant; actress Alyssa Milano; former representative (and unsuccessful Democratic candidate for the U.S. Senate) Donna Edwards; Center for Popular Democracy organizer Ady Barkan; and other activists. The website previously listed Center for American Progress vice president Topher Spiro among its co-chairs. Spiro's work as a senior staffer to former senator Ted Kennedy (D-MA) included helping to draft the Obamacare bill.

But let's zero in more closely at what is at stake in the politics of health care (including Obamacare and Medicare for All), who Arabella's left-wing lobbying allies are in this field, and how Arabella and its offspring have played their part.

Obamacare and the Alternatives

On July 19, 2017, at least 155 demonstrators were arrested by U.S. Capitol Police for creating a coordinated disturbance at U.S. Senate office buildings. The scofflaw infiltration was in response to lawmakers' planning to repeal and replace the Affordable Care Act (i.e., Obamacare).[2] The *Washington Post* reported the protesters hoped to "have more than 500 people occupy offices of 52 Republicans."[3]

Motivating the protest's intensity was the astounding amount of wealth and power at stake. The United States spends $11,600 *per person* each year on health care.[4] That adds up to well over $900,000 during an average lifetime of seventy-nine years.

Both before and after Obamacare, most of that cash was controlled by big insurance companies and big government. Obamacare didn't so much change our costly third-party-payment system as cram millions more people into it.

Excluding 64 million Medicare beneficiaries, the federal government alone spends more than $750 billion per year on health care, all of it tax dollars taken from Americans the government programs are supposed to help.[5] Setting aside the several hundred million dollars more chipped in by state governments every year for their share of Medicaid spending, the federal spending on health care comes to more than $2,700 per person each year.[6]

That's $10,800 in taxpayer health spending every year for every family of four. So the question arises, Who should control that money if not big government and big insurance bureaucrats?

One answer comes from the advocates of finishing the job and creating a full single-payer "Medicare for All" program in which government controls almost all health spending.[7] The opposing camp argues that we should empower patients with a much larger share of the control over government health dollars. In 2008, GOP presidential nominee Sen. John McCain (R-AZ) proposed dividing up a big chunk of the government health dollars into vouchers (known as refundable tax credits) of $2,500 per person and $5,000 per family ($3,300 and $6,600 in late 2021 dollars, respectively).[8]

These vouchers would have gone to everyone, providing universal health coverage. But this program would have been the opposite of single-payer, because it would have empowered every adult and family to decide for themselves the level of health coverage to purchase and what to pay for out of pocket. Call it a "multimillion-payer plan," the same kind of payment system Americans use for nearly everything else, including auto and home insurance.

A system biased heavily to patient control over spending has been in place in Singapore for decades. The average resident of Singapore is just as wealthy as the average American, but the Singapore citizen spends one-third of what we do on health care to get results as good or better than ours. In 2013 the Brookings Institution issued a report on the Singapore program: *Affordable Excellence: The Singapore Healthcare Story.*[9] In 2019 *Newsweek* ranked Singapore General Hospital as the third-best hospital on the planet.[10]

The opposing viewpoint was represented by those 155 lawbreakers arrested in the Capitol Hill office buildings back in 2017. They were a mix of those pushing for Medicare for All and those defending the Obamacare status quo.

According to the *Post*: "The demonstrations were to follow a meeting described as a National Town Hall Meeting on Health Care. . . . Organizers included the Center for Popular Democracy, Housing Works, National Nurses United and Health Care for America Now, among others." Nine days earlier, another incursion into congressional office buildings over the same issue resulted in eighty arrests.

As these incidents showed, the advocacy ecosystem promoting government control over health care resources is vast, wealthy, and even willing to use extralegal measures to get its way. This isn't surprising, because they are fighting over control of 18 percent of the U.S. economy.[11]

The Arabella Network

In terms of money totals and hence political influence, Arabella Advisors has established itself as a major player on the left in the health care battles. It is difficult to track the funding (as opposed to the total revenues) for many Obamacare advocates, but a number of them can be traced back to Arabella Advisors. For example, Health Care for America Now (HCAN), which joined in the 2017 protest at congressional offices, does not report its finances like a normal nonprofit, because it's a fiscally sponsored subsidiary of Arabella's Sixteen Thirty Fund.[12] HCAN provides an example of how difficult it is to calculate just how much is being spent to promote government control over health care dollars, let alone who is spending it and who originally gave the money.

The Safety Net Defense Fund is another good example of the coordination of educational and political missions in the Arabella universe. Safety Net Defense was jointly managed through New Venture (the "Safety Net Defense Fund Project") and Sixteen Thirty (the "Safety Net Defense Action Fund Project").[13] Fundraising memos produced by Arabella in June 2017 reveal that the purpose of Safety Net Defense was to prevent reforms to Medicaid and other federal poverty programs.

Together, the two Safety Net Defense Fund memos sought $10 million so the project could exploit "deep divisions among Republicans" in seventeen targeted states. The combined budget was to be for a two-year mission (i.e., through the 2018 midterm elections). Even as $8 million of the total was intended for New Venture Fund, the supposedly nonpolitical educational charity, both memos used this politically charged language: "We will direct intense pressure on selected House Republicans."

According to the memos, the project's real manager was Arabella Advisors. The first sentence of the donor appeal from the New Venture Fund educational arm stated that "Safety Net Defense Fund" is "a project through Arabella Advisors."[14] The language from the Sixteen Thirty Fund political advocacy arm memo is identical: "The Safety Net Defense Action Fund (SNDAF), a project through Arabella Advisors."[15]

According to the 2017 and 2018 IRS filings from New Venture and Sixteen Thirty, the two nonprofits paid more than $42.1 million in total consulting fees to Arabella Advisors, presumably to manage the Safety Net Defense Fund and other pop-up projects.

Because of the design of Arabella's network, the specific percentage of expenses used to operate each pop-up is difficult (often impossible) for the public to discover. An April 2021 *New York Times* report summed up the subterfuges by saying that Arabella was operating a "dark money" network that "obscures the identities of donors" and was "a leading vehicle for it on the left."[16]

Individually, Arabella's pop-ups are often misleadingly portrayed as independent grassroots advocacy groups, rather than as one among hundreds of messaging vehicles from the same lavishly funded left-wing network.

Arabella enhances this façade by creating redundant pop-ups promoting similar or identical messages. There have been at least two dozen different Arabella pop-up groups (including Health Care for America Now) with a major mission objective of promoting increases in government control over health care dollars.

Enhancing the confusion, some of the Arabella-managed pop-up projects are managing *other* left-leaning health care pop-up projects.

The webpage of Health Care Voter denounces Republicans for "trying to abolish the Affordable Care Act and eliminate vital protections that we rely on."[17] A careful look at the bottom of the page reveals: "Paid for by Health Care Voter, a Project of the Sixteen Thirty Fund." Similar anti-Republican messaging adorns the main page of the group Health Care Facts, which on close inspection of the fine print turns out to be a "Project of Health Care Voter."[18]

Following the Arabella Money

So, a dollar spent for a project such as Health Care Facts came from Health Care Voter. And Health Care Voter got that dollar from the Sixteen Thirty Fund. In many cases the dollar spent for a project such as this is really going to the *for-profit* Arabella Advisors.

Where did the dollar originate? That is even more complicated.

The Arabella nonprofits each operate as pass-through entities, connecting wealthy individuals and foundations to left-leaning projects and causes through Arabella. It is often impossible for the public to track the identities of the primary donors giving to the Arabella network. As a political advocacy nonprofit, the Sixteen Thirty Fund especially lacks transparency.

An additional layer of donor camouflage is sometimes created when the cash flowing into the Arabella nonprofits is sent by the original owner of the money through yet another large pass-through entity, such as the Fidelity Investments Charitable Gift Fund or the Silicon Valley Community Foundation.[19]

So, the money flowing into Arabella is difficult to track, and how the money is spent on a specific pop-up project is also obscure. Muddling the money flow still further, tens of millions of dollars are shuffled and cross-donated among the five Arabella nonprofits. In some cases, the subordinate status of the pop-up projects isn't clearly revealed or is hidden entirely.

For example, Lower Drug Prices Now is a pop-up that promotes price fixing for pharmaceuticals.[20] It claims an alliance with many left-leaning groups and labor unions, including other Sixteen Thirty front groups such as Health Care Voter. Many pages on the Lower Drug Prices Now website feature this disclaimer: "Paid for By Lower Drug Prices Now." Of course, this creates a perception that it is an independent group.

But in truth it is paid for by Sixteen Thirty. To find this out, a visitor to the website must find the "DONATE!" page and then read the fine print at the bottom: "Lower Drug Prices Now is a fiscally sponsored project of the Sixteen Thirty Fund . . . donations to Lower Drug Prices Now are made to the Sixteen Thirty Fund and then immediately restricted for use by Lower Drug Prices Now."[21]

The connection is far less clear for Small Businesses for America's Future.[22] This is a project of the Sixteen Thirty Fund that promotes itself as the voice of small businesses. It lists "strengthen the Affordable Care Act" as a major policy goal.[23] Yet the web page does not acknowledge the already large control government exercises over health care dollars—something painfully known to most small business owners—and instead blames rising health care prices on "market failure." Contrary to mainstream small business trade groups, Small Business for America's Future calls on Congress to increase corporate taxation rates via a "roll back" of the tax cuts enacted during the Trump administration.

Neither the Small Business for America's Future web page nor the Sixteen Thirty web page show any obvious connection between the two groups.[24] As a mysteriously funded front group in Arabella's network, Small Business for America's Future portrays itself as a grassroots collection of business owners.

Only an American who makes it through to the last page of the IRS filing of the Sixteen Thirty for 2018 will find that "Small Business for America's Future" is listed as one of dozens of trade names that Sixteen Thirty was using that year, in place of its own name, according to the group's corporate registry filing with the government of the District of Columbia.[25]

Arabella's Secretive 2018 Election Projects

These opaque arrangements and tactics are often entirely legal and for a very good reason; namely, to protect donor privacy and anonymous speech. But left-of-center politicians, political groups, and "charities" have been the most strident opponents of any such free speech protections. Arabella has also opposed them, despite being a prolific user and beneficiary of such structures. Sixteen Thirty actually hired lobbyists in 2019 to pressure Congress to pass a law that would have the government force the disclosure of donor names to charities and political nonprofits.[26]

During the 2018 federal elections, Arabella deployed more than a dozen state-specific political projects to agitate against Republicans who didn't support left-leaning health care policies. In late July 2018 (still three months before the election) *Politico* reported that groups "organized under the Sixteen Thirty Fund have spent $4.6 million on television ads criticizing GOP members of Congress on health care and taxes."[27] The analysis also revealed that, in addition to being "among the most prolific political advertisers" on television, the "network of secret-money nonprofit groups" had "also been one of the top political advertisers in the country on Facebook."

The news website tabulated each group's spending through the end of July 2018 by consulting information collected by the Federal Election Commission and Advertising Analytics. An analysis of these Sixteen Thirty projects by *Nonprofit Quarterly* was headlined, "Darker-than-Dark Money Targeting GOP House Candidates."[28]

The Sixteen Thirty pop-up projects identified in the *Politico* report were: Arizonans United for Health Care, Colorado United for Families, Floridians for a Fair Shake, Health Care Voters of Nevada, Keep Iowa Healthy, Mainers Against Health Care Cuts, Michigan Families for Economic Prosperity, North Carolinians for a Fair Economy, Ohioans for Economic Opportunity, SoCal Healthcare Coalition, and Speak Out Central New York.[29]

Two others were identified as trade names of Sixteen Thirty in the 2018 Sixteen Thirty Fund tax filing: New Jersey for a Better Future and For Our Families (a Virginia-focused project).[30] In keeping with the tactics used for Small Business for America's Future, at least eight of the websites for these state pop-ups, and the Sixteen Thirty website, do not reveal the financial collusion between them.

An October 2018 report in the *New York Times* characterized the collection as an "array of affiliate groups around the country, many with vaguely sympathetic names."[31] The objective was to present the appearance of being independent, local grassroots efforts. *Politico* interviewed an activist with Ohioans for Economic Opportunity who claimed each affiliate had "complete local control."

If so, the locals abruptly lost interest as soon as the November 2018 election ended. The website for Ohioans for Economic Opportunity does not appear to have been updated since the voting ended.[32]

Likewise, if the "complete local control" assertion is to be believed, then the local activists in Colorado, Florida, Michigan, New Jersey, North Carolina, Virginia, and New York all seem to have independently yet coincidentally stopped using their websites at the same time. And as of this writing the websites for the other five affiliates in Arizona, Iowa, Nevada, Maine, and California each direct to dead links.

Protect Our Care and Save My Care were also listed as projects (i.e., "trade names" used) on the 2018 IRS report submitted by Sixteen Thirty.[33] According to media accounts of the 2018 election, both pop-up groups were used to attack Republicans for failing to support left-leaning health-care policies such as the Affordable Care Act.

A February 2018 report from the *Washington Examiner* announced that the two groups were coordinating on a "six-figure TV and digital ad buy in seven states" that was "aimed at pressuring Republicans over their attempts to repeal Obamacare."[34] On May 7, 2018 (still six months before election day), an OpenSecrets analysis of TV ads showed Save My Care had already spent $2.2 million for nearly 7,000 TV spots in eight states.[35]

In October 2018 the *New York Times* reported that all of the Sixteen Thirty political front groups put together (those focused on health care, plus other issues) had spent a total of $30 million during 2017 and 2018 "with the goal of battering Republicans for their health care and economic policies during the midterm elections."[36]

The Capital Research Center's InfluenceWatch website found that spending during the 2018 election cycle (2017 and 2018 combined) by the four nonprofits then in the Arabella network exceeded $1 billion.[37]

It's Almost All of Them

Arabella's advocacy strategy for left-wing health care laws during the 2017-2018 election cycle provides a textbook example through which one can see how Arabella and its progeny operate on all the core leftist issues. Obfuscating; multiplying groups; creating multitudes of pop-up groups that, by their number and seeming independence, exaggerate the size and diversity of "grassroots" support; concealment, to the extent legally possible, of how money passes through the nonprofits—all this is Arabella "dark money" in action.

And it doesn't stop at particular public policy issues. As the next chapter documents, Arabella marches straight into the conduct of elections that decide who gets to decide all issues of public policy.

4

Center for Secure and Modern Elections

*Funding Election Administration or
Changing Election Outcomes?*

B Y N O W most Americans know that Big Philanthropy exercised significant influence over the 2020 election. In numerous groundbreaking reports, CRC revealed how billionaire and left-wing mega-donor Mark Zuckerberg channeled $350 million through a sleepy Chicago nonprofit, the Center
for Tech and Civic Life (CTCL), to thousands of local election offices.[1] These
so-called Zuck Bucks had the expected effect of boosting turnout for Democratic nominee Joe Biden in key battleground states under the guise of
COVID-19 "relief," a fact that has even appeared in the *New York Times.*[2]

What *isn't* well known about CTCL's election meddling is the close
involvement of Arabella Advisors.[3]

The "Dark Money" Connection

Enter New Venture Fund, the 501(c)(3) flagship of Arabella's multibillion-dollar network that the *New York Times* identified as "a leading ve-

hicle" for "dark money" on the left, because under the guise of fiscal sponsorship, New Venture Fund uses an intricate "system of political financing, which often obscures the identities of donors."[4] Given the long history of New Venture Fund's issue advocacy and the prominence of its foundation clients/project donors, it's clear that a donor goes to Arabella expecting a legislative or even election payoff.

Arabella's nonprofits move hundreds of millions of dollars each year from major foundations, unions, and Democratic mega-donors to activist groups pushing the Left's most radical agenda items, such as ending the Senate filibuster, abolishing the Electoral College, and packing the Supreme Court. But since 2016—long before COVID-19 created a unique crisis in the election process—a New Venture Fund project was designed to radically change how Americans vote.

Since the last election cycle, the Center for Secure and Modern Elections (CSME) has pushed for a host of election laws, including automatic voter registration to swell every state's election rolls, looser penalties for falsifying voter registration applications, and expanding or even requiring mail-in voting for all future elections, even though the blue-ribbon, bipartisan commission led by former Democratic president Jimmy Carter and former Republican secretary of state James Baker declared the well-known truth about mail-in voting: "Absentee ballots remain the largest source of potential voter fraud."[5] (This truth was even reported, some years back, by the *New York Times.*[6])

While CSME—and the reporters who cover the group—present it as a "bipartisan" and stand-alone activist organization, it's little more than a website run by its "dark money" master, New Venture.[7] But you won't find CSME's relationship to its fiscal sponsor on its ModernElections.org website.

The Louisiana Lawsuit, Part 1

That connection between the two groups came to light only when Louisiana attorney general Jeff Landry sued CTCL and the New Venture Fund (as the nonprofit behind CSME) in October 2020 for injecting "unregulated private money" into the state just before the November election that same year.[8] According to the attorney general, the two groups unlawfully targeted thirteen parishes (as Louisiana calls its counties) for grants, some exceeding $500,000, in exchange for detailed information about the "operations, conduct, and expenses" of local election offices. The exchange was facilitated by Dawn Maisel Cole, head of Full Circle Strategies, a Louisiana political consulting firm. She allegedly "directly solicited registrars and clerks of court to accept contributions from CTCL and New Venture for the operation of their respective offices."

The attorney general pointed out the obvious: Privatizing elections sows mistrust among the public toward its election officials, causes those officials to be beholden to unaccountable special interests, invites the opportunity for foreign governments to meddle in elections by funding those nonprofits ("charities," unlike political campaigns, may accept foreign funding), and encourages an arms race between left- and right-leaning groups for control over public institutions that are supposed to be strictly independent. At first, the Louisiana lawsuit was shot down by a state trial judge, but the 2020 case exposed the first known connection between CTCL and Arabella, and as we'll see, an appeals court came to a different decision.[9]

Just What Is CSME?

Again, because the Center for Secure and Modern Elections is a project of New Venture Fund, which resists such disclosure and transparency, exactly when the group was established is uncertain. But it dates back to at least 2016, when (now former) CSME staff member Tova Wang participated in an election panel for politically active grant-makers hosted by the Funders Committee for Civic Participation.[10] (This committee is yet another fiscally sponsored entity, this time via the left-wing pass-through group NEO Philanthropy.)[11] Since 1981, the Funders Committee has helped donors—

including George Soros's Open Society Foundations and his donor cabal of the Democracy Alliance, the Ford Foundation, teachers' unions, the AFL-CIO, and other left-wing mega-donors—to direct their philanthropy to "civic engagement," by which they mean things like get-out-the-vote efforts that benefit the Democratic Party.[12]

CSME seems to have started as "the Cities Project," according to some older grant reports.[13] It has a "charity" wing run by New Venture Fund, and a 501(c)(4) "dark money" wing run by Sixteen Thirty Fund, which is common among politically active nonprofits and front groups in the Arabella network.[14] This means all donations to either wing are *really* donations to Arabella's nonprofits, neither of which are mentioned on the CSME website. It also means that the center doesn't file its own Form 990 reports with the IRS, keeping its exact finances a secret. Still, foundations must disclose their donations to nonprofit organizations, and some filings include descriptions of the grants made.

Using those descriptions, the Capital Research Center traced grants to both New Venture and Sixteen Thirty to fund CSME from several donors, including the leftist Bauman Foundation (a Democracy Alliance member); eBay founder Pierre Omidyar's Democracy Fund and Democracy Fund Voice ($1 million); the Blaustein Fund ($200,000); the mysterious pass-through Wellspring Philanthropic Fund ($2.3 million in 2020–2021), which gave to expand mail-in voting; and the Joyce Foundation, where then senator Barack Obama (D-IL) was once a board member.[15]

The Joyce Foundation's $600,000 grant was meant to help CSME support "elections jurisdictions in WI [Wisconsin], MI [Michigan], MN [Minnesota], and OH [Ohio] for the November 2020 election," all of which were targeted by the Biden campaign after Trump unexpectedly flipped Wisconsin and Michigan in 2016 and came within 45,000 votes of winning Minnesota, a decades-old Democratic stronghold.[16] The professional Left and Big Philanthropy were intent on not letting that happen again in 2020.

Working with Zuckerberg

CSME's co-defendent in the Louisiana lawsuit was the Center for Tech and Civic Life (CTCL).[17] CTCL was an obscure Chicago-based nonprofit run by Democratic Party digital campaign operatives, but in 2020, the group received around $350 million in "charity" dollars from Facebook founder Mark Zuckerberg and his wife's donor-advised fund at the Silicon Valley Community Foundation.[18] In turn, CTCL launched a program to distribute the funds directly to local boards of elections as COVID-19 "relief funds," supposedly to make voting safer (though National Public Radio and other outlets found less than 10 percent of funds were spent on personal protective equipment and the like).[19] In reality, Capital Research Center reporting revealed strong partisan trends in CTCL's grant-making that favored Democratic cities in battleground states essential to a Biden victory.[20] Other documents suggest the Center funded a campaign to track and advocate changes to voting laws brought on by COVID-19 ahead of the 2020 election.[21]

Lawmakers in Louisiana weren't the only ones asking questions. An investigation by a Wisconsin special counsel appointed by the state House of Representatives produced a report finding that the CTCL collaboration and funding led to an improper, government-sanctioned, get-out-the-vote campaign that favored Democrats.[22]

Ashish Sinha, a former CMSE employee, was involved in an email chain between CTCL leadership, the National Vote at Home Institute, and elections officials in Green Bay, Wisconsin.[23] In the chain, they discussed the use of private drop boxes and "targeting communities" with absentee ballots in the coming 2020 election.

Why does this matter? Public record requests after the election revealed how Michael Spitzer-Rubinstein, a Vote at Home Institute staffer, practically ran Green Bay's election as the city's "de facto elections administrator" with access to voted absentee ballots *days before the election*.[24] Spitzer-Rubinstein had access to four of the five keys to the ballroom where early ballots were stored and counted, and he even asked the city clerk to "cure" problematic absentee ballots. Green Bay "went rogue" under the Vote at Home Institute, in the words of the Brown County clerk. Green Bay also received $1.1 million from CTCL, the third-largest grant the Center made in Wisconsin.[25]

Sam Oliker-Friedland, chief counsel for the Center for Secure and Modern Elections, previously worked for the digital campaign group that birthed CTCL: the New Organizing Institute.[26] Capital Research Center documented that group's history in a January 2021 report, showing how the now-defunct institute trained activists in registering voters and getting voters to the polls in order to elect Democrats.[27] The New Organizing Institute was so effective in its partisan work that the *Washington Post* declared it, "the Democratic Party's Hogwarts for digital wizardry." Three of the Institute's staffers—Whitney May, Tiana Epps-Johnson, and Donny Bridges—went on to found CTCL, where they perfected their craft to help win the 2020 election.

Todd Shepherd, an investigative journalist writing for the Pennsylvania outlet *Broad + Liberty*, has also documented the ties between the CTCL and Arabella's CSME.[28] Shepherd explained to Capital Research Center:

> Emails from Green Bay and Philadelphia clearly show the CSME was operating hand in hand with the CTCL at the earliest possible stages on these grants while calling it the Cities Project. . . . Even months after the election, persons working for the CSME were still talking to election officials about the CTCL grants while using the name Cities Project. Because of this evidence, I think it's a very fair question to ask to what degree the CSME may have actually been the originator of the entire effort, and whether the CTCL was just a better front for the project because they had 501(c)(3) status [of their own, independent from the Arabella network that is already known for its Democratic Party alignment].[29]

The full extent of these three groups' involvement in key states may never be known. But the evidence of their collective ability to manipulate voting laws and election procedures behind the scenes is only growing.

Automatic Voter Registration Campaigns

Csme also provides allies with model bill text for automatic voter registration, one of the Left's longtime goals.[30] Many Democratic groups (wrongly) believe that high turnout always helps Democrats, so they fight to pass laws that push voter registration on as many people as possible.

Csme has pushed automatic voter registration in Connecticut, Oregon, Maine, and Maryland.[31] It popped up again in a confidential "Statement of Work" contract between New Venture Fund and Dickinson & Avella PLLC, an Albany, New York–based political consultancy, to cover election work from February to June 2020:

> In partnership with Marc Solomon and the Center for Secure and Modern Elections (Csme) staff, represent New Venture Fund's Csme project *in support of Automatic Voter Registration and other provoter [sic] modernizations* before the New York State Legislative, Executive and Administrative branches of government [emphasis added].[32]

New York's governor at the time, Democrat Andrew Cuomo, signed automatic voter registration into law in December of that year.[33]

Shepherd adds that Marc Solomon is a principal at Civitas Public Affairs, a nominally Republican-led consulting firm in Washington with clients that include such left-wing groups as Voto Latino, Campaign Legal Center, Voter Participation Center, and the Center for Secure and Modern Elections.[34] Solomon and his colleagues led the gay marriage campaigns of the early 2000s (Freedom to Marry) and seem to specialize in deception.[35] Capital Research Center also documented Civitas's role in secretly infiltrating the conservative movement with a global warming, pro-carbon tax group run by staffers with résumés full of time at far-left organizations.[36]

The Louisiana Lawsuit, Part 2

In April 2022, a Louisiana state appellate court reversed the lower court's decision of October 2020 that threw out the state attorney general's lawsuit against the Center for Tech and Civic Life (CTCL), New Venture Fund, and a Democratic consultant who helped funnel millions of dollars from billionaire Mark Zuckerberg into thirteen Louisiana parishes.[37] CTCL and friends had argued that Attorney General Jeff Landry had no grounds to sue them for privately funding local elections, because state law didn't explicitly prohibit the practice. The lower court judge agreed and dismissed the case with prejudice.

Since then, facts have emerged that reveal *much* more about how CTCL spent its "Zuck Bucks" to boost turnout in Democratic counties across the country, particularly in battleground states.[38] Across the nation, over half the states have permanently limited or prohibited private funding of election offices, keeping election funding where it belongs, under the control of the citizenry and their elected representatives.[39] Louisiana alone received more than $1.1 million from the shadowy left-wing CTCL, prompting the state's Republican-led legislature to pass a bill banning private funding for elections, which Democratic governor Bel Edwards vetoed, thereby proving the partisan nature of the scheme. (Every governor who has vetoed such a law has been a Democrat.)

So it's no surprise that Louisiana's Third Circuit Court of Appeals reversed and remanded the lower court's dismissal of the suit, finding instead that the state had a clear legal "cause of action" to bring the lawsuit.[40] In its appeal, the state argued that even if "the defendants here may be well-intentioned, private money in any amount, but particularly the amount of money offered by the defendants to select clerks and/or registrars, has an inherently insidious and corrupting effect."[41]

More Details Emerge

Court documents have revealed more about Ctcl's offer of Covid-19 "relief" grants to local elections officials.[42] In exchange for five- and six-figure grants, Ctcl allegedly demanded officials provide it with:

- the election office's 2020 budget;
- number of "active registered voters" in the county;
- number of "full-time staff (or equivalent)" employed by the county;
- copies of its W-9 contractor tax forms;
- information on which officials and/or agencies were responsible for approving Ctcl grants.

Far from constituting "free money," Ctcl's Zuck Bucks appear to include plenty of strings attached.

Ctcl and New Venture Fund will soon be defending themselves in court again. As the lawsuit progresses, perhaps answers to some of the following questions will come to light:

- What is the relationship between Ctcl and New Venture Fund beyond a $25 million grant in 2020 from New Venture to Ctcl? In which states did Ctcl and New Venture Fund perform the same or similar operations as in Louisiana?
- Who initiated first contact about Covid-19 relief grants: Ctcl, New Venture Fund, or local election officials?
- Did New Venture Fund or Ctcl receive information or public documents from local officials about their offices' operations, conduct, and expenses in exchange for a contribution?
- Did New Venture Fund perform "voter education" services, encourage the deployment of ballot drop boxes, or provide funds in support of mail-in/absentee ballots in its pass-through grants to Ctcl?
- What is the Csme budget? Who sits on its board of directors and advisory board, assuming they exist? Who are its donors (via New Venture Fund)?
- What was the role of Csme Action, a front for Arabella's Sixteen

Thirty Fund, in CSME's communications and coordination with CTCL? What role did the $1.5 million in grants from liberal mega-donor Pierre Omidyar's Democracy Fund Voice play in this coordination, and were those funds passed on to election officials?[43]

History Repeats Itself: The U.S. Alliance for Election Excellence

Around the same time Louisiana's appeal was granted to allow its lawsuit against the New Venture Fund and CTCL to proceed, CTCL's executive director Tiana Epps-Johnson announced the Chan Zuckerberg Initiative would no longer be donating to CTCL to fund election administration. Almost immediately, CTCL moved on to its next project: The U.S. Alliance for Election Excellence, called by critics, "Zuck Bucks 2.0."[44] Here, too, Arabella plays a role.

While the Alliance presents itself as a "nonpartisan collaborative," it was launched by CTCL as an $80 million, five-year initiative, and it's entirely controlled by its parent, CTCL, for whom it's just a project (cynics would say, "a rebranding of the original project"). It's called "Zuck Bucks 2.0" because instead of having election administration offices apply for and then quickly receive direct grants, as in the 2020 Zuck Bucks scheme, the Alliance lets local election offices apply to receive training on the election process and to be certified as "U.S. Centers for Election Excellence."

In the "Frequently Asked Questions" portion of the website, the Alliance admits that election officials may well recall the criticism stirred up by its original Zuck Bucks program, and so one frequently asked question it responds to is, "What if an election office receives backlash by participating"?[45] Never fear, the Alliance responds, because it will provide "guidance and resources" to election officials criticized for joining the scheme. In addition, "As part of the alliance, centers will receive training, mentorship, and resources, and serve as a support system for each other and election departments across the country."

Besides the formerly Zuckerberg-aligned CTCL and the Arabella-sponsored CSME, whose collaboration with CTCL continues in this new incarnation, the other "partners" in the Alliance share left-leaning ties. (The entire "Partners" page was deleted from the Alliance website somewhere between May 24, 2023, when it still showed up in a web archive as present, and June 27, when it had disappeared. But a November 2022 announcement still on the site lists these partners.[46])

One partner is the Elections Group, a consulting firm run by two former Democratic county elections officials to give "guidance" for election offices on ballot curing, all-mail elections systems, and ballot drop boxes.[47]

The Center for Civic Design, another partner, advocates for making the expanded mail-in voting used in 2020 a permanent feature of all future elections and has advised the National Vote at Home Institute whose outrageous meddling in 2020 in Wisconsin was described earlier.[48] With funding from liberal billionaire Pierre Omidyar's Democracy Fund, this group focuses primarily on redesigning ballots to make voting easier for perceived Democratic constituencies, such as recent immigrants, ethnic minorities, and young people.[49]

Other partners are the Hasso Plattner Institute of Design at Stanford University; the Prototyping Systems Lab at the University of California, Davis; and U.S. Digital Response, which was started during the pandemic to help with state and local governments' digital needs and has worked with CTCL and fellow Alliance partner Center for Civic Design to create a reusable election website template.[50] U.S. Digital Response also received a "multimillion-dollar" grant from CTCL in 2022, though it declined to state just how many millions when asked by the press.[51]

Finally, there is another partner in the Alliance, the Institute for Responsive Government, which the Alliance combines in the "partner" entry for the Center for Secure and Modern Elections, as if the two are one. Which doesn't appear far from the truth: both are pop-up groups under the Arabella New Venture Fund umbrella, and Sam Oliker-Friedland claims to be executive director of the Institute and chief counsel of the Center, and as noted earlier he's an alumnus of the group—the "Democratic Party's Hogwarts of digital wizardry," according to the *Washington Post*—that gave birth to Ctcl.[52] He served that partisan (c)(4) group as deputy director of data of technology, helping Democrats win elections, but now we're supposed to believe his work for the Institute for Responsive Government, and Csme, and the Alliance will be blissfully nonpartisan.

Yet given the backgrounds of these organizations and their respective staffing, it's hard to believe their motives are purely benevolent. The groups generally support more mail-in voting, automatic voter registration, and same-day registration, whereas no partner groups seem concerned about election security measures such as voter ID. This makes the perfect cocktail for left-wing manipulation of elections to maximize victories for the Democratic Party.

A report by the election integrity watchdog Public Interest Legal Foundation characterized the Alliance as an expansion of Ctcl's work.[53] "The U.S. Alliance for Election Excellence . . . promises an $80 million grant fund for local election officials to tap for aid," the report says. "This represents only a shallow representation of the parallel ecosystem of left-leaning nonprofits standing ready to financially support and augment government administration of elections."

The Alliance has identified a handful of localities already selected to participate in the program, but recruiting members has not gone smoothly. In both Greenwich, Connecticut, and Brunswick County, North Carolina, contentious debates erupted after election officials announced they had been designated by the Alliance as a "U.S. Center for Election Excellence."[54] Greenwich, after much controversy, agreed to accept funding from, but not to join, the Alliance. In Ottawa County, Michigan, officials eventually declined the chance to receive $1.5 million from the new Ctcl program.[55] Ottawa County Clerk Justin Roebuck explained, "While I value the overall stated goals of the Alliance, I firmly believe that funding for election administration must come from federal, state and local governments."

In short, even with the help of Arabella's vast empire, sometimes the schemes of the Left fall flat, especially when local citizens learn just what those schemes entail.

Our next chapter, however, recounts an area where Arabella and one of its billionaires have had considerable success controlling public policy—abortion.

5

CASE STUDY

Hopewell Fund

*How Warren Buffett's Wealth Funds
the Nation's Abortion Infrastructure*

T HE SUSAN THOMPSON BUFFETT FOUNDATION is possibly
the biggest anti-people funder on the planet. For decades, the Buffett Foundation—endowed by business magnate Warren and named for
his late wife—has poured incredible sums into the most powerful abortion
lobbies in the world. From pushing unrestricted abortion access to testing
experimental abortion pills on impoverished Africans, these groups are advancing an extremist agenda with billions of dollars from one of America's
most-celebrated philanthropists—and with almost no scrutiny from the
media. But with significant help from the Arabella empire, as we'll see.

Warren Buffett and the Teeming Hordes

He's not exactly the face of abortion activism. When most Americans think
of Warren Buffett—the famed Wizard of Omaha and fifth-richest man on
Earth—other things come to mind: the brilliant investor and founder of

mega-conglomerate Berkshire Hathaway, outspoken Democratic Party donor, and accomplished philanthropist.[1]

It's his charity that's earned this notoriously frugal arch-capitalist (he still lives in the house he bought in 1958 for $31,500) the most acclaim from the media who are otherwise great skeptics of free markets.[2] Liberal pundits and philanthropists gushed over Buffett's 2006 "Giving Pledge," an oath to gradually give away 99 percent of his wealth. (Other elites such as Bill and Melinda Gates, Paul Allen, and Michael Bloomberg have also taken the pledge.) In 2011, President Barack Obama even hosted Buffett in the White House for an "update" on the Giving Pledge's progress.[3] CNBC has celebrated Buffett as America's "most charitable billionaire."[4]

But there's a darker side to Buffett's multibillion-dollar philanthropy. For decades, he's donated vast sums to a foundation created to address what one biographer called Buffett's "Malthusian dread" of overpopulation—the thoroughly debunked idea that humans will reproduce themselves into mass starvation and death, named for the nineteenth-century British author Thomas Malthus. Given his enormous wealth and single-minded commitment, Warren Buffett may be the biggest funder of abortion in history.

Billions for Millions of Abortions

According to my colleagues' analysis, over roughly the past two decades—from 2000 to 2020—the Susan Thompson Buffett Foundation has poured an incredible $4.7 billion into pro-abortion, pro-population-control groups, easily making Warren Buffett the single most important supporter of abortion-on-demand in our day. That includes $785 million to Planned Parenthood and $525 million to Marie Stopes International, which provides abortions in developing countries, and $114 million to the Guttmacher Institute.[5] In that same period (2000–2020), the foundation's grants to all groups totaled $7.6 billion, meaning 62 percent of the Buffett Foundation's grant money went to anti-life groups.

To put that in perspective, Buffett's billions are enough to pay for 9.4

million abortions, according to data from the Guttmacher Institute, a pro-abortion think tank, at an average cost of roughly $500 per aborted child.[6] That's more than the entire population (in 2023) of New Jersey or roughly the equivalent of the people in ten states combined: Wyoming, Vermont, Alaska, North Dakota, South Dakota, Delaware, Rhode Island, Montana, and New Hampshire.[7]

It's a stunning revelation from a foundation so shadowy that even its liberal admirers call it "secretive" and "publicity-shy."[8] But these are understatements. A favorable profile by the left-leaning *Inside Philanthropy* commented on the difficulty in simply contacting the Buffett Foundation: "Trying to penetrate this place is like being a tourist asking around for the Mafia in Little Italy."[9]

The Buffett Foundation is one of the largest grant-making foundations in America. In 2020, it gave away $647 million in grants, enough to earn Warren Buffett infamy as the "King of Abortion" in pro-life circles. The president of Students for Life, a center-right college group, once deemed Buffett the "sugar daddy of the entire pro-abortion movement."

Through 2020, the foundation has given $259 million to DKT International, a nonprofit that sells inexpensive contraceptives to poor countries, and $57 million to Pathfinder International, a little-known juggernaut for aborting Africans founded in 1957 by Clarence Gamble of the Procter & Gamble fortune, a close friend of Margaret Sanger, the founder of Planned Parenthood who advocated for eugenics.[10] But that's far from the whole. More recipients include:[11]

- $140 million to Guttmacher Institute[12]
- $99 million to Engenderhealth (formerly Sterilization League of New Jersey)[13]
- $91 million to Society of Family Planning Research Fund[14]
- $53 million to Center for Reproductive Rights[15]
- $49 million to Population Council[16]
- $46 million to the National Campaign to Prevent Teen and Unplanned Pregnancy
- $39 million to NARAL Pro-Choice America and affiliates[17]

- $36 million to Gynuity Health Projects LLC, which conducts horrifying abortion research on impoverished women in Africa as well as Armenia, Nepal, Vietnam, Moldova, Uzbekistan, and Ukraine[18]
- $30 million to Catholics for Choice[19]
- $25 million to National Network of Abortion Funds[20]
- $22 million to Catholics for the Right to Decide

Buffett's largesse has also won him acclaim in the pro-abortion camp. "Have an IUD? Thank Warren Buffett," the *Washington Post* pronounced in 2015, referring to grants his foundation gave in the first decade of the twenty-first century to develop modern intrauterine devices for preventing pregnancies.[21]

Even far-left *Vox*—whose writers often disparage the very existence of billionaires as "a policy failure"—grudgingly praises Buffett. "If you could snap your fingers and rid the world of billionaire philanthropists instantly," it wrote in 2019 of Buffett's philanthropy, "hundreds of millions of women worldwide would lose access to contraception."

Yet the Buffett Foundation is almost nonexistent in the mainstream news. Although it's been in operation since 1964, the group's simple, out-of-date website offers information about scholarships for college freshmen in Nebraska (Buffett's home state), nothing more.

Perhaps left-leaning NPR summarized it best in 2006: "You mean you didn't know Warren Buffett's foundation has been funding abortion rights organizations? Well, that's just the way the Buffetts wanted it."[22]

Abortion's Underground Railroad

Buffett's involvement in pro-abortion activism predates the *Roe v. Wade* decision in 1973 and is largely attributable to Charles Munger, Buffett's close friend and second-in-command at Berkshire Hathaway. Munger, a Republican, described his views in a 2000 interview: "It was emotionally hard for me to become pro-choice because I do have reverence for human life, but when I thought through the consequences, I found it necessary to overrule that part of my nature."[23]

Munger convinced Buffett to join him in paying for the legal defense of Leon Belous, a California doctor convicted in 1967 of administering an illegal abortion; Belous's appeal in that case led the California Supreme Court to declare the state's ban on abortion unconstitutional in a four-three vote two years later. The Left still hails Belous as a hero for advancing the nation's abortion laws, and his case was cited in the pro-abortion brief in *Roe v. Wade* four years later.

At the same time as the Belous case, Munger and Buffett organized a "church" run by a minister who had broken with his congregation over his own pro-abortion views. By the pair's own admission, the so-called Ecumenical Fellowship was far from a religious institution; instead, it acted as a roving counselor on "family planning," aiding women in obtaining abortions outside the United States in the late 1960s. Munger explains,

> Warren and I were revolutionaries. We created a church that was used as an underground railroad. We supported the Clergy Counseling Service [a group of liberal ministers who arranged abortions for women outside the U.S.]. The minister running it was cashiered by his own church for helping women get abortions. First I tried to persuade the church to let him continue. That failed. I called Warren and asked him to help me establish our own church. That we did. For years this minister ran the thing. That was our contribution, trying to help so that society didn't force women to give birth—to be held in a system [overpopulation alarmist and abortion activist] Garrett Hardin called "mandatory motherhood."

Although this "underground railroad" lost its purpose after abortion was legalized nationwide with the Supreme Court's 1973 decision in *Roe v. Wade*, Munger continued his activism for years as a trustee and chief financial officer for the Los Angeles chapter of Planned Parenthood. He merged the Ecumenical Fellowship into the chapter and advised it on getting into the abortion business. Munger later bragged that "we were way ahead of the national office of Planned Parenthood in arranging abortions." Munger did not just quote Garrett Hardin, either. He financially supported Hardin, a white nationalist who was an avowed eugenicist in his "scientific" and popular works. [24] In one of his most famous essays, Hardin declared, "Freedom to breed is intolerable." [25]

A Quiet Malthusian

Unlike his business partner, Buffett himself hardly speaks publicly about abortion, perhaps (as some have speculated) out of concern that it would damage his investments and public image. Population control was more the domain of his first wife, Susan (née Thompson), an outspoken population control advocate who regularly attended meetings on reducing global population growth around the world.

The two had a curious relationship. They were married in 1952 and had three children; in 1977, the sometime-cabaret singer Susan left her husband in Omaha to pursue a singing career in San Francisco, though they remained married and apparently on good terms. One year after leaving Nebraska, Susan introduced Warren to Astrid Menks, who soon moved into his house; Astrid married him after Susan died from a stroke in 2004.

In a 1988 interview with the Omaha *World-Herald*, Susan relayed the Buffetts' shared interest in addressing the world's "population problem":

> Success that can be shown statistically appeals to her husband, Mrs. Buffett said. "Warren likes numbers . . . he likes to see concrete results, and you can see them [population figures] change," she said.

As president of the Buffett Foundation, which was giving away over $1 million annually in the mid-1980s, Susan Buffett directed spending toward two goals: "preventing nuclear war and limiting population growth."

In 1986, that meant grants totaling $300,000 ($708,000 in 2020 dollars) to various Planned Parenthood affiliates, and another $250,000 to the Population Institute (run by Rodney Shaw, a minister who pushed for population control policies in the United Methodist Church in the 1970s).

After Susan's death, her estate bequeathed $2.9 billion to the Buffett Foundation over four years, which Warren rechristened the Susan Thompson Buffett Foundation. Between 2006 and 2018, Warren gave the Buffett Foundation another $2.6 billion, nearly all of it in the form of Berkshire Hathaway shares.

Funding population control and abortion has become a Buffett family specialty. The family controls four foundations besides the Susan Thompson Buffett Foundation, all of which contribute to center-left political issues ranging from immigration to higher taxes to LGBTQ interests.

In a 1997 interview with the *Chronicle of Philanthropy*, Suzie Buffett—the couple's eldest daughter and Buffett Foundation chair—said that funding population control is "what my father has always believed was the biggest and most important issue, so that will be the [foundation's] focus. I feel as his child that it's important to carry out his wishes. It's his money."[26]

That fidelity to her parents' donor intent also extends to Suzie's ex-husband, Allen Greenberg, a former lawyer for Public Citizen (one of the litigation groups created by arch-activist Ralph Nader in the 1970s) and staffer for then Representative Chuck Schumer (D-NY).[27] Greenberg has quietly directed the Buffett Foundation since 1987 (2021 compensation: $784,313) and was *Inside Philanthropy's* 2019 Foundation President of the Year for "leading the pushback" against abortion-on-demand with massive grants to pro-choice groups.[28]

The Gates-Buffett Population Cabal

In his 2006 "Giving Pledge," Buffett promised to donate 99 percent of his wealth to four Buffett family foundations, including $3 billion to the Susan Thompson Buffett Foundation. He also bought himself a seat on the board of trustees for the Bill and Melinda Gates Foundation with what observers noted was the largest donation in history.[29] While the Gates Foundation does support genuine philanthropy—especially fighting disease in developing nations—it's also one of the world's largest funders of abortion activism and research. Buffett's gift of 10 million shares in Berkshire Hathaway effectively doubled its assets and ability to push global "family planning" schemes.

There's reason to suspect that the sudden influx of Buffett money encouraged the Gates Foundation to engage in abortion funding. While Bill and Melinda Gates have expressed personal support for abortion programs—they've criticized President Donald Trump's ban on federal funding of abortions, and Bill Gates's father was a longtime Planned Parenthood board member—pro-abortion activists observed as late as 2006 that the Gates Foundation was "shyer of abortion rights funding" than the Susan Thompson Buffett Foundation, although it had no qualms about funding "family planning and sex education programs."[30]

Whatever prompted its change of heart, the Gates Foundation's newfound support for abortion programs was most obvious at a 2012 conference in London it organized with the British government and United Nations. Dubbed "Family Planning 2020," the conference outlined a plan for elites and major governments to extend "reproductive health and rights" to 120 million people in poor countries by the end of 2020. While that includes less controversial things such as birth control and education for girls, the plan chiefly aims to loosen abortion restrictions for low-income persons around the world.

Funding At-Home Abortions

Even acting alone, the Buffett Foundation is the unrivaled terror of the unborn. In the early 2000s it bankrolled efforts to legalize the abortifacient mifepristone (also called RU-486 or Mifeprex) for sale in the United States through grants to the drug's developers, the Population Council and the pharmaceutical firm Danco Laboratories.[31]

Although it was designated to be used to end pregnancies before the ten-week mark, according to the World Health Organization mifepristone is safe through 12 weeks, and there is strong pro-abortion agitation to extend the window further—in the case of some activists, *much* further. This push to extend the window of opportunity and ease of access (including online access) for mifepristone has accelerated since the Supreme Court's *Dobbs* decision overturned *Roe v. Wade*, producing near hysteria in pro-abortion circles.

Once taken, the drug, and its counterpart, misoprostol, induce a miscarriage. "Excessive bleeding" is a common side effect that, according to a *RealClearInvestigations* report, requires large quantities of blood bags to avoid lethal hemorrhaging.[32]

In September 2000, the FDA-approved mifepristone, to the enthusiastic applause of the pro-choice camp, with one Planned Parenthood board member hailing the drug as a "literal lifeline for abortion rights . . . because it's trained a whole new generation of doctors to perform abortion at a time when the first pioneering generation of doctors" was retiring.[33] Since then, innovative abortion advocates have attempted to market mifepristone and misoprostol over the Internet.

Groups such as TelAbortion and Aid Access now offer online "consultations" and mail-order drugs for women looking to administer their abortions at home—a practice pro-life critics call a "chemical coat hanger."[34] TelAbortion brags that it's induced 3.5 million abortions this way across the United States. Pro-choice activists see it as a way to bypass abortion restrictions, particularly since the U.S. Supreme Court's *Dobbs* decision gave abortion policy back to state legislatures. Meanwhile, litigation involving the circumstances of the FDA's original approval of the drug for abortion—and attempts by lower courts to ban or limit its use—is now reaching the Supreme Court.

Arabella Gets in on the Gynuity Action

Clinical trials of the refined abortifacient are run by Gynuity Health Projects (also called Gynuity Institute), a New York–based company-turned-nonprofit that ultimately wants to sell the drugs online. Gynuity is well connected to the professional abortion industry: Beverly Winikoff, a Gynuity co-founder and board member, was a Population Council staffer for twenty-five years.[35]

Gynuity opted to test it overseas in Armenia, Burkina Faso, Nepal, Vietnam, Moldova, Uzbekistan, and Ukraine—all poor countries.[36] For example, Burkina Faso is a small, utterly destitute, landlocked country of 20 million people in West Africa; almost 44 percent of its people were living at or under the global poverty rate ($1.90 per day) in 2014.

The experiment's subjects were given repeat doses of the drug "every three hours" to induce the "complete evacuation of fetus and placenta . . . within 24 hours."[37] Children were also eligible for the study, and it stopped recruiting only in December 2019.

Gynuity continues to research many aspects of this medication, its composition, administration, follow-up protocols, and complications in less prosperous parts of the world. Recent research posted on its website include a 2021 study with the title "Postpartum Infection, Pain and Experiences with Care among Women Treated for Postpartum Hemorrhage in Three African Countries: A Cohort Study of Women Managed with and without Condom-Catheter Uterine Balloon Tamponade." (The African countries identified in this study are Uganda, Egypt, and Senegal). The website also lists recent research in Mexico and India.

So who's responsible for Gynuity's funding? Gynuity's website reports funding from the Population Council (a population control group) and Planned Parenthood.[38]

Gynuity's research has also received your tax dollars. In 2012, the Obama administration's Department of Health and Human Services awarded Gynuity a $368,000 grant for research into "misoprostol for treatment of fetal death at 14–28 weeks."[39]

And in 2017, Gynuity received $288,000 from the Hopewell Fund, the abortion advocacy arm of the Arabella empire run.[40] (It was given another $217,000 in 2017 from the Wellspring Philanthropic Fund, a little-known "dark money" donor, backed by obscure billionaires, that Capital Research Center has also investigated.)[41]

Between 2003 and 2017, Gynuity raked in $74 million in donations from five foundations (most of it in the last seven years), nearly half of which came from the Buffett Foundation.[42] Its second-biggest foundation donor, at $26.4 million, was the Gates Foundation.

Funding Arabella Advisors' "Dark Money" Activism

We've just seen that Arabella's Hopewell Fund has chipped in to help Gynuity, as has Buffett independently. But what does Buffet's abortion blood money have to do more directly with Arabella? In March 2020, CRC learned that the Buffett Foundation was the single biggest donor to the Hopewell Fund in 2018—which, again, is the abortion arm of the $635 million "dark money" empire run by Arabella Advisors.

When the Hopewell Fund started in 2015, the Buffett Foundation was its second largest donor that year, behind whatever donor(s) were hiding behind a large donation Hopewell was given that year by its "sister" Arabella group, the New Venture Fund. (And the hidden donor could have been the Buffett Foundation, which gave New Venture over $20 million the same year.) In 2016, Hopewell's second year, the Buffett Foundation provided it with half its income, and Hopewell's Form 990 shows it received the other half of its income from a single contribution of $8.5 million in publicly traded securities, which may well have been a gift of Berkshire Hathaway stock from Warren Buffett or Charles Munger.

More recent information indicates that the Hopewell Fund has pulled in nearly $66 million from the Buffett Foundation since 2015.[43] These funds were almost certainly used to support pro-abortion "pop-up" groups—websites that appear to push policies and then pop out of existence—Hopewell's specialty. Buffett has also donated $70 million to Hopewell's "sister" group New Venture Fund.[44]

Under IRS rules, foundations are required to publicly disclose to whom they make grants, though 501(c)(3) charities such as Hopewell *aren't* required to name their donors (only the amounts of their largest donations) in their annual Form 990 filings. This often obscures the money trail, making it nearly impossible for watchdog groups such as Capital Research Center to expose the funders behind an activist group.

In its 2018 IRS Form 990, the Hopewell Fund reported just two anonymous donors: One gave the group $2.3 million, and the other nearly $29 million.[45]

The Buffett Foundation donated $27 million in grants to Hopewell in 2018, making the foundation the largest donor to Hopewell in 2018. (The remaining $2 million may have been gifted after the foundation filed its own Form 990 with the IRS.) The description for each Buffett Foundation grant is the same: "project support," likely referring to one of Hopewell's nine then known "pop-up" groups. But which one?

Obscuring which donor paid for which project is one strength of the Arabella "dark money" system, which is why its biggest clients are the biggest left-wing foundations in America. But considering the Buffett Foundation's deep-pocketed support for abortion on demand, one Hopewell pro-abortion group stands out as the likely 2018 recipient: Resources for Abortion Delivery (RAD).[46]

Almost nothing concrete is known about RAD. Its website is a one-page, seventy-three-word, vague description of its mission: "improv[ing] access to quality abortion care in the United States . . . by supporting the abortion care delivery system" against outside challenges and restrictive laws.[47]

A $200,000 grant in 2017 from the Tara Health Foundation, an abortion funder, indicates that RAD advocates against "burdensome laws" and the "stigmatizing" of abortion.[48] A job listing from earlier in 2020 notes that the group has eight employees and "provides legal and regulatory compliance advice to abortion providers" as well as loans to "independent abortion providers."[49]

RAD was created in 2016 by Bonnie Scott Jones, an abortion movement veteran previously at the Center for Reproductive Rights (also a Buffett grantee). Its leadership includes Meagan Cavanaugh, the former national director of affiliate services for Planned Parenthood. Before that, she was a research manager for the Guttmacher Institute, Planned Parenthood's think tank for abortion research.[50] As noted, the Buffett Foundation has shown its generosity to Guttmacher over the years, donating more than $112 million to it in the last two decades.

RAD co-manages (along with the ACLU, National Abortion Federation, Planned Parenthood, and other aligned organizations) the Abortion Law Project, a public database of abortion laws and regulations across the country.[51] While many of the group's activities remain shrouded, what is known about Resources for Abortion Delivery further reveals the Left's massive network of overlapping abortion groups—and the billions of dollars they receive from secretive mega-donors such as Warren Buffett.

And That's Not All!

Hopewell's pro-abortion outreach is not confined to RAD. At the federal level, during the Trump administration, one front group for a secret money network attacked political appointees at the Department of Health and Human Services (HHS) for opposing the left-wing abortion agenda.

That group was Equity Forward, and the name of its campaign was HHS Watch.[52] Behind them was Arabella Advisors and the Hopewell Fund, according to online job listings.[53]

So, what did "HHS Watch" watch? During Donald Trump's term as president, HHS Watch published opposition research on the Trump administration's appointees, focusing on their work for social conservative groups, especially those smeared by the Southern Poverty Law Center.[54] The campaign further attacked the administration appointees' efforts to overturn provisions in Obamacare that compel religious dissenters to pay for birth control and abortifacient drugs. With the election of Biden in 2020 (as described on Equity Forward's website), HHS Watch pivoted to ensuring that "the Biden-Harris administration is restoring our nation's health department and advancing rights for all people." In other words, more of the same, but for an administration that can be trusted to be working for the same "reproductive health" goals as Equity Forward.

Because Equity Forward is a fiscally sponsored "project" of the Hopewell Fund, identifying its funders definitively is impossible. One of the key perks of donating to Equity Forward, or any other project housed by Arabella's three 501(c)(3) funds, is that donors can make tax-deductible donations while maintaining their anonymity. Watchdogs can see some grants and donations made *to* Hopewell, but after Hopewell has it, the precise route that money takes is at best a matter of educated guesswork.

But the ideological motivation behind the campaign is clear from the résumé of Equity's Forward's first executive director, now senior advisor, Mary Alice Carter.[55] Carter worked for the national Planned Parenthood Federation of America, Physicians for Reproductive Health, the National Institute for Reproductive Health, and the NARAL state affiliate in New York before heading up this Hopewell pop-up campaign.[56]

Arabella "Dark Money" Turns to Funding Dark Humor

Though Hopewell is the abortion "specialist" fund in the Arabella network, it is not the only member of the group to be involved in promoting abortion. Consider the case of Lizz Winstead's unusual outreach over the past seven years. Since 2016, Winstead has led a "dark money" pro-abortion comedy troupe and advocacy organization called Abortion Access Front.[57] It runs a comedy tour—the Vaginal Mystery Tour—to raise awareness for abortion access, and it also maintains a strong social media presence.[58]

Abortion Access Front is a rebranded name: Winstead's brainchild was originally christened Lady Parts Justice League, but in the era of sensitivity to gender fluidity, this name became an embarrassing liability. As their website's "About Us" page explained, "the name was narrow, alienating, and just plain hurtful to many. I want to apologize to all who felt excluded or othered by it. . . . Let's be clear: not all ladies have uteruses. And not everyone with a uterus identifies as a lady. Full stop."

This "coven of hilarious badass feminists who use humor and pop culture to expose the haters" aims to increase awareness of their radical pro-abortion agenda.[59] Winstead herself is proud of her abortion and wants to "normalize" the practice.[60]

While the Abortion Access Front appears to be a stand-alone charity, it is actually a project of NEO Philanthropy where it is a drop in the vast ocean that is NEO's budget.[61] NEO is here using a fiscal sponsorship model similar to the one used by Arabella Advisors and, as we saw in chapter 2, pioneered by the Tides Foundation in the late 1970s.[62] What is unusual about NEO Philanthropy—a pass-through nonprofit created in the 1980s and funded by foundations on the left—is that it often launches these projects without intending to release them from incubation into adulthood. Organizations like Abortion Access Front just work under NEO's IRS designation as a "bona fide 501(c)(3) nonprofit with funding and employees."[63] This circumvention of IRS standard procedures for independent nonprofits helps hide the donors to these more radical activists and allows "charities" like NEO to maintain a positive, more moderate public image.

Winstead's group is structured as two separate organizations: Abortion Access Front and Abortion Access Force.[64] Abortion Access Force (the previously named Lady Parts Justice League) is the advocacy arm of the group. For a while they also shared the same managing director, Kat Green.

My colleagues discovered that, in its dual-organization structure, the group has ties to not one, but *two* enormous left-wing "dark money" networks. Aside from NEO Philanthropy, Abortion Access Force was incubated as a project of an obscure group—Creative Majority—and transferred to the Sixteen Thirty Fund, the lobbying arm of Arabella Advisors' "dark money" empire.[65] Like members of a modern-day blended family, Abortion Access Force and Abortion Access Front are "dark money" siblings with separate mothers. No doubt the hilarious ladies of Abortion Access would find that funny too.

A Victory for Life

Warren Buffet and his Susan Thompson Buffett Foundation have the wealth to keep the pro-abortion camp afloat for years. But here's one positive anecdote for those rooting for the unborn.

In the 1980s and 1990s, a significant portion of the Buffett Foundation's funding came from Berkshire Hathaway itself, which for decades made donations to nonprofits at the direction of the company's shareholders. Between 2002 and 2003, for example, that totaled $18.5 million. And since Warren Buffett himself has always maintained a plurality control of the company, that's translated to tens of millions of dollars given to pro-choice and population control groups over the years.[66]

But the scheme ended in 2003 in a curious set of circumstances.

In 2002, Steven Mosher, president of the pro-life Population Research Institute, gave a lecture before gathered Berkshire Hathaway shareholders that culminated in a resolution that would have barred the company from donating to abortion and population control groups. "What sense does it make for you to be eliminating future Berkshire Hathaway customers? The success of Berkshire Hathaway depends on having customers to buy its products." (The conglomerate owns dozens of name brand companies, including GEICO, See's Candies, Dairy Queen, and Fruit of the Loom.)

Shareholders voted the resolution down. But the next year, Berkshire Hathaway acquired Pampered Chef (a kitchen tool manufacturer) and its network of 67,000 independent sellers, many of them stay-at-home mothers. One of these "kitchen consultants," Cindy Coughlon, objected to association with Berkshire Hathaway since part of the profits from her sales for Pampered Chef would invariably benefit the conglomerate's pro-abortion donations.

Coughlon drafted her own resolution barring Berkshire Hathaway donations to abortion and population control groups, and incredibly, it passed in July 2003. (Aghast, Buffett ceased making corporate contributions entirely.)

Looking Ahead

The abortion activism industry is one of the most powerful pillars of the Left. With a virtually bottomless well of cash to draw upon, it isn't hard to see why. But (almost) all the money in the world wasn't enough to prevent the Supreme Court from overturning *Roe v. Wade* in 2022, sending the issue back to the states in what looks to be a prolonged and contentious battle in state legislatures. Barring a road-to-Damascus conversion, we know which side the Buffet Foundation will be subsidizing, whether through Arabella Advisors' Hopewell Fund, or abortion industry behemoths like Planned Parenthood. But at least the Supreme Court has told Americans that they—not nine robed masters in Washington—now control their own state's laws on this issue.

If only our laws on the environment were controlled by each state, rather than through murky Washington maneuverings by Arabella and megadonors, as we'll see in the next chapter.

6

Co-Equal

Funding Congressional Staff to Attack
Their Environmental Opponents

THROUGHOUT President Donald Trump's time in the White
House, "dark money" activists ran a coordinated campaign to sab-
otage and undermine his administration from the offices of Arabella Advisors in Washington, D.C. After four years of this relentless onslaught,
Trump was ousted, ushering in the most extreme environmentalist regime
in our history under President Joseph Biden. This chapter examines the
Arabella network's funding of the professional Left's years-long campaign
to undermine President Trump's Department of the Interior, which laid
the groundwork for the Biden administration's crusade for environmental
policies so radical that they involve not merely the loss of Americans' gas
stoves but also their gas-powered cars and trucks.[1]

"Keep It in the Ground"

The U.S. Department of the Interior is primarily responsible for managing roughly 450 million acres of federal land and conserving the natural

resources there, most critically, vast reserves of oil and natural gas.[2] The department oversees the *majority* of land in states like Alaska, Idaho, Nevada, and Utah, and more than a third of the land in states like California and Wyoming.[3] Interior manages hundreds of dams and reservoirs, regulates drilling on public lands, runs the National Park Service, and maintains public monuments.

The department also plays a role in foreign diplomacy and national security. Under President Trump, that role included international wildlife trafficking bans, encouraging trade of precious metals and rare earths, and promoting his Indo-Pacific security and economic strategy.[4]

But the Trump-era Interior's openness to expanding oil and gas production brought the sharpest attacks from the Left. Since the department and its lands are entirely under the president's purview, halting all drilling on public land is far easier than attempting to halt private oil and gas production nationwide—the radical Left's expressed ultimate goal.

"The natural place to start phasing out supply is on our public lands and oceans where a ban on new leasing will keep up to 450 billion tons of carbon pollution in the ground," Center for Biological Diversity director Kieran Suckling said in 2015.[5] Bill McKibben, founder of the far-left 350.org, agrees, "public lands are one of the easiest places for us to control the flow of carbon into the atmosphere."[6]

Unsurprisingly, that's been the policy of Democratic presidents and their activist allies for years. President Barack Obama canceled lease sales in the Arctic and Atlantic offshore sites and banned the leasing of coal on federal lands. Phasing down "extraction of fossil fuels from our public lands" was in the Democratic Party's 2016 platform.[7] That same year a 350.org activist asked Democratic presidential nominee Hillary Clinton what she meant by "extraction on public lands is a done deal?" Clinton replied, "That's where [President Obama] is moving: No future extraction. I agree with that."[8] Her running mate, Virginia senator Tim Kaine, later assured another 350.org activist that "I actually am now in that position."[9]

But even "phasing down" is too conservative for today's "keep it in the ground" Left. No fewer than twenty Democratic presidential hopefuls vowed to ban drilling on public lands outright during their party's 2020 primary.[10] On January 27, 2021—exactly one week after his inauguration—President Biden indefinitely suspended development of new oil and gas wells on public lands, which the left-leaning *San Francisco Chronicle* cheered as "a first step to halting the granting of federal drilling leases permanently."[11]

Why does this matter? Federal lands account for roughly 24 percent of America's oil, natural gas, and coal production.[12] In 2019, when Trump was still in office, total crude oil production reached an all-time high of 4.471 billion barrels, with a significant chunk of that growth coming from oil drilled on federal lands.[13] Biden's ban blocks future development of these key resources, removing them from the supply stream and hampering the energy independence the United States struggled to achieve in recent years. This means higher gasoline and household electricity prices, an estimated $11.3 billion in lost federal royalties and rental fees, and the elimination of hundreds of thousands of jobs across the economy.[14]

So, going back to January 2017, as Trump assumed office, the stakes for the Left couldn't have been higher. Thus Arabella turned its guns on Trump's Department of the Interior using a pair of pop-up organizations: Western Values Project (WVP) and its "sister," Western Values Project Action (WvPA).[15]

According to their websites, WVP and WvPA were created in 2013 in Helena, Montana, to expose corrupt corporate lobbyists preying on public lands in the West. In reality, WVP is run by the 501(c)(3) "charity" New Venture Fund in Washington, D.C., while WvPA is run by the 501(c)(4) nonprofit Sixteen Thirty Fund, Arabella's in-house lobbying shop. Whatever staff the groups actually have were likely paid by one of Arabella's nonprofits or possibly by Arabella Advisors itself; we're unlikely ever to know. But in its 2018 Form 990, New Venture Fund revealed that it is the "paymaster" for Sixteen Thirty Fund (which reported zero employees on its own 2018 Form 990) and "pays the salary and immediately invoices Sixteen Thirty Fund, which reimburses the full amount."[16]

Case Study: Co-Equal

As we've repeatedly seen in this book, it's common for groups to use both kinds of nonprofits to maximize their ability to lobby through the 501(c)(4) and fundraise through the 501(c)(3) "charity," since donors may deduct donations to the charity from their taxes. Arabella takes that tactic to another level, using pop-up fronts for its nonprofits that can take advantage of the New Venture and Sixteen Thirty Fund's respective tax advantages without disclosing their relationship to one another. Donations to WVP and WvPA in fact benefitted the Arabella-run nonprofits behind the projects.

Until late 2019 the website for WVP and WvPA revealed a handful of staffers, including Chris Saeger, ex-communications director for the Montana Democratic Party and former Service Employees International Union (SEIU) staffer; Jayson O'Neill, a Democratic staffer for Montana's legislature and Gov. Brian Schweitzer (D); and Yetta Stein, a staffer for the left-wing political action committee End Citizens United and staffer for the 2018 reelection campaign of Sen. Jon Tester (D-MT).[17] The archived website also showed a small advisory board consisting of:[18]

- Kjersten Forseth, a former chief of staff for Colorado State Senate Democrats, former director of the left-wing strategy group ProgressNow Colorado, political director for the Colorado AFL-CIO, and chief political strategist for Rocky Mountain Voter Outreach, a Denver-based get-out-the-vote and ballot initiative firm.[19]

- Kent Salazar, an environmental health manager for Albuquerque, New Mexico, former New Mexico State game commissioner for Gov. Bill Richardson (D), and a board member for the left-wing National Wildlife Federation.[20]

- Pat Smith, a lawyer representing Indian tribes in Montana, member of the 2010 Montana Redistricting Commission, and appointee of Montana gov. Steve Bullock (D) to the Northwest Power and Conservation Council.

WVP's advisory board also included Caroline Ciccone, who in 2019 was executive director of the New Venture Fund pop-up and anti-Trump "oversight" group Restore Public Trust.[21] Ciccone is a former communications director for the Democratic National Committee (DNC), Obama appointee to the U.S. Small Business Administration, and Democratic strategist. From 2014 to 2017 she led Americans United for Change (AUFC), a top left-wing strategy group whose national field director, Scott Foval, was recorded in late 2016 by undercover journalists from Project Veritas bragging that AUFC had paid mentally ill and homeless people to instigate violence at Trump campaign rallies.[22] Within days of the video's release, Foval was fired.

Also on the WVP advisory board was Kyle Herrig, a former New Venture Fund board member who sat on the advisory boards of at least five New Venture Fund projects, including American Oversight, a judicial activist and litigation group; Allied Progress, which attacked Trump cabinet officials; and the Ciccone-run Restore Public Trust.[23]

In early 2020 it was announced that Western Values Project and these three Arabella "pop-ups" were being rolled into one new organization: Accountable.US, *itself* a former New Venture Fund project established as an independent nonprofit sometime later that year, headed by president Kyle Herrig and executive director Caroline Ciccone.[24] (Sixteen Thirty Fund listed Western Values Project Action as a trade name in its Form 990 for fiscal years 2017 and 2018.[25] 2018 was the last year that the Sixteen Thirty Fund listed trade names as required.) In other words, far from being a grassroots group, Western Values Project is enmeshed in a deeply networked, highly coordinated cabal of professional activists.

Anatomy of an Arabella Campaign

From 2017 to 2018, WVP ran an all-out attack against Trump administration secretary of the interior Ryan Zinke, publishing post after post savaging Zinke and his staff.[26] (We introduced readers to native Montanan Ryan Zinke in chapter 1, where we told the story of Arabella's original proof-of-concept project: Responsible Trails America.) WVP even published a massive website, DepartmentofInfluence.org, which compiled boatloads of data on nearly every appointee to the Trump administration's Department of the Interior.[27] The group's goal was clear: drive Ryan Zinke out of office and undermine the department's policies. They finally succeeded in December 2018, and Zinke resigned in early January 2019, amid ethics complaints alleging he had misused public funds during official travel and spent large sums on frivolous things.[28]

My colleagues at the Capital Research Center have counted nine Freedom of Information Act (FOIA) cases filed by WVP between April 2017 and Zinke's resignation, all sporting WVP's supposed address: a UPS store in Whitefish, Montana (704C 13th St. E., #568, Whitefish, MT 59937).[29] As investigative reporter Dave Skinner points out, "'Suite 568' is actually a $150-per-year private mail box, snugged next to a sales placard touting a 'street address, not a P.O. box number.'"[30]

In these complaints WVP describes itself as "a not-for-profit public interest organization" and "a tax-exempt organization within the meaning of Section 501(c)(3) of the Internal Revenue Code," never mentioning its status as a project of the New Venture Fund or its connection to Arabella Advisors.[31] At least one FOIA request was co-filed with American Oversight, another former New Venture Fund pop-up run by Kyle Herrig that also used a UPS Store address in its filings (1030 15th St., NW, Suite B255, Washington, D.C. 20005) and describes itself as "a nonpartisan, non-profit section 501(c)(3) organization."[32]

These FOIA complaints exclusively targeted the Department of the Interior. Highlights include:

- requesting Zinke's travel receipts, "a daily schedule of the Secretary's events, meetings and activities including locations and attendees";[33]
- seeking correspondence between department heads and members of various oil and gas interests, such as the American Petroleum Institute, Colorado Oil and Gas Association, and Independent Petroleum Association of America;[34]
- demanding access to all records, emails, and expenditures pertaining to Lolita Zinke, Ryan Zinke's wife;[35]

- asserting that Zinke threatened Alaska Republican senators Lisa Murkowski and Dan Sullivan for voting against the 2017 effort to repeal Obamacare;[36] and
- multiple FOIA complaints complaining that the department had not complied with prior FOIA complaints.[37]

On October 22, 2018, the Department of the Interior's Office of Inspector General released its investigative report into Zinke's alleged ethics abuses and referred the matter to the Department of Justice.[38] The office noted that it "initiated this investigation" in December 2017, "based on information we received while investigating [Zinke's] use of noncommercial aircraft for U.S. Governmental travel." The source of that information isn't named, but it isn't a stretch to believe it originated with Western Values Project.

Eight days later on October 30, 2019, WVP released its statement on the probe, calling on Zinke to resign.[39] It also launched a website (Has-RyanZinkeBeenFiredYet.com) demanding the same.[40] On November 9, WVPA released a $30,000 attack ad in seven Montana newspapers accusing Zinke of having "priorities" that were "upside down" and calling for his resignation—all presumably paid for by the Sixteen Thirty Fund, which controls WVPA's finances.[41] One month later Zinke resigned.

Big Green's Campaign Rolls On

Joining WVP and WVPA was the Center for Western Priorities (CWP), a front for the California mega-activist group Resources Legacy Fund— by Capital Research Center's count the sixteenth-largest environmentalist group in the country, spending over $42 million in 2018 alone.[42] CWP painted Zinke as a feckless tool of the oil and gas industry, accusing him of "following President Trump's marching orders to attack our public lands" and fomenting an "illegal attack on America's national monuments."[43] When Zinke resigned in December 2018, CWP labeled him "the most anti-conservation Interior Secretary of all time."[44]

Almost immediately after Zinke's resignation, CWP and WVP turned their guns on Deputy Secretary of the Interior David Bernhardt, who became acting secretary on January 2, 2019, and was officially confirmed in April.

Bernhardt had served in the George W. Bush administration's Department of the Interior, leaving in 2009 as the department's solicitor.[45] After that he led the Denver firm Brownstein Hyatt Farber Schreck's natural resources law practice, where his clients included Halliburton Energy Services and the Independent Petroleum Association of America, and he lobbied for Cobalt International Energy and Samson Resources.[46] Before his appointment to the Trump administration, Bernhardt was also registered as a lobbyist for the Westlands Water District in California's San Joaquin Valley.[47]

On December 17, CWP policy director Jesse Prentice-Dunn published a long hit piece calling Bernhardt a "walking conflict of interest" who would continue "Ryan Zinke's culture of corruption" and accusing the department of shilling for big oil.[48] That same day WVP published the website DavidBernhardt.org, calling Bernhardt "the ultimate DC swamp creature" and an "ex-lobbyist who is too conflicted to be Interior Secretary," while detailing a laundry list of ethics charges in an attempt to derail his confirmation to the post.[49] Memos about Bernhardt's background and conflicts of interest and more FOIA requests followed from WVP and Center for Western Priorities, including one from Democracy Forward, a leftist litigation group created in 2017 by Clinton crony Marc Elias (of Perkins Coie and Steele dossier fame) to target the Trump administration.[50]

In February, the Campaign for Accountability, a former "pop-up" of the Arabella-run Hopewell Fund, petitioned the Interior Department inspector general to investigate Bernhardt's ties to Westlands Water District as a conflict of interest and urged the Senate to reject his confirmation.[51] Campaign for Accountability, which specialized in targeting Trump political appointees, was founded by alumni of another left-wing litigation group, Citizens for Responsibility and Ethics in Washington (CREW), and has been represented by the ex-Arabella pop-up American Oversight in past lawsuits.[52]

The Center for American Progress joined in, labeling Bernhardt "the most conflicted Trump Cabinet nominee."[53] Greenpeace and the Center for Biological Diversity urged the department's inspector general to investigate those conflicts of interest, melodramatically declaring him "the most dangerous man in America for endangered species and public lands."[54] The Sierra Club demanded that the Senate reject his confirmation, as did the National Parks Conservation Association and the Natural Resources Defense Council.[55]

In March, WvPA launched a six-figure television ad buy targeting Democratic senator Martin Heinrich (NM) and moderate Republican senators Cory Gardner (CO) and Martha McSally (AZ) to oppose Bernhardt's confirmation.[56] The assault continued until the Senate confirmed Bernhardt in April 2019. From then on, the group's crusade against Trump's Department of the Interior focused on thwarting its agenda.

Harried Until the End

WVP filed another five FOIA requests against the Department of the Interior between 2019 and 2020, almost certainly with the intent of discovering ammo for future ethics complaints. Among its requests were all communications between the department and Bernhardt's former clients from Brownstein Hyatt and the Westlands Water District as well as copies of all text messages sent by Secretary David Bernhardt from July 1, 2017 through February 2020. The leftist website *Outside Online* even set up a "David Bernhardt Scandal Tracker" days after his confirmation.[57]

But much of the Left's campaign shifted to halting Trump's supposed war on public lands until he left office in January 2021. "Yes, Trump really is coming to take your public lands," WVP howled in late 2019, claiming the administration was selling off federal land to oil interests bent on pillaging it.[58] In reality, the Bureau of Land Management (which is part of the Interior Department) continued to *lease* lands to drilling companies in five-to-ten-year options, a decades-old practice. As a result, oil and gas production soared in 2019, particularly in New Mexico and Wyoming, which sit atop massive deposits.

The Department of the Interior disbursed a staggering $11.69 billion to the states in 2019 alone from energy production on federal and Indian-owned lands, a $2.76 billion increase over 2018.[59] Gasoline prices dropped from a nationwide average of $2.813 in 2018 to $2.691 in 2019 to $2.258 in 2020.[60] And the United States achieved energy independence in 2019, with energy production exceeding consumption for the *first time* since 1957.[61] In a single year, energy production increased by an impressive 5.7 percent, with so-called fossil fuels accounting for 80 percent of all energy production and consumption that year.[62]

WVP harried Trump and his cabinet out of office, blasting "Secretary David Bernhardt's Wildly Destructive Track Record" in December 2020—after the 2020 election had prompted Trump's political appointees to begin packing up.[63] The list of Bernhardt's supposed destructive acts included such silly accusations as Bernhardt's staging Trump's May 2020 Fox News town hall inside the Lincoln Memorial, allowing national parks to be used as "centerpieces" for his reelection campaign, and holding "expensive military-infused Independence Day rallies on the National Mall" (the horror!).

Targeting Trump's energy and environmental policies was among Biden's first moves in office. He canceled a planned expansion to the Keystone oil pipeline, pledged to protect 30 percent of U.S. land and water by 2030, and froze new leases for oil and gas development on federal land.

Biden's nominee for the department, Rep. Debra Haaland (D-NM), was confirmed in March 2021, in a nearly party-line vote (four Republicans joined with every Democrat in the Senate).[64] Haaland has been criticized by conservatives as a far-left extremist with a perfect 2020 score and 98 percent lifetime score from the League of Conservation Voters, which ranks politicians for their fidelity to leftist environmental legislation (and is one of the most powerful "dark money" operations on either side of the aisle).[65] Incidentally, Haaland also received a 100 percent score from the pro-abortion groups Planned Parenthood and NARAL Pro-Choice America.[66] While Haaland told Congress during her confirmation process that fossil fuels "will continue to play a major role in America for years to come," she's a global warming ideologue who during her 2018 reelection campaign trumpeted her commitment to "keep fossil fuels in the ground," voting "against all new fossil fuel infrastructure," and transitioning to "100% clean energy."[67]

In May 2021, the Biden administration proposed ramping up the Interior Department's 2022 budget by $2.5 billion (17 percent) to $17.6 billion in order to "address the climate crisis" and create "good-paying union jobs."[68] Biden stated that he wants to conserve 30 percent of U.S. lands and waters by 2030 (it's currently about 26 percent), a plan proposed by liberal groups in the states as "30 by 30"—using the justification that the measure would "slow climate change" by storing carbon dioxide in plants and soil.[69] He has also proposed spending $86 million on the "Civilian Climate Corps," a reboot of Franklin Roosevelt's New Deal–era Civilian Conservation Corps. And he sought $300 million for "plugging orphan oil and gas wells" and $249 million to boost renewable energy production on public lands.

Science Moms

Not surprisingly, climate activism is another target for streams of Arabella "dark money." One good example of how this operates is Science Moms. You might know them from the ads on streaming services and YouTube bearing the same message of doom-and-gloom fanaticism: "Climate change (aka global warming) is real, and our kids' future is at risk," while "real climate science is not up for debate." The clear message is that mothers must elect politicians who support the Left's extreme climate agenda—or else.

Science Moms, whose name certainly suggests an outfit run entirely by women, is really a front for the Potential Energy Coalition, an activist group founded by two men: John Marshall and Daniel Schrag.[70] Marshall's background is in brand design and advertising. Schrag—a professor of geology and environmental science at Harvard—supports the abolition of coal and total electrification of all vehicles in the United States.[71] He also served on President Obama's (heavily politicized) science advisory council from 2009 to 2017.

But Potential Energy Coalition is itself apparently operated by the Windward Fund, one of Arabella Advisors' in-house nonprofits.[72] In 2019 Windward Fund reported paying the Coalition $1 million for unspecified "consulting services." That same year, however, the William & Flora Hewlett Foundation paid Windward Fund $1.5 million "for the Potential Energy Coalition project," and Windward received another $75,000 "to support the Potential Energy Coalition" from the McKnight Foundation.[73] Both are regular donors to the Arabella network and liberal political causes. And in 2021, the KR Foundation—which makes grants to address "the root causes of climate change" and fight "misinformation"—gave Windward Fund $822,456 for the "Potential Energy Coalition pilot phase."[74]

Yet Potential Energy Coalition reported revenues of just $100,100 in 2018 and less than $50,000 in 2019. Where did the rest of the money go?

The answers no doubt connect to its strange relationship with the Windward Fund. Job listings misleadingly presented the coalition as "a small, flexible nonprofit," yet noted it's a project of the decidedly not-so-small Windward Fund (2020 revenues: $158 million).[75] The coalition's Form 990 said in 2020, "The Chairman and Treasurer/Secretary of potential energy are employed by the Windward Fund, a 501(c)(3) public charity organization that incubates new and innovative public interest projects and grant-making programs. Their salaries are paid by and reported on the Form 990 of the Windward Fund. A portion of these salaries are included in in-kind donated services within this 990."[76] So Windward "donated" the services of two of the coalition's officers. One of them, secretary/treasurer David Wigder (who has since departed), is listed as one of Windward's top employees earning $210,000. Windward's Form 990 for 2020 also says it paid $1 million to the coalition for "consulting services." Another $950,000 was paid for "consulting services" in 2021, when Windward also provided the coalition with a $4.5 million grant.

Although the coalition's privacy policy (current as of September 2021) calls the group a 501(c)(3) nonprofit, its address is a multimillion-dollar private home in the tony Boston suburb of Newton, Massachusetts (median household income: $151,068).[77]

When my colleagues wrote about the Potential Energy Coalition in 2022, it couldn't be reached for comment on its affiliation with Windward Fund or questions about how its staff and leadership are compensated.

Potential Energy Coalition is only one of Windward's environmental initiatives, and it has plenty of money to play with. Windward Fund pulled in $274 million in 2021 and paid $4.2 million to Arabella Advisors in consulting fees.[78] Windward's top anonymous donor contributed $59 million to the environmental group. Major grants from Windward in 2021 included:

- $1.4 million to the League of Conservation Voters;[79]
- $725,000 to Blueprint North Carolina, an anti-voter integrity policy group;[80]
- $10 million to Carbon Mapper, which seeks to "accelerate local climate action";[81] and
- $4.5 million to Potential Energy Coalition, which runs the global warming alarmist group Science Moms.[82]

In addition, Windward engaged in the usual circle of payments to its sister funds: In 2021, it paid $225,000 to New Venture Fund, $150,000 to North Fund, $500,000 to Sixteen Thirty Fund, and $25,000 to Hopewell Fund. All told, the five nonprofit sisters paid almost $47 million in consulting fees to the for-profit Arabella Advisors in 2021. The nonprofits and Arabella shuffled an amazing $98 million among themselves the same year.

Pebble Mine

Although Windward Fund has been engaged in much of Arabella's specifically environmental-themed campaigning, other members of the Arabella network have also pushed a left-wing environmental agenda. In recent years, an Alaska mining project called Pebble Mine has garnered intense scrutiny from the environmental Left, which is desperate to kill it in the cradle. Arabella entities have piled on here as well.

Pebble Mine is a mineral exploration project in southwest Alaska that's been locked in intense legal battles for nearly fifteen years. It has the potential to supply as much as 25 percent of the United States' copper needs over the next century—a critical metal used in everything from refrigerators and smart phones to the electric cars and wind turbines so beloved by environmentalists.[83]

In fact, copper is *essential* to electric vehicles; according to the Copper Development Association, up to 49 pounds of copper are used in the construction of petroleum-powered cars, whereas electric cars can require as much as 183 pounds of copper to build.[84] And copper is even more valuable in the construction of wind and solar power sources, which couldn't exist without the metal. Each wind turbine, for example, requires some 800 pounds of copper to be built.[85]

Considering its value to the construction of renewable energy sources like wind and solar, one might expect left-wing groups to be the loudest voices in support of the Pebble project. But there's little consistency from the "keep-it-in-the-ground" crowd, which happily demands renewable energy production while protesting the means to generate it.

Washington, D.C.–based mega-lobbying groups, including the Natural Resources Defense Council (NRDC), Sierra Club, and Greenpeace, aided by front groups for D.C. "dark money" funders, are all aligned against the project. The NRDC has claimed the mine would pit an "eternal supply of food against an eternal supply of poison," absurdly casting Pebble as a scheme by money-grubbing miners to pump toxins into Bristol Bay.[86]

Bizarrely, the League of Conservation Voters even painted the mine as an insidious effort by Pebble to *intentionally* pollute Alaskan waters.[87] (Pebble's primary backer is based in Canada, our friendly neighbors to the north).

The Left has coalesced its efforts to halt Pebble around the so-called Save Bristol Bay campaign, which alleges that Pebble will destroy the venerable salmon fishing industry. But once again, names can be deceiving:

Save Bristol Bay isn't even headquartered in Alaska; it's a front for also-inappropriately named Trout Unlimited, a D.C.–based group run by radical eco-activists masquerading as "conservationists."[88]

Trout Unlimited is a classic decoy funded by left-wing foundations to fool viewers and the gullible media into thinking it's a sportsmen's group. Although it's true the group's original founders in the 1950s were conservation-minded fishermen, it's since been taken over by liberals closely connected to the professional Left. The group is led by Chris Wood, a member of President Barack Obama's 2008 transition team.[89] Nowadays it receives tens of millions of dollars from the Nature Conservancy and the Gates, Hewlett, and Wyss Foundations.[90]

The Save Bristol Bay campaign is being waged alongside SalmonState, where we arrive at the Arabella connection: SalmonState is an Arabella "pop-up" group for one of Arabella's 501(c)(3) nonprofits, the New Venture Fund.[91] So donations to SalmonState in reality go to the New Venture Fund—something the group's website failed to mention in 2019, when my colleagues called them out on it, though now the "Donate" page is more honest.[92]

Another player in the campaign against Pebble Mine is the deceptively named Alaska Center, another eco-activist group that wants you to know "Alaskans deserve a fair process" when it comes to Pebble, "not one hijacked by D.C. lobbyists and foreign companies."[93]

But by its own admission, the Alaska Center's top three donors in 2019 were the Sixteen Thirty Fund (Arabella's lobbying shop), the League of Conservation Voters, and the Tides Advocacy Fund.[94] The first two are headquartered in D.C., the last in San Francisco (in other words, very much *not* Alaska), and all are prominent "dark money" advocacy groups responsible for funding the activists behind the eco-Left's increasingly radical agenda at the expense of the everyday Americans who benefit from cheap energy and abundant minerals.

The Alaska Center also supports an economy-killing carbon tax similar to the Canadian carbon tax passed in 2018, which has become increasingly unpopular as its burdens on families increase.[95] (In 2023, the Parliamentary Budget Officer released figures showing net losses for Canadian households after accounting for taxes, a tax rebate, higher fuel charges, and lowered incomes. The household losses vary by province but are currently in the hundreds of dollars per year, rising to $1,000 to $2,000 by the decade's end.)[96] In short, the Alaska Center pushes the kinds of extremist policies favored by its rich donors in Washington, D.C., but not necessarily by ordinary Alaskans or any other strapped-for-cash Americans.

Pebble Mine is an opportunity to tap into The Last Frontier's vast abundance, bringing much-needed prosperity to the state, as well as American mineral independence from countries like communist China that have gruesome environmental records. It's a decision Alaskans—not wealthy Beltway activists—need to make, but in January 2023, the Biden administration had the Environmental Protection Agency take what even the Associated Press called, "an unusually strong step" to block the mine, a step others called legally indefensible.[97] The project at this writing remains mired in red tape and litigation.

"Dark Money" behind "Electrification"

Another environmental incursion undertaken by the Democrats during the Biden administration—and generously funded with Arabella dollars—is directed at something disarmingly called "electrification." It may sound innocuous, but it is strongly anti-consumer, and along with other major players in "green" left-wing politics, Arabella Advisors is behind this campaign to cut off every house in America from natural gas and make Americans dependent on electric-only appliances. The campaign is run through Rewiring America, which itself is powered by Arabella's Windward Fund.[98]

Rewiring America—which has received at least $300,000 from the left-wing Rockefeller Brothers Fund since 2020—wants to weaponize the federal budget to subsidize construction of "electrified" houses (including special wiring and electric-only appliances), and pushing "loan-loss guarantees" and "direct assistance to low-to-moderate income households, including renters" to advance its agenda.[99] In other words, it's advocating classic command and control policies that would redistribute wealth to preferred groups and force top-down housing policies on communities.

Soon after the Biden administration moved in, Democrats began pushing their climate bill, the Build Green Act—a $500 billion plan to fight "environmental racism." The legislation included a call for the country to shift entirely to renewable energy and to replace all vehicles with electric cars. Rewiring America praised the legislation for "decarbonizing our economy and meeting the climate challenge."

Many of the bill's provisions, however, were not even related to the climate or the environment. The legislation would redistribute wealth to low-income and minority communities, as well as communities "facing environmental injustice." It would also institute "strong labor provisions" for union workers and establish a $15-per-hour minimum wage.[100]

Liberals frequently use "environmental racism" to justify a host of radical policies. The bill's sponsors claim that "environmental racism" justifies everything from racial reparations payments to single-payer health care. The left-wing Sunrise Movement, which endorsed the legislation, supports abolishing "police and prisons" in order to achieve "climate justice."[101]

President Joe Biden himself invoked "environmental justice" on the campaign trail, calling to have the Justice Department prosecute fossil fuel companies "to the fullest extent permitted by law."[102] The legislation was endorsed by left-wing groups like 350.org, Greenpeace, and Zero Hour, which claims the world has less than nine years left until it's made uninhabitable by global warming.[103]

In January 2021, the Windward Fund hired AJW Inc., which lobbies for environmental groups including the Clean Air Task Force and the Environmental Defense Action Fund.[104] After months of legislative debate and negotiation, many elements of the original Build Green bill (combined with Biden's touted "Build Back Better" framework) were included in the Infrastructure Investment and Jobs Act signed into law in November 2021.

Electrification Rejects What Already Works

Electrification's stated goal is to ward off climate change by minimizing natural gas use. But natural gas is among the least carbon dioxide–intensive energy sources in the world. Increased use of natural gas has lowered the U.S. carbon dioxide emissions over the past few years, far beyond the reductions in most industrialized countries, as the United States switches from oil to cheaper gas—a benefit of the fracking revolution so hated by the Left.

Even the United Nations recently credited rapidly falling U.S. emissions to this widespread adoption of natural gas—*after* President Trump withdrew from the Paris Climate Agreement—which ironically enabled the United States to meet 2020 emissions reduction targets.[105] Yet the sprint to electrification continued to intensify. Rewiring America's June 2021 report detailed the "One Billion Machines" required to reach net zero emissions in time for the United States to comply with the Intergovernmental Panel on Climate Change's global warming goals. The machines identified ranged from space and water heaters to vehicles to cooking appliances.

When the Infrastructure Investment and Jobs Act (IIJA) passed in late 2021, Ari Matusiak, the CEO of Rewiring America applauded the legislation while acknowledging that "much must still be done to decarbonize the supply side of our energy sector." He continued, "Our mission in the year and change that Rewiring America has existed has been to electrify everything, starting with our homes, in a way that helps all Americans." Then, the organization and over sixty left-wing groups hailed the August 2022 Inflation Reduction Act and its $391 billion in spending on energy and climate change to "decarbonize our buildings and homes."

Fast forward to January 2023, when Richard J. Trumka, a U.S. Consumer Product Safety commissioner, stated in an interview with Bloomberg that gas stoves were a safety hazard and banning them could be an option (based on a study by another electrification advocacy group, the Rocky Mountain Institute).[106] The backlash from consumers was so fierce that Trumka walked back his comments within three days. Corporate media rushed to the Biden administration's defense, epitomized by this dishonest headline in the *Philadelphia Inquirer*: "Calm Down, the Government Isn't Coming for Your Gas Stove."[107] Or *Rolling Stone*'s "No, the Government Is Not Seizing Your Gas Stove."[108] Yet the "decarbonation" activism of Arabella's Rewiring America and similar groups stands in stark contrast to the media's claims, giving an entirely new definition to the term, "gaslighting."

In March 2023, Renewing America announced that failed Georgia gubernatorial candidate Stacey Abrams would become its senior counsel and launch an awareness campaign to help America go electric.

And in one more contradiction of the media's claims that activists aren't aiming to overturn Americans' lives, New York governor Kathy Hochul signed the state's fiscal year 2024 budget—including a ban on the use of natural gas in new building construction as soon as 2025.

Arabella's Origins Conveyed Its Future Agenda

It's not surprising that environmental issues have garnered such attention over the years from Arabella Advisors and its nonprofits, given how closely Eric Kessler's early career arc tracked with environmentalist schemes. After all, he started out with the League of Conservation Voters and followed its head to Clinton's Department of the Interior. As we have seen, he now maintains close ties with Biden's Interior appointees.

Wherever the Left builds up government power and assaults the liberties and way of life of ordinary Americans, there you will find Arabella, its donors, and its activists. Of course, this requires considerable efforts at propaganda, which we will explore in the next chapter.

7

CASE STUDY

The Hub Project

How a Foreign Billionaire Uses Front Groups to Intervene in Elections

IT'S A STORY that goes to the very heart of the Left's mountain of shadowy funding and professional activism: a foreign billionaire infamous for illegally funding Democrats, enriched by selling ghoulish medical treatments that resulted in multiple deaths, and bankrolling a multimillion-dollar "dark money" campaign to transform America.

Meet Swiss-born Hansjörg Wyss (pronounced "Hans-yurg Veese"), perhaps the most important mega-donor you've never heard of. His Wyss Foundation, founded in 1998, quietly commands a stunning $2.7 billion in assets (as of 2021) and annually pours out tens of millions of dollars to activist groups—around a billion dollars between 2002 and 2021—so it's little wonder he's been called the "new George Soros."[1]

Wyss is one of the best-connected mega-donors on the left. He's a member of the Democracy Alliance, a cabal of the rich and powerful that meets regularly to strategize funding to leftist activists (see chapter 9).[2] He's also a substantial contributor to and sits on the board of the Center for American Progress, a leading liberal think tank founded by John Podesta, who chaired Hillary Clinton's failed 2016 presidential campaign.[3] Podesta has reportedly advised Wyss on his funding of public policy efforts, and Podesta and Wyss Foundation president Molly McUsic have collaborated on stealthy nonprofit schemes to win elections for the Democratic Party.[4]

To the degree Wyss is known, it's for his contributions to green groups, such as the Wilderness Society, where he sits on the board along with top lieutenant, McUsic.[5] In the past two decades Wyss has made substantial contributions to environmental groups on the center-left and far-left, including the Sierra Club, Defenders of Wildlife, Trout Unlimited, National Religious Partnership for the Environment, and Natural Resources Defense Council.[6]

But his money extends beyond environmental advocacy. For years Wyss has backed groups involved in getting out the vote for Democratic politicians, such as the League of Conservation Voters, Environment America, and even the infamous ACORN successor group Project Vote (defunct since 2017).[7]

This brand of "philanthropy" has made this billionaire a hero to the same Northeastern Corridor liberals who loathe the very *idea* of billionaires and who howled over foreign meddling in U.S. politics for years after the 2016 election. But the Left's hypocrisy aside, Wyss is the wrong horse to back.

He's declined to tell even the *New York Times* whether he holds U.S. citizenship and as recently as 2014 stated that he does not hold a green card granting permanent residency—and the legal ability to donate to U.S. election campaigns.[8] In 2016 Wyss got into trouble when it was revealed he had contributed $41,000 to Democratic political action committees (PACs) in violation of the federal government's strict ban on foreign nationals giving to U.S. political campaigns.[9] Since 2018, this foreign national has also donated at least $1 million through his foundation to States Newsroom, a bundle of partisan attack sites posing as impartial news outlets but actually spawned by Arabella Advisors.[10]

So it was refreshing in April 2022, when a *New York Times* reporter revealed Wyss's efforts to purchase the parent company of the *Chicago Tribune* and other failing newspapers around the country for $100 million.[11] This reporter's display of genuine investigative journalism came at a time when so many were busy framing Wyss as a liberal white knight bent on saving a venerable American industry.[12]

It's worth recalling that same crowd's horror when the libertarian Koch brothers announced they were considering buying *the same parent company* in 2013: It could "serve as a broader platform for the Kochs' laissez-faire ideas," insisted the Gray Lady; could help the brothers "take on media reports they dispute," groaned the *Washington Post*; and could even "spark [a] 'culture clash,'" warned National Public Radio.[13]

Mute liberals probably played no role in Wyss's rapid change of heart when—just days after the *Times'* exposé—he quietly withdrew his bid for the newspapers, supposedly after reevaluating the *Chicago Tribune's* financial troubles.[14]

The eighty-eight-year-old Wyss will probably never achieve his goal of becoming a media mogul. His *true* legacy will be constructing a key "dark money" group created to help Democrats win elections and enact policy, situated within Arabella's multibillion-dollar network.

No Love for the Limelight

Hansjörg Wyss is famously secretive. The few public interviews he's given largely concern the environment and his deep interest in conservation, prime targets for his giving.

The future Swiss billionaire first came to the United States as a graduate student in 1958 and took a job as a surveyor for the Colorado Highway Department. The Rocky Mountains reminded him of the Swiss Alps, he explained in 2017, and he was particularly impressed with America's system of national parks compared with Europe's, where many natural areas are "privately owned, developed, or otherwise off-limits to the public."[15] Besides environmental activism, Wyss funds genuine philanthropy and is a major donor to universities, including Harvard's Wyss Institute for Biologically Inspired Engineering.[16]

Wyss made his fortune as the head of Synthes USA, a major medical implants and biomaterials manufacturer that he built from practically nothing and sold to Johnson & Johnson in 2012 for $19.7 billion. Today, Wyss is worth an estimated $9.4 billion.[17]

Yet his success is marred by the macabre. In 2009, Synthes—with Wyss at its head—was charged by Philadelphia's U.S. attorney with running illegal clinical trials on humans: injecting them with a cement that turns to bone inside the human skeleton. The Food and Drug Administration (FDA) reportedly told the company not to use the cement during spine surgeries, but Synthes ignored the warning, and five people died as a result. Four of Synthes's top executives were ultimately sentenced to prison. One wonders if liberal billionaire privilege saved Wyss from sharing the blame—he wasn't charged by prosecutors—since he's been accused of purposefully ignoring clinical trials and of being a "hands-on," "forceful," "800-pound gorilla" who allowed little dissent in the ranks.[18]

Add to that allegations of sexual assault in 2011 leveled against Wyss by a female former employee in New Jersey in late 2017, while the pair were staying at a hotel in Morris County.[19] It's unclear how the case was resolved.

Whatever the truth may be, it's hard to shake the sense that Wyss is both a genuine conservationist and a liberal technocrat, using his vast wealth to try to control a country to which he refuses allegiance. Nothing better illustrates Wyss's brand of paternalism than his longstanding relationship with the largest "dark money" network in politics.

The Hub Project: Born in "Dark Money"

The story begins in 2015, when the consulting firm Civitas Public Affairs Group—whose clients include the pro-gun-control Brady Campaign and the Voter Participation Center, a Democratic get-out-the-vote "charity"—produced a private report for the Wyss Foundation outlining a plan for a "communications hub."[20] (It's unknown exactly how much the foundation paid for the report, but from 2015 to 2018 it paid over $442,000 to Civitas.)

Seventeen members of the professional Left were interviewed for the report, representing such groups as Pew Charitable Trusts, the attack group Media Matters for America, the Center for American Progress (where Wyss is a board member), American Civil Liberties Union (ACLU), abortion giant NARAL Pro-Choice America, the Brennan Center, and the Center for Popular Democracy (famous for assaulting Arizona Republican senator Jeff Flake in an elevator during a Supreme Court nomination battle).[21]

This hub would support the foundation's "core issue areas," creating "research-based message frames" to "drive measurable change" and achieve "significant wins," which in turn would "dramatically shift the public debate and policy positions of core decision makers," "leading to implementation of policy solutions at the local, state, and federal level." In other words, it would elect Democrats and make public policy.

The IRS strictly prohibits 501(c)(3) nonprofits from contributing to or intervening in political campaigns "on behalf of (or in opposition to) any candidate," period.[22] Foundations, which fall under the 501(c)(3) rules, are subject to even stricter rules concerning funding of voter registration and lobbying activity than 501(c)(3) charities.[23]

From the start, the hub was "solely funded by the Wyss Foundation," yet its ties to the foundation were intentionally hidden. The Civitas report even recommends it be dissociated from the Wyss Foundation so as to "give the foundation appropriate separation from the hub's work" and "allow the hub to engage in a more robust way than it could if it was based within the foundation." In other words, the hub was designed to be hidden, precisely *to allow the foundation to bypass the IRS prohibition on intervening in elections.*

Instead, the hub would be set up as an "independent organization with a fiscal sponsor." Its advisory board would consist of Wyss Foundation officials, who would receive quarterly reports on its progress. These arrangements made the hub a front group for an established liberal nonprofit that specializes in incubating new advocacy groups. That sponsor, the plan explains, would need to have the "flexibility to work across the spectrum of 501(c)(3), (h) election, and 501(c)(4) activities"—references to the lobbying caps the IRS places on different kinds of nonprofits. And the sponsor would need to set aside "15 to 25 percent of the budget for (c)(4) work funded by The Wyss Action Fund" (more on that later).

Not many fiscal sponsors fit that description in 2015. One stands out: Arabella Advisors, the then obscure consultancy whose network of (then) four in-house nonprofits already commanded a staggering $332 million in revenues in 2015 alone.[24]

As we've explained earlier, each of these nonprofits manages a host of "pop-up" groups, websites designed to fool viewers into believing they're grassroots activist groups. The New Venture Fund alone claims to have launched close to 500 "projects," with more appearing all the time.

So it isn't difficult to guess the kind of results the Wyss Foundation expected when it began funneling millions of dollars ($57 million from 2007 to 2020) into the New Venture Fund, Arabella's flagship 501(c)(3) "charity."[25]

The "communications hub" described in the 2015 Civitas report is strikingly similar to an existing Arabella group launched in January 2017—the Hub Project.[26] The Hub Project consists of two organizations: an action arm fronting for the Sixteen Thirty Fund, Arabella's 501(c)(4) lobbying wing, and a research arm fronting for the "charity" New Venture Fund.[27] Many of Arabella's groups use this kind of pairing scheme, maximizing their respective tax status advantages for lobbying and fundraising.

The Hub Project has been busy trying to flip Congress and the White House since its founding. As the *New York Times'* reporter puts it, "the Hub Project came out of the idea that Democrats should be more effective in conveying their arguments through the news media and directly to voters."[28]

Early on the group organized a series of marches in 2017 to demand President Trump's tax returns. *Politico* reports the group and its fellow Sixteen Thirty allies aided Democrats on "health care, taxes and the economy" in the 2018 midterm elections.[29] The *Atlantic* cheerfully credits the Hub Project with doing "remarkable damage" to President Trump's reputation among Wisconsin voters in the lead-up to the 2020 election.[30] In April 2021, the group hired a campaign director whose last job was flipping the Senate in 2020 for a top Democratic PAC.[31]

An Indirect Strategy

The Hub Project doesn't contribute directly to campaigns. As its name implies, it provides messaging strategies and research to *other* groups involved in elections and issues like D.C. statehood and abolishing the filibuster.

But in good Arabella fashion the Hub Project links up with *other* Arabella-run groups to form a constellation of make-believe grassroots advocacy organizations: Arizonans United for Health Care, Floridians for a Fair Shake, Keep Iowa Healthy, New Jersey for a Better Future, North Carolinians for a Fair Economy, and Opportunity Wisconsin have been identified so far.[32] Each of these groups is, in reality, run by Arabella's Sixteen Thirty Fund, but acts like a tentacle of the Hub Project, further obscuring the network's connection to Arabella.

The Hub Project's staffers come from the Obama administration, Democratic PACs, and a panoply of activist groups. Its founding director, Arkadi Gerney, is an old Arabella hand who has held senior positions with New York mayor Michael Bloomberg's administration, the Bloomberg-funded Everytown for Gun Safety, and the Center for American Progress Action Fund (the lobbying arm of the think tank where Wyss is a board member).[33] Between 2016 and 2018 (and possibly before) he was a project director for the New Venture Fund (2018 compensation: $339,517), and he's also listed in Sixteen Thirty Fund's 2019 Form 990 (total compensation: $145,468 to work eight hours per week, amounting to just under $350 per hour).

A Foundation with a Lobbying Arm?

Enter the Berger Action Fund, founded in 2007 with the name of Wyss Action Fund.[34] It is perhaps the most unusual piece of the puzzle. Foundations are typically wary of associating themselves with 501(c)(4) advocacy nonprofits because of the strict limits the IRS places on foundations' political activities. But the Berger Action Fund is *formally listed* as the

Wyss Foundation's advocacy arm on its Form 990—a phenomenon rarely if ever seen, though regular (c)(3) charities, as opposed to (c)(3) foundations like Wyss, often operate with a (c)(4) arm—because the two groups share "personnel and facilities," for which the foundation reimbursed the lobbying arm with $173,012 between 2017 and 2018.[35]

It was formally renamed in 2016, presumably after Wyss's sister Susi Berger (née Susanna Ottilia Franziska Wyss, 1938–2019), a notable graphic artist and furniture designer in Switzerland. It's unclear what triggered the change, but it's possible that greater scrutiny of Wyss and his foundation in 2015–2016 led to this distancing of his foundation from its action arm.

No donors to Berger Action Fund are known, but between 2017 and 2018 the Wyss Foundation paid $173,012 to the lobbying group as "payment from organization for shared personnel and facilities." Berger paid out nearly $272.5 million in grants to leftist groups between 2008 and 2021, including six- and seven-figure grants to the League of Conservation Voters (called a "'dark money' heavyweight" by a left-leaning watchdog), Planned Parenthood Action Fund, and the Center for Popular Democracy Action Fund, the lobbying wing of an ACORN agitation group successor funded by labor unions and a favorite of the Democracy Alliance.[36]

Berger's most notable grants are $12.4 million to Arabella's Sixteen Thirty Fund and $1.3 million to the New Venture Fund (2010–2017). Berger didn't specify how those funds were spent in its Form 990, but the grants likely bankrolled the Hub Project. We may never know, though, because officials from Arabella Advisors, the Hub Project, the Sixteen Thirty Fund, the New Venture Fund, the Wyss Foundation, and the Berger Action Fund declined to comment to the *New York Times* about their finances.

Leadership Ties to the Arabella Network

The ties connecting Wyss to the Arabella network—and possibly Arabella's very origins—began in the Clinton administration. Wyss Foundation president Molly McUsic (2021 total compensation: $565,679) and Arabella

Advisors' founder Eric Kessler both worked for Clinton administration interior secretary Bruce Babbitt (1993–2001), the former Democratic governor of Arizona (1978–1987) and aggressive environmental regulator.[37]

As discussed in chapter 1, it's unclear how closely McUsic and Kessler worked together, but both were political appointees from the broader activist world. Kessler came from the League of Conservation Voters, where he directed field operations.[38] McUsic, who served on Babbitt's legal counsel team, clerked for the liberal U.S. Supreme Court justice Harry A. Blackmun (author of the Court's opinion in *Roe v. Wade*) and U.S. Ninth Circuit Court of Appeals judge Dorothy W. Nelson, a Carter appointee.[39] McUsic now sits on the League of Conservation Voters' board.[40]

Add to this pair McUsic's predecessor at the Wyss Foundation, John Leshy. Leshy—an ex-staffer from Carter's Department of the Interior and a Natural Resources Defense Council lawyer—was solicitor general to Babbitt's Interior (1993–2001), which would've made him McUsic's boss.[41] Leshy may have headed the Wyss Foundation in its infancy in 1998 (information before 2002 is scarce), but he was certainly its president from at least 2002 until 2008, when then chief operating officer McUsic succeeded him. Leshy—a professor of real property law at the University of California College of Law, San Francisco, since 2001—co-chaired President Obama's transition team for the Department of the Interior in 2009 and led the Interior transition team for the Clinton-Gore administration.

Although Kessler didn't start Arabella Advisors until 2005, it appears his ties to McUsic connected him to Hansjörg Wyss as the Wyss Foundation began making six-figure annual grants to the New Venture Fund (then the "Arabella Legacy Fund") in 2007, just one year after the fund's creation. As noted earlier, Wyss could be described as the progenitor of the Arabella network. His foundation's 2007 grant accounted for 55 percent of New Venture Fund's revenues for that year (see chapter 1).

As also noted, Wyss Foundation staffer Kyle Herrig left Wyss for Arabella.[42] Herrig has ostensibly been on the New Venture Fund's board since 2014 (although that cannot be verified in its Form 990 filings with the

IRS) and was a Wyss Foundation staffer from 2012 to 2013. Interestingly, he was one of the individuals interviewed in the 2015 Wyss Foundation report leading to the creation of the Hub Project. He now runs the left-of-center activist group Accountable.US, a former New Venture Fund project that controls a number of anti-Trump groups that began life as New Venture Fund projects: Restore Public Trust, American Oversight, and Western Values Project (which ran an attack site on Trump's interior secretary, David Bernhardt).[43] In early 2021 American Oversight got into trouble for trying to blacklist, in McCarthyite fashion, former Trump administration officials so they wouldn't be hired by big corporations.[44] This earned the group a critical letter from the House Committee on Oversight and Reform, which condemned it for "trying to deny Americans the opportunity to earn livelihoods simply because they made the sacrifice to serve on behalf of the President."[45]

Wyss's Meddling

Wyss's efforts to influence American policy debates and election outcomes has not gone unnoticed. In May 2021, the right-leaning Americans for Public Trust filed a complaint with the Federal Election Commission, arguing the evidence already available indicates "Mr. Wyss indirectly funded federal electoral advocacy through his nonprofit organizations, the Wyss Foundation and the Berger Action Fund. The intended recipient of these funds was ultimately a variety of organizations whose primary purpose is to engage in electoral advocacy."[46]

The complaint observed that "the law prohibits foreign nationals from making contributions to political committees whether directly or indirectly," because of the near-universal view that foreign interests should not intervene in American elections. Unfortunately, the Federal Elections Commission (FEC) rarely does much to enforce the law, so after waiting a year, Americans for Public Trust filed a lawsuit in late April 2022, aiming to prod the Commission to investigate Wyss's alleged illegal donations to left-wing groups and various Democratic politicians, including Sen. Dick Durbin (D-IL) and former Rep. Jay Inslee (D-WA)—now governor of Washington State—and former Rep. Mark Udall (D-CO), who was later elected to the Senate.[47] Wyss has bragged to Swiss media about his contacts in the White House and support for Democrats.[48]

Federal law prohibits foreign nationals from making contributions of any kind "in connection with any federal, state, or local election," according to the FEC.[49] It's also illegal for campaigns, PACs, and other such organizations "to knowingly accept such donations from a foreign national."

With the lawsuit pressing it, the FEC general counsel finally produced a document with recommendations for what the commission should do regarding Wyss and his relations with the Arabella network. The general counsel said an investigation into Arabella's Sixteen Thirty Fund's relations with its largest grant recipients in the 2018 and 2020 election cycles should be conducted, to see if the group should have been registered as a PAC, rather than a 501(c)(4) nonprofit. Even with evidence already available, the general counsel found grave violations and recommended that the FEC "Find reason to believe that the Sixteen Thirty Fund and The Hub Project"—the latter launched and sustained through the Arabella network by Wyss and his nonprofits—had "violated 52 U.S.C. §§ 30102, 30103, and 30104 by not registering as a political committee and meeting the Act's organizational, recordkeeping, and reporting requirements."

The complaint to which the FEC general counsel responded alleges the Hub Project has served as a vehicle for the political spending of Mr. Wyss. This is demonstrated by the fact that Mr. Wyss has not publicly disclosed his role in founding the Hub Project. Neither his influence nor his financial support can be found anywhere on the group's website. Indeed, the intrepid *New York Times* reporter only learned of Wyss's connection to the Hub Project with the help of "interviews with five people with knowledge of The Hub Project, an internal memo from another liberal group that was obtained by the *New York Times*, and the appearance of The Hub Project's business plan in a tranche of data made public by WikiLeaks."[50]

But as the *New York Times* makes clear, it is no right-wing "conspiracy theory" that this foreign donor is shaping our politics in powerful ways, especially in the area of environmental policy close to his heart. For example, the *Times* observes, the Hub Project appeared in 2015 "as a sort of incubator for groups backing Democrats and their causes," and it "created more than a dozen groups with anodyne-sounding names that planned to spend $30 million attacking Republican congressional candidates before the 2018 election."[51]

And the inauguration of Joseph Biden as president only led to more influence for Wyss. "Several officials from the Hub Project were hired by the Biden administration," the *Times* reports, "including Rosemary Enobakhare, a former Environmental Protection Agency official in the Obama administration who returned to the agency under Mr. Biden; Maju Varghese as director of the White House Military Office; and Janelle Jones as chief economist for the Labor Department." Then there's Wyss's top aide, Wyss Foundation and Berger Action Fund president (and former Sixteen Thirty Fund board member) Molly McUsic: she "was a member of the Biden transition team that reviewed Interior Department policies and personnel."

The Man Behind the Curtain

Especially given the FEC's slowness to respond to complaints and eventual decision to ignore its own general counsel's recommendations, Wyss's fortune will continue to influence public policy debates for many years. Wyss still commands billions of dollars that will exist in perpetuity in his tax-free private foundation. As with so many of the big left-wing donors, his death will likely not liberate America from the reach of his money.

And just as billionaires yearning to control Americans seem to keep multiplying, so do Arabella's nonprofits keep proliferating. Our next chapter deals with the latest major nonprofit to be created in Washington by this ambitious empire.

8

CASE STUDY

North Fund

Birth of Another Massive Political Pass-Through

In OCTOBER 2020, Addie Slanger, a journalism student writing for the *Community News Service*, worked to understand the funding source of Montana's marijuana legalization effort. She found that something called the North Fund provided at least several million dollars of the funding for the New Approach Montana, or 70 percent of the total money behind the ballot initiative campaign.[1] But it wasn't until the following year that Hayden Ludwig at Capital Research Center exposed the North Fund as yet another orb in the Arabella constellation.[2] While this newest of the Arabella network's sister nonprofits originated in 2019, it was our digging that placed this mysterious group squarely in the Arabella camp.

Now we know quite a bit about the once obscure funding source.[3] Like Sixteen Thirty Fund, North Fund is a 501(c)(4) nonprofit designed to carry out Arabella's most politically charged advocacy campaigns, including numerous state ballot initiatives (like the one in Montana on marijuana) and the effort to grant D.C. statehood. In 2019, its first year of operation, North Fund brought in close to $9.4 million—all given to it from Arabella's Sixteen Thirty Fund.[4] According to North Fund's 2020 IRS Form 990, from 2019 to 2020 the group's revenues exploded to over $66 million, a single-year increase of 613 percent. If it were a private company, North Fund's success would have skyrocketed it to the front of *Forbes* magazine.[5]

Where did that $66 million come from? At least 46 percent—nearly half—flowed in from two "sister" Arabella nonprofits, the Sixteen Thirty Fund and New Venture Fund.[6] The rest of the seven-figure donations came from a handful of anonymous donors.

Just Passing Through

The North Fund acts as a cousin to Arabella's four in-house "sister" groups, and it effectively functions as a pass-through for Arabella's nonprofits and other as-yet-unidentified left-wing funders. In 2020 it paid out $34 million in grants to dozens of groups, nearly all of them politically active 501(c)(4)s, which are allowed to engage in political spending and electioneering far beyond what their (c)(3) counterparts may legally do.[7]

North Fund bankrolled activist groups pushing gun control, amnesty for illegal aliens, fracking and "fossil fuel" bans, federally funded abortions, and targeted get-out-the-vote campaigns to boost Democratic turnout.

For example, Future Forward USA Action is a 501(c)(4) nonprofit with an affiliated super PAC, Future Forward PAC.[8] The (c)(4) nonprofit arm received nearly $7 million from North Fund, which likely joined the tens of millions of dollars that that arm gave to the super PAC, which in turn spent $74 million boosting Biden in 2020.[9] Since so much of the super PAC's funding came from its nonprofit arm, in all likelihood that nonprofit served as a double-blind pass-through for North Fund cash. In other words, donors gave to North Fund, which anonymized their gift as it passed the cash on to Future Forward USA Action, which likely passed it on to Future Forward PAC. (Other donors to Future Forward PAC in the

2020 cycle included the disgraced crypto-billionaire Sam Bankman-Fried and his now-bankrupt Alameda Research firm, each of which gave $5 million or more alongside North Fund's millions.)[10]

Planned Parenthood and various affiliates received nearly $1.5 million in North Fund cash for "civil rights, social action, [and] advocacy"—North Fund's and Arabella's standard line—while the State Policy Institute, a group so obscure it doesn't even have a website, netted another $1 million from the fund. This institute is run by Roshan Patel, a consultant for the D.C.-based Democratic firm 50 State and a former finance director of the Democratic Governors Association.[11]

North Fund gave $250,000 to Yes on National Popular Vote, a group pushing states to ignore the Electoral College and give their electoral votes to whichever presidential candidate wins the most votes nationwide.[12] In the 2016 elections, this scheme would have had *every* state sending its votes to Hillary Clinton, even though Trump won the most votes in thirty states versus Hillary's victory in twenty states.

North Fund even gave $100,000 to LUCHA, the far-left Arizona group whose staffers harassed Democratic senator Kyrsten Sinema in an Arizona State University bathroom in October 2021 for not toeing the "progressive" Left's line in Congress.[13]

Pulling States Leftward

The North Fund was behind multiple Colorado ballot initiatives in 2020. It funneled $1.35 million to Abortion Access for All, the campaign to defeat a proposed twenty-two-week abortion ban (Prop. 115).[14] The initiative was rejected 59–41 percent. North Fund and Sixteen Thirty Fund together provided $7 million of the $9 million campaign to pass paid family medical leave (Prop. 118), which won by 58–42 percent.[15] In contrast, opponents of this ballot initiative spent less than $800,000.

In Missouri, North Fund poured at least $1.1 million into a campaign to defeat Republican-proposed changes to the state's redistricting process and campaign finance laws (it lost) and an unknown amount into Missouri's pro-Medicaid expansion campaign, which passed.[16]

In Ohio, the group sent $1.7 million to Ohioans for Raising the Wage for its campaign to hike the state minimum wage to $13 per hour.[17] (It failed to make the ballot.)

Multiple lobbyists for North Fund on "voting and election policy" have also been traced to Virginia, though the details remain unclear.[18] They may be linked to the Voting Rights Lab, a North Fund project that supports changes to voting laws across the country that weaken election fraud measures.

Trouble in Montana

North Fund and its various fronts have received flak for declining to disclose their donors, a free-speech right nonprofits enjoy under federal law.[19] But in December 2020, Montana's commissioner of political practices ruled that the fund's excessive political spending in the state—it dumped nearly $5 million into a successful marijuana legalization campaign between January and October—makes it an independent political committee under state law, forcing it to publicly disclose its donors and spending.[20] (It was this activity that caused the group to be exposed by local reporters.)

"In 2020, North Fund made 83 different grants or contributions to 70 different organizations," the resulting document notes, each ranging "from $500 to over $1 million."[21] But "many of the recipients do not participate in any political activity at all," the fund claims, and are instead *educational*. Really?

Like most politically active nonprofits, North Fund defines "educational" differently from the way John Q. Public does. Among the group's examples of its supposedly *apolitical* activities are:

- $6 million for "public outreach educational services regarding Wisconsin economic policies, voter education, and nonpartisan GOTV [get-out-the-vote] efforts";

- $2 million for "Black Lives Matter and other racial equality issues," a "program to eliminate the filibuster," and "DC statehood"; and
- $1.2 million for "nonpartisan polling access" and "gender and reproductive equity."

Recall that this was all presented as "evidence" for the fund's defense that its activities were essentially *charitable*. The fund vigorously defended its donors' right to privacy under the First Amendment—a wildly hypocritical position, given that the North Fund spent at least $200,000 lobbying Congress to pass the Democrats' For the People Act (H.R. 1), which would have forced nonprofits to disclose their donors.[22]

Through its brief life, the North Fund has quickly morphed into one of Arabella's more active funds. North Fund's top grants in 2021 (the most recent year available) included:

- $300,000 to Common Cause, which lobbies on everything from redistricting to campaign finance law;[23]
- $500,000 to NARAL Pro-Choice Ohio, part of one of the pro-abortion Left's top advocacy groups;[24]
- $222,000 to Our Voice Our Vote Arizona, which elects non-white "champions into office" in Arizona;[25]
- $1 million to Run for Something Action Fund, which trains Democratic political candidates;[26] and
- $1 million to Secure Democracy, an election "reform" group currently engaged in a whistleblower lawsuit over alleged racial discrimination, as well as violations of civil rights and nonprofit law.[27]

Undeniably Connected to Democrats

If the North Fund was indeed initially formed with the intention of becoming a kind of decoy that would direct attention away from Arabella, the fact that—alone among its siblings—it has an address different from Arabella's suggests Arabella's displeasure and frustration at the attention its activities have garnered in recent years. But the quickness with which my colleagues at Capital Research Center traced it back to its origins would also seem to indicate that the secrecy Arabella and its many clients—whether self-created or independent—are seeking will be increasingly hard to come by, now that investigative journalists know what to look for.

As with all the other Arabella entities, the North Fund has been unquestionably tied to Democrats since its founding. North Fund's board of directors is led by Jim Gerstein, founding partner of the Democratic polling firm GBAO Research and Strategy.[28] Gerstein is a former campaign advisor to multiple Democratic politicians and the 1996 Democratic National Convention, and he led James Carville's Democracy Corps, a nonprofit polling group that services the Left.[29]

Notably, GBAO's clients include Pierre Omidyar's Omidyar Network, the Rockefeller Foundation, Center for American Progress, Sierra Club, Service Employees International Union (Seiu), Planned Parenthood, and Arabella's Hub Project—among dozens of other Democratic committees, politicians, ballot measures, and "progressive" advocacy groups.

Other North Fund board members include Christina Uribe, a union organizer with the National Education Association, and Melanie Beller, a Texas consultant who works on "voter enfranchisement" and "health care reform," among other issues.[30] Beller is a former vice president of government affairs for the environmentalist Wilderness Society.[31]

North Fund contracted with two of the Democratic Party's top law firms for legal services in 2021: Perkins Coie ($1.9 million) and its spinoff, Elias Law Group, run by the Democratic superlawyer Marc Elias.[32] The Elias Law Group is also counsel to Arabella Advisors, which is another reason to laugh at Arabella's protests that it is nonpartisan.[33] The firm's lead attorney, Mr. Elias, has publicly declared that if you don't help Democrats win, "we are not the law firm for you."[34] (In an April 2023 move that shocked many political observers, the Democratic National Committee and Elias's firm parted ways, perhaps due to his deep involvement with the Steele dossier that was central to the now-exposed Russiagate hoax.)

The Big Shuffle

As mentioned above and unlike Arabella's other nonprofits, North Fund doesn't share Arabella's L Street address in Washington, D.C., but lists the address of a virtual-office-space provider, Carr Workplaces, two blocks away. Still, North Fund's books and records are in the care of Arabella Advisors, with which the nonprofit "contracts" to provide "administrative support, accounting services, and legal guidance" according to multiple tax filings. This mirrors the close relationship between Arabella Advisors and the other members of its non-profit network, which are legally distinct entities that contract with the company for compliance, grant-making guidance, and staffing support and typically use Arabella's office space. This kind of arrangement isn't uncommon. What is unusual is the role Arabella senior leadership played in founding each of these nonprofits—in effect creating the company's own "clients."

North Fund is no exception.

One of the network's key phenomena is the way Arabella nonprofits shuffle millions of dollars among themselves each year. In 2020 alone, North Fund gave $500,000 to the network's biggest 501(c)(3), New Venture Fund, which gave $11 million back to North Fund. Similarly, Sixteen Thirty Fund distributed $30 million to North Fund, which gave the former $800,000. And Arabella itself collects millions in management fees: North Fund paid Arabella $942,000 in 2020 for its services, and $552,000 in 2021.

Arabella's structure and lack of transparency mean that we're largely left to conjecture when it comes to discerning the purpose of these intra-network grants, much less their original donors. The most likely explanation is that they both further obscure the Arabella network's donors and also fuel its complex "pop-up" campaigns, using 501(c)(3) "charitable" dollars to free up (c)(4) funds for advocacy purposes, since money is fungible.

Other Notable North Fund–Related Pop-Ups

North Fund's involvement in this intricate money flow further highlights its place in the network. That includes funding *former* Arabella pop-up groups, such as States Newsroom, a set of left-leaning websites pretending to be local newsrooms, incubated by Arabella's Hopewell Fund under a previous name: Newsroom Network. In 2020, North Fund funneled $85,000 to States Newsroom for "capacity building."

We've also identified North Fund's involvement in at least one (c)(3)-(c)(4) pop-up pair: Voting Rights Lab Action, the (c)(4) advocacy arm of the (c)(3) New Venture Fund front Voting Rights Lab, a self-described "campaign hub" designed to "supercharge the fight against voter suppression" and "transform our voting systems." (As of mid-2023, the Voting Rights Lab is at the center of the first of two lawsuits filed against New Venture Fund by former employees.[35])

It's common for public policy groups to maintain a 501(c)(3) research and fundraising arm that pairs with a 501(c)(4) lobbying arm, often with overlapping staffers and leadership. The goal is to maximize funding and advocacy capacities by combining the advantage of the tax deduction donors receive for giving to (c)(3) groups with the higher lobbying capacity enjoyed by (c)(4)s. For example, the conservative Heritage Foundation and left-wing Center for American Progress are (c)(3) think tanks that both have (c)(4) "action funds" for this reason. But because all these groups are independent nonprofits, they report their activities annually through public tax filings.

Arabella runs the same model for many of its pop-up groups, but they hide under the 501(c)(3) and (c)(4) tax status of Arabella's in-house nonprofits, instead of each obtaining their own independent status. This "project of" an umbrella nonprofit denies the public information on the groups' boards of directors (if any), campaign activity, finances, and other disclosures commonly available.

What We Don't Know

We don't know *why* Arabella chose to add a fifth nonprofit—and a second 501(c)(4) political nonprofit—to its network. Again, the most likely reason is obfuscation. Since we began reporting on Arabella and its nonprofits in late 2018, Sixteen Thirty Fund has become a target for investigative reporting and now is described as a "dark money" group even by friendly outlets like *New York Times*.[36] Funneling cash through a new (c)(4) would provide cover for at least a short period before journalists catch on. This isn't a crazy theory, given the huge amount of money North Fund pumped into independent expenditures meant to aid Democratic Senate candidates as well as numerous ballot initiatives in the 2020 election.[37]

Still, we know enough to include North Fund among the other Arabella "sisters." And after more than two years with no Internet presence, the North Fund finally launched a basic website at www.NorthFund. org.[38] (The earliest Internet Wayback Machine capture of the site occurred in December 2021. Capital Research Center ran four articles about the North Fund before the website launched.)

As with the other Arabella-related entities, we expect more information to reveal itself in time. Meanwhile, we now turn to one of Arabella's most important coalition partners, a George Soros–created cabal of megadonors.

9

CASE STUDY

Democracy Alliance Funds

How Soros and Other Billionaires
Pool Money for Politics

SINCE AT LEAST 2005, the nonprofit tail has wagged the Democratic Party dog. If you're trying to understand American politics and the Left, it is much more important to look at who heads Arabella Advisors, or the Ford Foundation, than it is to see who happens to be chairing the Democratic National Committee this afternoon. While the Left is always hungry for power and money, the party of big government it supports is the last stage in a campaign effort that begins with megadonors and their tools for distributing cash, especially Arabella and its pet nonprofits.

I focus on 2005 because two momentous entities were born that year: Arabella Advisors and the Democracy Alliance. Admittedly, Arabella's birth was smallish and not dramatic, as we saw in chapter 1, while the unrelated creation of the Democracy Alliance—a cabal of left-wing megadonors—received much more notice. Yet the two were fated to find each other and intertwine, as this chapter will show. Nothing better demonstrates the way Arabella's numerous tentacles reach into every organ—and the preferred political party—of the Left.

The Democracy Alliance's Origin Story

Back in 2003, an informal group of donors looking to defeat President George W. Bush coalesced into an informal coalition called the Phoenix Group—rising, no doubt, from the ashes of the "stolen" 2000 election of Bush vs. Gore. These folks began giving tens of millions of dollars to liberal candidates and 527 political committees, but unfortunately for them, 2004 still ended in humiliating failure. So, in December 2004, a small group of wealthy donors met in San Francisco. George Soros, Progressive Insurance billionaire Peter Lewis, savings and loan tycoons Herb and Marion Sandler, and a few others gathered to gripe about what one called "our Pearl Harbor" and how best to respond.

In April 2005, their response began in earnest. A larger group of donors—around seventy billionaires and millionaires—met in a secret, long-term planning session in Phoenix, Arizona. Three-quarters of the members voted that this "Democracy Alliance" should not "retain close ties to the Democratic Party," whom they blamed for the Left's defeat in the elections of 2002 and 2004.

Some former Clinton officials were there, too; the most important was the attorney Rob Stein. He had been an evangelist of sorts among this group, showing them a famous PowerPoint presentation, "The Conservative Message Machine's Money Matrix," which featured donors like the Bradley Foundation and the Sarah Scaife Foundation, and think tanks like the American Enterprise Institute and the Heritage Foundation, and so forth.

He credited conservatives' electoral success to four decades of conservatives' long-term investments in ideas and institutions. "Perhaps," he said, "the most potent, independent, institutionalized apparatus ever assembled in a democracy to promote one belief system." Later, Stein would recall "an unbelievable frustration, particularly among the donor class . . . with trying to one-off everything—with every single one of them being a single, 'silo' donor and not having the ability to communicate effectively with a network of donors."

Now whether Stein was correct that the Right had been outspending the Left on culture-shaping intellectual institutions is open to question—he didn't count little things like the Ford Foundation and Harvard, or ABC and the *New York Times*, institutions that set intellectual trends across America! But the donors bought what he was selling. As a Capital Research Center report from more than a decade ago put it:

> the [Democratic] party had become a top-down organization run by professional politicians who cared little about donors' concerns. [Stein] was convinced that the Democratic Party's hierarchy had to be turned upside-down: Donors should fund an ideological movement that would dictate policies to the politicians.[1]

Similarly, the party's activists were "fed up with perceived Democrat dithering and were demanding more say." One of the most important new groups, which was perhaps the true beginning of the Left 2.0, was Move-On.org, an online outlet born out of grassroots activists' fight to keep Bill Clinton in power. One of its young activists insisted in 2005: "Now it's our party: We bought it, we own it, and we're going to take it back."

Of course, where these forces were really going to take the party was further to the left. A good insider's account of this period comes from Matt Bai, a left-leaning writer for *Yahoo News*, in his book *The Argument: Billionaires, Bloggers, and the Battle to Remake Democratic Politics*:

> The Democracy Alliance continues to this day, a shadowy and sometimes bickering group of big-money leftists who have channeled we don't know how much money—it's somewhere in the hundreds of millions—to a couple dozen groups, mostly nonprofits. Some but not most of that money has flowed through the Alliance's official entity, which is a "taxable nonprofit" incorporated in Washington, D.C., but mostly the Alliance serves as a place to strategize with fellow donors and hear pitches for private money from approved groups. It's not very different from the much-maligned donor seminars held by Freedom Partners and the Koch Network.

As Stein described it, the Alliance is a "gathering place," "learning environment," "debating society," and "investment club." Members of the Alliance must pony up initiation fees and promise to send at least a couple hundred thousand dollars a year into Alliance-approved groups. The Alliance's legal status, of course, means it provides no financial disclosure— even though most of these donors pumped a lot of money into the fraud known as "campaign finance reform."

Donors Take the Reins

Another aspect of the Democracy Alliance worth noting: it quickly included unions—first, the SEIU (Service Employees International Union), which is itself a Left 2.0 entity thanks to longtime leader Andy Stern's reshaping of it, and then, afraid to be left behind, the AFL-CIO joined.

The Alliance's agenda spelled out the nature of the Left 2.0. Briefly, the Alliance provided some guidance on its web site for groups hoping to receive a grant. The form listed the following priorities:

- *Building power and capacity in key constituencies:* primarily Latinos and young people, as well as African Americans and unmarried women.
- *New media and technology:* content generators, aggregators and distributors that disseminate and amplify progressive messages.
- *Law and legal systems:* working to advance progressive values at all levels of the legal system.
- *Early-stage idea generators:* including journals, academic networks, books, and *nontraditional* think tanks.
- *Content generation:* traditional and new media vehicles capable of effectively promoting progressive ideas.
- *Civic engagement coordination:* achieving greater efficiency and effectiveness through collaboration and creating economies of scale.
- *Civic engagement tools:* increasing capacity and availability of data services, including online organizing services for civic engagement groups.

- *Election reform:* structural reforms of our democratic process that will increase voter participation among progressive constituencies.
- *Youth leadership development:* the youth part of the leadership pipeline, especially organizations targeting young people that work at scale.
- *Mid-career nonprofit leadership development:* again, they want to strengthen the "leadership pipeline," especially "organizations working at scale."

The consequences of the Democracy Alliance's emphasis on building a nonprofit network of progressive activism was clear by 2014. Donors on the left, inside the Alliance and out, have poured stunning amounts into "charities" active in public policy. My colleagues' research identified that in the $9.6 billion universe of "traditional public policy nonprofits," left-of-center organizations—environmentalist groups like the World Wildlife Fund, social liberal groups like Planned Parenthood, and think tanks like Center for American Progress—outraised conservative organizations by 77 percent to 23 percent. An analysis of foundation grant-making on the Right and the Left came to a similar conclusion; the nonprofit cash on the Left far outstrips that on the Right.

The methods the Left employs to make this vision a reality have undergone some streamlining. Project incubation and fiscally sponsored projects of preexisting organizations—such as Arabella's network specializes in—add an element of spontaneity and flexibility to the Left's operations.

While organizations like the Tides Center have been around for a long time, offering incubation services and back-office support to new campaigns and movements, an explosion of new, Potemkin-esque groups arose in resistance to the Trump administration. And some of the organizers are making a pretty profit while pushing the Left's agenda.

The Importance of the Alliance Conferences

The Democracy Alliance doesn't make grants itself. Instead, it's an invite-only strategy group for leftist luminaries to coordinate the best ways for environmentalists, foundations, labor unions, and their allies to spend resources and reshape America. The Alliance hosts semi-annual conferences that connect left-leaning donors with like-minded activist groups.[2] In secret strategy sessions, the groups pitch themselves and everyone discusses "investment recommendations" for where donations will have the strongest political effect.

Though Democracy Alliance closes the meetings to the media, works to keep the conference agendas confidential, and discourages attendees from speaking to reporters, news outlets have often obtained and published conference materials, and Capital Research Center's InfluenceWatch has a page devoted to what is known about the speakers and participants.[3] The conference themes are telling:

- A New Progressive Era? (spring 2014)
- Honoring the Past, Shaping the Future (spring 2015)
- Vision Strategy Victory (spring 2016)
- Seizing Opportunity & Building Power (fall 2016) (It's worth noting that this conference was planned prior to the results of the 2016 election that shocked the Left and ushered in the Trump administration.)
- Beyond #Resistance: Reclaiming our Progressive Future (fall 2017)
- Charting the Course for Progressive Power (spring 2018)
- Taking Our Democracy Back (fall 2018)
- Focus|Strategy|Victory (fall 2019)

The materials outline the group's sophisticated, multipronged approach to securing enduring political power, and their conference participants read like a who's who of the Democratic Party.

Following the fall 2016 conference, held a week after the election that former Alliance president Julie Kohler deemed the "most shocking and disturbing in recent history," the Alliance scrambled to reexamine its strategy in its "Democracy Alliance 2020 Investment Portfolio Progress & Updates."[4] Note that this report, appearing in November 2016, was explicitly looking toward the 2020 election. According to the report, in 2016 alone, the Democracy Alliance's 113 "partners" (read: *coordinated donors*) pledged to invest $146 million in "Progressive infrastructure map organizations" and promised close to $72 million to other 2020 efforts (recommended organizations, state funds, and leveraged investments).

In her introduction to the report, Kohler promised it would explain the ways the left-wing groups it recommended be funded "are collectively moving the needle towards ambitious, movement-wide goals." She added that

> Accomplishing these and many other aligned goals requires us *not only to win elections* but to advance policy and *build power* in a way that realigns complex economic and democratic systems that currently serve the interests of the privileged few. [Emphasis added.]

The report illustrated fifteen funding streams moving money to battleground states ahead of the 2016, 2018, and 2020 elections to avoid attention. Fourteen of those streams were made up of seven matching pairs of groups, an Arabella specialty: each pair has a 501(c)(3) "charity" tied to a (c)(4) political nonprofit. The (c)(3) maximizes fundraising, because it's easier for foundations to give to (c)(3)s and individual donors are incentivized by a tax deduction, while the (c)(4) maximizes political power, because these nonprofits have much greater latitude to lobby, to purchase political ads, to endorse candidates, and the like. These groups let the Democracy Alliance pool donor funds for distribution to the places where cash would have the strongest effect on elections. The seven pairs were

- Climate Fund / Climate Action Fund
- Democracy Fund / Democracy Action Fund
- Inclusive Economy / Inclusive Economy Action Fund
- New American Majority / New American Majority Action Fund
- Black Civic Engagement / Black Civic Engagement Action Fund
- Latino Engagement Fund / Latino Engagement Action Fund
- Youth Engagement Fund / Youth Engagement Action Fund

Every single one of these streams ran directly through Arabella Advisors. Page 28 of the report details precisely where contributions to the funds should be directed. While each fund's director was affiliated with Democracy Alliance (evidenced by the fund directors' email addresses), donations were directed to Arabella organizations. For example, under Democracy Fund/Democracy Action Fund, the directory states:

> Checks for 501(c)(3) donations must be written payable to: New Venture Fund
>
> * Check Memo Line: Democracy Fund EIN: 20-5806345
>
> Checks for 501(c)(4) donations must be written payable to: Sixteen Thirty Fund
>
> * Check Memo Line: Democracy Action Fund EIN 26-4486753[5]

The Alliance, in its 2016 report, identified states to target as a part of its strategy to mobilize the various voter cohorts identified by the seven activist pairs. One of those states was Pennsylvania, and the Keystone State showed up as a target for five separate campaigns (Climate Fund/Action, Youth Engagement Fund/Action, and the State Engagement Initiative).

The group entrusted with the plans developed under the Climate Fund/ Climate Fund Action strategy was One Pennsylvania (styled as One PA).[6] One PA is virtually a subsidiary of the SEIU, which is one of the largest institutional donors on the Left. The Climate Action Fund raised roughly $1.3 million and gave One PA at least $188,000 in 2018 through the Arabella-run Sixteen Thirty Fund for "fighting a proposed refinery and dirty energy port facility in a low-income African-American community, *educating voters on U.S. Senate candidate positions* on climate change, and *mobilizing them to vote*" (emphasis added).

Similarly, the Democracy Alliance's Youth Engagement Fund raised $3.5 million to bolster youth turnout, which the report calls the Left's "long-term competitive advantage against the political Right." Almost all of that was intended for youth turnout in elections—ideally "doubling" it in "high impact states."

The New American Majority Fund and its 501(c)(4) arm, the New American Majority Action Fund, raised over $1 million in 2016 to target left-wing outreach to likely Democratic-leaning constituencies in North Carolina, Virginia, Florida, Ohio, and Arizona. The funds especially targeted "Asian and Pacific Islanders Americans, women, the LGBTQ community, and white working class"—the so-called New American Majority. The pair's spending is overseen via an advisory board staffed by Democracy Alliance employees, the teachers' union operative Daaiyah Bilal-Threats, and an SEIU representative.[7]

Similarly, the Black Civic Engagement Fund and Action Fund—with oversight from the Ford Foundation and three unions (AFSCME, NEA, and SEIU)—directed spending toward Blueprint NC and groups in other key states "to build political power and activism within the Black community." In 2016, the pair raised close to $5 million. They're joined by the Latino Engagement Fund and Action Fund pair, which also directed money to Blueprint NC. That pair raised over $2 million in 2016.

The State Engagement Initiative, another Democracy Alliance front group run through Arabella, raised $6.7 million in 2016 to create "donor tables" in battleground states, aiming to increase left-wing spending on elections and activist nonprofits supporting the Left. In North Carolina, the initiative directed funds to a group mysteriously called Put NC First, possibly a front for the liberal news aggregator Real Facts NC. (Hilariously, on one map, the report mistook South Carolina for its northern sibling—a shining example of how less-than-grassroots these megadonor operations run by Arabella actually are. Their puppetmasters are not merely from another state; they can't even recognize the state for which they presume to speak on a map.)

America Votes

Another example of the dramatic overlap between Democracy Alliance and the Arabella network is America Votes. (America Votes was covered briefly in chapter 2.) America Votes emerged from the Democrats' defeat in the 2004 presidential election as the brainchild of a group of influential operatives.[8] These operatives—Clinton official Harold Ickes, SEIU president Andy Stern, Sierra Club executive director Carl Pope, EMILY's List founder Ellen Malcolm, and Partnership for America's Families president Steve Rosenthal—quickly gained the support of major labor unions, litigation nonprofits, abortion groups, environmentalist groups, and professional activists to put together a huge $95 million war chest for churning out likely Democratic voters in key battleground states.

That's considered a "charitable" act by the IRS, by the way, so long as tax-exempt nonprofits like America Votes don't engage in *partisan* efforts—that is, overtly supporting members of a political party.

While IRS rules don't require America Votes to report its donors, past grants to the group show substantial funding from the League of Conservation Voters, Atlantic Advocacy Fund, Tides Advocacy Fund, Patriot Majority USA, Rockefeller Philanthropy Advisors, and the National Education Association.[9] The grant-making organizations in George Soros's foundation network alone gave a combined $30 million to America Votes in 2021.[10]

Little wonder that America Votes' coalition includes just about every leftist standby imaginable, including the AFL-CIO, EMILY's List, Indivisible, Planned Parenthood, and the Sierra Club. The list also includes ACRONYM—the nonprofit owner of Shadow, Inc., the tech firm run by Clinton and Obama cronies that was responsible for the debacle at the 2020 Iowa Democratic caucuses that caused delays in counting votes.[11] (Chapter 2 documented how Arabella's Hopewell Fund directed $8.6 million to ACRONYM in 2020 and 2021.)

Chapter 2 also showed that America Votes received $191 million in (combined) funding from New Venture Fund and Sixteen Thirty Fund from 2019 through 2021. During the same period, America Votes had revenue totals of $339 million, so Arabella nonprofits provided 56 percent of the group's income.

A Giant Money Funnel

America Votes is also a donor to aligned state-level groups. Consider North Carolina. In 2017, it gave $25,000 to NC Citizens for Protecting Our Schools, an education lobbying group that gave $1.1 million in 2017 to NC Families First—a group that spent millions of dollars attacking Republicans in the state legislature.[12]

In 2016, America Votes gifted $175,000 to Make North Carolina First, which despite having no website nonetheless raked in $4.1 million in 2016 and another $2.7 million in 2017. It's a good example of how the Left weaponizes nonprofits to achieve political aims—entirely in secret.

Among the activities listed in Make North Carolina First's 2017 IRS Form 990 are "voter registration and voter representation." Its three-person board is headed by Adam Abram, owner of an insurance group and a board member for the left-wing groups Human Rights First and the Urban Institute. In November 2019, Abram was appointed to the state Housing Finance Agency by the governor.[13] Also on the board are Dean Debnam, who runs the highly successful polling firm Public Policy Polling, and Michael L. Weisel, a legal expert in independent expenditure activities—the domain of partisan super PACs.

In 2017 alone, Make North Carolina First made eight (mostly six-figure) grants to groups such as North Carolina Latino Power, Progress North Carolina Action, Advance Carolina, and NC Citizens for Protecting Our Schools. In 2018, it granted $1.3 million to NC Citizens for Progress, a PAC that spent some $1.6 million in attack ads during the midterm elections.[14] Mainstream media reporting about Make North Carolina First and similar groups has been nonexistent—and it will almost certainly stay that way.

The Democracy Alliance Windfall

The first thing to remember about the Democracy Alliance is the central role partisan politics and electoral outcomes have always played in it. The second is that nonprofits have always been the primary types of organizations that the Alliance has recommended to its funding partners. Nearly all the groups identified in Matt Bai's 2007 left-leaning analysis *The Argument: Billionaires, Bloggers, and the Battle to Remake Democratic Politics* were nonprofits.

There are critical (though not always clear) legal restrictions on how nonprofits may involve themselves in elections. Private foundations and charities—the 501(c)(3) world—are categorically prohibited, in the IRS's language, from "directly or indirectly participating in, or intervening in, any political campaign on behalf of (or in opposition to) any candidate for elective public office."[15] Voter registration, get-out-the-vote, and other voter "education" activities are permitted, but must not "have the effect of favoring a candidate or group of candidates." By contrast, 501(c)(4) nonprofits (groups like Democratic Socialists of America and the National Rifle Association) may engage in substantially more direct political activities—endorsing candidates, making independent campaign expenditures, and so on—as long as these do not become their "primary" activity (legally, that ends up meaning no more than 49 percent of the budget goes to these efforts).

Nothing proves the Democracy Alliance's activities have violated any of these restrictions. Documents indicate that the Alliance is attentive to the requirements of applicable nonprofit law.[16] Yet even with these requirements in place, the Alliance certainly sees nonprofits as playing an important role in America's political landscape and in electoral outcomes. It's also a role that appears to be growing. Funding directed toward ideologically left-of-center nonprofits has swelled since at least the 2004 election cycle. The Democracy Alliance is one notable part of this trend.

Consider the budgetary growth of the Alliance's recommended groups during that time. The Center for American Progress, the Center on Budget and Policy Priorities, the Economic Policy Institute, and Media Matters for America are all technically charities identified in *The Argument* as among the earliest recipients of Democracy Alliance funding. All remain core Alliance-recommended groups to this day. Organizations highlighted by the Democracy Alliance are often assured of future resources—which can have lasting effects. In 2004, these four nonprofits had combined revenues of about $37.6 million. Adjusted for inflation, based on the Consumer Price Index, that would have come out to just over $60.5 million 2021 dollars. But the actual combined 2021 revenues of those four groups exceeded $139 million.

This trend is consistent across many Alliance-recommended groups. Faith in Action (formerly known as PICO National Network) had 2004 revenues of about $5 million.[17] By 2021 its annual revenue exceeded $31.6 million (a drop from $37.4 million in revenues in 2020). The National Employment Law Project brought in less than $1.6 million in 2005, but $28.4 million by 2021.[18] The Brennan Center for Justice, which among other things fights to overturn voter ID laws, went from about $4.4 million in 2003 to $101.3 million in 2021.[19]

Note, too, that many of the nonprofits the Democracy Alliance recommends today didn't even exist when the Alliance was founded or were brand new. America Votes, the Center for American Progress, ProgressNow, Re:Power (formerly known as Wellstone Action), and Working America were all founded in 2003—the same year that Rob Stein started showing his PowerPoint presentation.[20] Media Matters for America and Color of Change popped up between 2004 and 2006—roughly the period chronicled in *The Argument*.[21] Others came about even later: the 501(c)(3) Center for Popular Democracy was established in 2012, merged with another group in 2014, and brought in almost $173 million total from 2017 to 2021.[22]

The Alliance, while steering vast sums of money into groups like these, was not solely responsible for their creation, or for their revenue growth. More money has simply been flowing through the ideological nonprofit sector in general. But wherever that money flows, it is never far from the Arabella empire.

What all these Democracy Alliance and Arabella groups have in common is their support for more and more centralized government in Washington, including ever more burdensome regulation of all facets of American life. We turn now to one especially disturbing Arabella effort to control lives through regulation, and by no coincidence, it has advanced through the near-unlimited checkbook wielded by George Soros.

10

Governing for Impact

Darkness within Darkness to Shape the Biden Administration and America's Schools

ONE OF THE MORE NOTABLE examples of the coordination between the Soros philanthropic network and Arabella Advisors—and the Biden administration—came to light in mid-2022, despite extensive efforts to keep it hidden.

Governing for Impact

In early 2022, Capital Research Center alerted Fox News to the existence of a secret 501(c)(3) "charity" called Governing for Impact.[1] The research organization and its sister (c)(4) "dark money" group, the Governing for Impact Action Fund, exist to research, write, promote, and defend new federal regulations for the Biden administration to issue. These two groups, sponsored by Arabella's New Venture Fund and Sixteen Thirty Fund, respectively, received a combined $17.4 million in funding from Soros grant-makers from 2019 to 2021.[2] Most surprisingly, the group intentionally operated far under the radar from its launch in 2019 (long *before* the 2020 presidential election) because its website was carefully set to be invisible to Google and other search engines. That's right; it was hidden from the public, who couldn't find it even by accident. But friends, including in the Biden administration, could reach it if they were told the site's URL, GoverningForImpact.org, and typed that into their computers. (After news reports based on our research "outed" the site, it became visible to search engines.)

Once the Biden administration took power, Governing for Impact exploited its high-level contacts within the administration (illustrated in previous chapters), ultimately enacting "more than 20" of the group's policy recommendations in the first couple years of the administration.

The regulations the secret group helped shape and make law aren't obscure or minor. A case study of just one of those policies illustrates how Arabella's infrastructure empowers the Left (particularly when endowed with Soros-level funding). But before we examine that particular case, observe the breadth of influence this secretive Arabella-Soros group has achieved.

The group's internal presentations to donors in 2022 state that it has drafted more than sixty policy memos designed to shape federal department after federal department, specifically:

- Education
- Interior
- HHS
- Labor
- Environmental Protection Agency
- Justice
- Housing and Urban Development
- Agriculture
- Energy
- Treasury

The sweeping agenda of specific radical policies in those agencies is breathtaking. At the Labor Department, for instance, they want to change the rules of independent contracting (likely to shut down the "gig" work industry, which means shuttering Uber, Doordash, and more). The Education Department agenda involves a half dozen specific issues, some of which we will examine more closely below, but in addition to those, the secretive radicals want to regulate "school discipline guidance," which likely means making schools even less safe. For the Environmental Protection Agency, the schemes involve things like regimens for government permits that hinder the building of factories and other industrial facilities where so many Americans have jobs. At the Agriculture Department, existing "work requirements" for food stamps are in the crosshairs for destruction—another policy where strong majorities of the public, and even half of all Democrats, support the opposite of what Arabella-Soros is pushing the Biden administration to do.[3]

"Transgender shelter protections" are among the items on the Department of Housing and Urban Development list, while the Department of Energy is being urged to increase "energy efficiency standards," which will raise prices on items within every American family's budget: refrigerators, furnaces, dishwashers, air conditioning, and much more. At the Department of Health and Human Services, there's an especially long to-do list, including, it appears, ditching work requirements for Medicaid benefits, getting rid of short-term health insurance plans that let people escape the costly insurance regulations of Obamacare, and of course, here as everywhere, expanding federal antidiscrimination requirements for sexual orientation and gender identity (the administration did the group's bidding on this in July 2022).[4]

The Treasury Department has an ominous checklist of a half dozen memos with titles like, "executive compensation" and "strengthening Dodd-Frank," the latter an Obama-era law that among other things has hurt small banks across the country, many of them serving rural voters whose political views differ from Governing for Impact's Harvard Law types and from those of the rich Wall Street financiers running the big banks that benefit from such regulation.[5]

Waging Culture War over Gender and Women's Sports

On its secret website, Governing for Impact prioritized six policy areas, with education policy listed at the top. One of the policies involved Title IX, the 1972 education law passed to protect women and women's sports on college campuses. So when in April 2022, Biden's Education Department announced it was seeking radical changes to Title IX—changes matching what Governing for Impact "research" supported—my colleague Parker Thayer sounded the alarm:[6]

> Governing for Impact is the ultimate example of the "dark money" the Left pretends to hate. It works totally in secret, it's funded by one billionaire, it's run by that billionaire's cronies, and it directly influences policy from the shadows. The idea that a group so deeply in Soros's pocket is calling the shots on regulations that will affect the education and safety of almost every child in the country is deeply disturbing and should be investigated at once.

As predicted, the Biden administration *did* announce sweeping changes to Title IX, and the proposed changes seem to pull directly from Governing for Impact policy papers. As Fox News reported:[7]

> The Education Department is set to announce a new regulation that will change Title IX rules on anti-transgender bias in schools, reversing Trump-era guidance.[8] [Governing for Impact] appears to have worked on the issue, as its site contains a November 2020 legal memo on the matter.[9]

The Education Department, like Governing for Impact, originally sought to make two key changes to Title IX. First, it would have changed the rules for investigations of sexual assault allegations in ways that seriously weaken the due process rights of accused young men. Second, it would have required schools, colleges, and universities to allow men and boys to compete in women's and girls' athletics based on their perceived "gender identity." Governing for Impact gave the administration policy papers recommending both changes.[10]

Creating Kangaroo Courts

In "Addressing Sexual Violence under Title IX of the Education Amendments of 1972," Governing for Impact advised the Education Department to repeal a regulation that required colleges to provide students accused of sexual harassment with in-person hearings, the opportunity to cross-examine accusers, and written summaries of the evidence presented against them.[11]

The Biden administration and its Soros-funded Arabella allies are trying to reverse Title IX regulations promulgated by then education secretary Betsy DeVos in 2020. Those regulatory reforms were needed because, as KC Johnson (he spells his name sans periods), professor of history at Brooklyn College, explains: "A well-intentioned policy initiative designed to ensure that survivors of sexual assault would not lose their access to education had wound up producing an entirely separate class of victims—students who were punished after dubious or false findings of guilt."[12] Johnson adds that these reforms had "survived five court challenges—from blue states, from professional and campus activist organizations," and from the ACLU.[13]

In response, Biden's proposed changes would implement almost every action item in Governing for Impact's memorandum and (if enacted) return campus Title IX procedures back to glorified kangaroo courts. KC Johnson and other academics have warned the changes would create a "Title IX Inquisition" on college campuses from which no one would be safe.[14]

Destroying Women's Sports

In a second memo, "Protecting the Rights of LGBTQ+ Students under Title IX of the Education Amendments of 1972," Governing for Impact also advises the Education Department to issue a regulation stating it will interpret Title IX protections so they extend to a student's gender identity.[15] The Biden administration's proposed rule changes include this item, citing the same court cases, providing comparable justifications, and using language similar to what's found in the Governing for Impact memo.

Opponents argue that this kind of regulation lacks any basis in law and would spell disaster for women's sports and women's on-campus opportunities.[16] Robert Eitel, the president of the Defense of Freedom Institute which has produced detailed rebuttals of the administration proposed regulations,[17] warns of how much damage those changes will produce: "By commandeering Title IX, progressives seek to force all educational institutions that receive federal funds to heed their ideological agenda on issues of gender identity, family, free speech, religious liberty, and abortion."[18]

Sarah Perry, senior legal fellow at the Heritage Foundation, warns that women's opportunities in college would be "jeopardized by the inclusion of biological males in their chosen athletic programs. How backward it is to take a women's movement 'win' and subjugate it to a 'loss' to the agenda of the radical few."[19]

Perry's phrase *agenda of the radical few* is apt, as the Governing for Impact memos reveal. The Biden administration's rule isn't responding to the American public, which by a large and growing majority oppose its policy.[20] No, the administration was following written instructions—from the Arabella network and its billionaire backer—and also, as we'll see, two other wealthy special interests on the left.

Uniting Soros, Teachers' Unions, and the Biden Administration

Although it worked in secret, Governing for Impact did not work alone. At the head of every single education policy memo it issued are two names: Governing for Impact and the National Student Legal Defense Network.[21] The Network is a left-of-center "charity" focused largely on college-debt forgiveness. The group helped write a policy memo proposing student-loan forgiveness for the permanently disabled, which the Biden administration appears to have acted on in its first year.[22]

It turns out the Network doesn't exactly work for students. It works for teachers' unions. In 2019, precisely when the Network began co-writing education policy memoranda with Governing for Impact, the American Federation of Teachers, the country's second largest teachers union, paid the Network $100,000 for "advocacy."[23] A year later, the National Education Association, the largest teachers' union, paid the Network another $150,000.[24]

During this period, we now know, the Network was hard at work with Governing for Impact, secretly developing educational regulations for the incoming administration. Meanwhile, the teachers' unions were loudly calling—and paying—for the exact policy changes that these two groups would co-create.

In 2020, American Federation of Teachers president Randi Weingarten publicly declared her union was fighting the pre-Biden regulatory reforms that reined in the Title IX kangaroo courts, and she baselessly accused Secretary DeVos of promoting a "boys will be boys" culture.[25] The National Education Association union also strongly opposed the reforms.[26] Then, seemingly coincidentally, both unions paid a combined $250,000 to the group that helped write the very policy that repealed the regulation.

The two teachers' unions have also been vocal supporters of allowing biological males to compete in women's sports and of canceling student loan debt, other areas that Governing for Impact policy memos have addressed.[27]

An Unholy Alliance

Biden's Title IX reforms were years in the making and were developed through a commingling of cash from teachers' unions and George Soros. As of this writing, however, the proposed rules are stalled. A coalition of twenty Republican state attorneys general—led by Tennessee attorney general Herbert Slatery—have sued the Biden administration, arguing that their states stand to lose significant federal funds because of statutes and policies that their states lawfully enacted.[28] In July 2022, federal district court judge Charles Atchley blocked the Education Department's Title IX guidance regulations. The administration has since issued new proposed Title IX rules, breaking its controversial proposed regulation of 2022 into two new proposed regulations.[29] The first focuses on sexual harassment proceedings for students and expanding rules that earlier prohibited only *sex* discrimination to now include discrimination against *gender identity*. The second proposal, issued in April 2023, addresses the issue of biological males participating in girls' and women's sports.

Reports that showed the Biden administration allowed teachers' unions to write the CDC's school-reopening guidelines during the COVID-19 pandemic exposed Big Labor's domineering influence over the administration and made that collusion "common knowledge."[30] But the combination of union influence with Soros influence via a once-underground think tank is a new and disturbing development. Together, two of the most powerful forces on the Left set their sights squarely on an important part of nearly every student's life, and—thanks to Arabella's sophistication and robust resources—nearly went unnoticed and unreported.

While the legal battles rage on, it is more important than ever to understand and investigate where these radical ideas come from, who is behind them, and the troubling amount of influence that left-wing megadonors seem to wield over the current administration, boosted by Arabella's little-known network.

Yet disturbing as all this growing power and control are, Arabella also faces new challenges as its operations become better known. As we'll see in the next chapter, it's harder to manipulate people when you're forced out of the shadows.

11

The End of Anonymity

Exposure and the Organizational Fallout

W HEN DEMAND JUSTICE first launched protests against President Trump's Supreme Court nominee (before Brett Kavanaugh
was even named as the nominee) in June 2018, the group was barely more
than a website. My colleagues at Capital Research Center immediately began digging. Within twenty-four hours, researchers posted a detailed profile
on our InfluenceWatch.org website—think Wikipedia, but for thousands
of advocacy groups, think tanks, foundations, activists, unions, and more
that work to influence public policy debates. The InfluenceWatch profile
on Demand Justice provided the only resource for everyone asking the same
question posed at the start of this book: "What is Demand Justice?"

The page was so successful that, for about six weeks in mid-2018, the
InfluenceWatch page outranked the group's own website in a Google search.

More importantly, Capital Research didn't stop digging. We waded
through the information about the Sixteen Thirty Fund and fiscal spon-
sorships. We noted the similarities in board members and contributions to
and from the group's other nonprofits. Eventually, our investigators uncovered promotional materials used in a presentation to funders by represen-

Demand Justice - Influence Watch
https://www.influencewatch.org/non-profit/demand-justice/ ▾
Jul 2, 2018 - Founded in early 2018, **Demand Justice** is a left-of-center 501(c)(4) advocacy group that
aims to influence the political leanings of America's ...
Media Campaigns · People · Director · Legal Counsel

Demand Justice
https://demandjustice.org/ ▾
Yes, I want mobile alerts from **Demand Justice**. Periodic messages. Msg & data rates may apply. Text
STOP to 738674 to stop receiving messages. Text HELP to ...

tatives from Arabella Advisors, which exposed how activists could utilize a joint 501(c)(3)-(c)(4) campaign model to provide "cohesive . . . messaging."

In April 2019, Capital Research completed its first major report on Arabella Advisors, documenting all of its activity through fiscal year 2017.[1] "Big Money in Dark Shadows: Arabella Advisors' Half-Billion-Dollar 'Dark Money' Network" earned significant coverage in center-right media outlets. At that point, the network's nonprofits were pulling in revenues of over $581 million.

Later that year, *Politico* covered a "little-known nonprofit called The Sixteen Thirty Fund" and observed that it "pumped $140 million into Democratic and left-leaning causes."[2] *Politico* named many of the "pop-up" groups Sixteen Thirty had concocted, carefully explained their state-level activities, and finally noted that Arabella Advisors provided "business and administrative services." (*Politico* had covered the Sixteen Thirty Fund's activity in 2018, but neither that coverage—nor a *New York Times* story that followed—uncovered Sixteen Thirty's relationship with Arabella Advisors or its connection to many other groups that operate through Arabella's other nonprofits.[3]) While *Politico* didn't acknowledge Capital Research Center's work, the coverage was similar.

The *Politico* article triggered dismay from none other than the *Washington Post* editorial board. In a house editorial decrying the lack of transparency regarding donors to social welfare organizations, the *Post* recounted a list of large anonymous donations. "According to the Politico report, a single donor to the Sixteen Thirty Fund gave $51.7 million, a second donor gave $26.7 million, and a third donated $10 million. Who are these donors?" Capital Research Center answered in a letter to the editor that the *Post* published two days later:

> In its 2018 Internal Revenue Service Form 990, a related nonprofit, New Venture Fund, showed a $26.7 million grant to the Sixteen Thirty Fund for "capacity building."
>
> The editorial also asked if Sixteen Thirty's donors are "part of a larger network of dark money." CRC has that answer, too. The Sixteen Thirty Fund is managed by Arabella Advisors, as is New Venture Fund and two more politically active nonprofits. To see their interlocking nature, note that Sixteen Thirty Fund claims zero employees on Page 1 of its 2018 Form 990. On Page 59, a footnote reveals "New Venture Fund (NVF) is the paymaster for Sixteen Thirty Fund payroll. NVF pays the salary and immediately invoices Sixteen Thirty Fund, which reimburses the full amount."

Arabella Finally Responds

Once Capital Research Center's response appeared in the *Post*, the references to Arabella's connections to the managed nonprofits only increased—and became widely noticed. At the beginning of 2020, *Inside Philanthropy*, a left-leaning online news outlet covering the world of grant-making, published a 3,000-word profile of Arabella Advisors that covered both its political and non-political clients; indeed, the profile seemed designed to provide a subtle defense of Arabella's hyper-political work from our criticism by stressing Arabella's more traditional philanthropic activities.[4] I suspect *Inside Philanthropy*, led by a co-founder of the left-wing Demos think tank, didn't like the tarnish that Arabella's empire was acquiring as its true nature became better known. Who knows? Perhaps Arabella even sought it out for friendly coverage. At the same time, *Inside Philanthropy's* profile was constrained by its commitment to fairly honest reporting and also by its admiration of what Arabella achieves for the team, as it were:

Beyond its impressive numbers and copious offerings, what makes Arabella interesting is what it's doing to build and shape the field. "In a philanthropy world that talks a lot about big bets, we do the big builds. We find that the field needs support in going from idea to impact," said CEO Sampriti Ganguli. Whether it's providing back-office support or playing a more frontal role, Arabella's fingerprints are all over any number of philanthropic projects. Yet while the firm is best understood as one of the sector's top workhorses, its public profile—shaped by a steady stream of articles by places like the Capital Research Center and Breitbart—can suggest something quite different, with conservatives criticizing Arabella for channeling unaccountable funds to politically sensitive causes.... These two narratives aren't necessarily in conflict.

The article acknowledged the increased scrutiny of Arabella and its overall activities:

Because its work is so varied, Arabella doesn't position itself in the ideologically pointed terms of some of its peers. But it hasn't escaped scrutiny. In particular, the magnitude of anonymous funds flowing through entities like the New Venture Fund and the Sixteen Thirty Fund have attracted negative attention for the political influence they may exert. Although most of that attention originates in conservative circles (the Capital Research Center, a think tank funded in part by major conservative philanthropies, has been especially adamant in its investigations), other outlets have picked up the story.

The *Inside Philanthropy* coverage represented the first time that anyone from the Arabella network acknowledged its large-scale, multifaceted political efforts to the press, in an attempt to reshape the narrative about this amazing beast.

Unpersuaded by that reshaping, my colleagues at Capital Research released a September 2020 update on the Arabella empire, documenting its 2018 activities, with $635 million in nonprofit revenue. This second study focused on the ways that the nonprofit organizations, particularly the Sixteen Thirty Fund, engaged in the 2018 midterm elections through ads, voter turnout, and state-based "pop-up" groups.

Around this time (at least according to the Internet Archive's WayBackMachine), Arabella Advisor acknowledged Capital Research's reporting by posting a long page on its website entitled, "A Note on Our Work."[5] This "note," over 630 words, begins by claiming that Capital Research Center "has promoted misleading stories regarding leaders in the philanthropic space that it believes do not support its ideology, including Arabella Advisors." In addition, it claims, "CRC's stories are filled with factual errors and inexplicable mischaracterizations."

If Capital Research's claims are lies, why has Arabella and its many tentacles never once contacted us about factual errors or mischaracterizations? Nor has Arabella ever responded to claims we've made in any public forum that has published those claims, including the *Washington Post* and the *Wall Street Journal*. Needless to say, we invite corrections, including of the exhaustive entries on our InfluenceWatch.org site that cover Arabella's many parts. And I'd enjoy nothing more than having a public debate with any Arabella leader on the nature of its work and our reporting on it. Capital Research Center would happily cover all costs for such a debate—say, at the National Press Club, where media friendly to Arabella and its left-wing agenda could join in. If Arabella were speaking the truth, rather than lies, in its complaints, it would welcome the chance to expose our errors before the press. (An interesting footnote on Arabella's "Note on Our Work": the page is dated October 2019, but it appears to have eluded search engines until August 2020.)

The Left's Equivalent of the Koch Brothers?

Capital Research continued to cover Arabella well into 2021, spurred by ever-more discoveries concerning their involvement in major campaigns.

Members of the Arabella network took positions in the Biden administration, showed up in *Time* magazine's amazing story on "The Secret History of the Shadow Campaign That Saved the 2020 Election," and directed the nomination debate over Justice Ketanji Brown Jackson.[6]

In April 2021, attention to Arabella Advisors increased dramatically. Reporter Ken Vogel of the *New York Times* uncovered the connections between Swiss billionaire Hansjörg Wyss and the Hub Project (covered in chapter 7) in the midst of Wyss's bid to purchase the *Chicago Tribune*'s newspaper chain.[7] Vogel followed that article three weeks later with a more in-depth profile of Wyss and his giving through both his foundation and its sister 501(c)(4) group—focusing special attention on the funding passed to Arabella-related nonprofits: "Between the spring of 2016 and the spring of 2020," the reporter noted, Wyss's (c)(4) "donated more than $135 million to the Sixteen Thirty Fund, which has become among the leading dark money spenders on the left."

Later that year, *Sludge*, a left-of-center investigative news outlet focusing on money in politics, ran its own exposé on how the "Gates Foundation Was [a] Major Donor to Pro-Biden 'Dark Money' Network."[8] The article spotlighted Gates' contributions to New Venture Fund, but it covered the entire "Arabella Umbrella." According to the piece, "Even though the Arabella network states its support for campaign finance reform, it also brandishes dark money in politics at very high levels."

But the biggest hit came in November 2021. The *Atlantic*'s Emma Green sat down with then Arabella CEO Sampriti Ganguli for an interview.[9] The introduction to the interview begins:

["Dark money" groups] tend to have innocuous-sounding names and promiscuously spawn mini-organizations that take up particular state and local causes. [Arabella's] North Fund, for example, spent nearly $5 million trying to legalize marijuana in Montana last year. [Arabella's] Sixteen Thirty Fund—the indisputable heavyweight of Democratic dark money—was the second-largest super-PAC donor in 2020, according to the investigative organization OpenSecrets, giving roughly

$61 million of effectively untraceable money to progressive causes. The organization that connects many of these groups—what a critic might call the mothership—is called Arabella Advisors.

Arabella hates this narrative. The organization's CEO, Sampriti Ganguli, insisted to me that she runs a relatively small business-services organization that does HR, legal compliance, accounting, etc., for clients such as the Sixteen Thirty Fund. Ganguli comes from a consultant background, and she talks like it: Arabella's mission is to make philanthropy more efficient, effective, and equitable, she told me.

The interview became steadily more uncomfortable:

GREEN: Do you think your clients and donors should have to put their names on those efforts?

GANGULI: I have an appreciation for why donors need to be able to choose whether they disclose that information or not. And I think it's a low likelihood that the laws will actually change in this area. Our laws protect individuals and their privacy around causes they believe in.

GREEN: You say you think donors should have the right to choose. Just to zoom out, what we're talking about is people with a lot of money, who want to channel that money into changing the way our society is structured. Why should people with a lot of money be able to do this anonymously?

GANGULI: There are a lot of actors involved in changing American civic life. I just have to be honest with you: You're zooming in on such a small part of what Arabella Advisors does. I'm struggling with your question.

GREEN: Yeah, but: 530 grants. That's not nothing.

• • •

GREEN: The Koch network is perhaps the biggest example [of philanthropic efforts that work in the opposite political direction of

Arabella Advisors]. I wonder: When you look out across the horizon and you see your Dark Spider-Man, do you think, Okay, well, that's the system we have, and as long as they're legally compliant, fair game?

GANGULI: There definitely are organizations that work in opposition to the Sixteen Thirty Fund and other clients. I think the rules have to be the same for all sets of actors and agents.

GREEN: But the rules are the same, right? The Koch brothers live in America; they're operating in the American tax system. Assuming they try as hard as you do to comply with the laws as they stand, they are able to put lots of money and energy into what you probably see as making America a worse country.

Are you okay with that?

GANGULI: I love that you're pushing me on my beliefs and values. I have a job to do, just like everybody else has a job to do. You're giving me more credit for systems-level thinking than I, candidly, spend. Let me just make sure I understand your question. Is it fair that the Koch brothers get to do what they do?

GREEN: Right. You both take advantage of similar legal structures, federal regulations, and the ability to put lots of money toward politics, little p. They just work on the opposite side, for opposite causes.

Do you feel good that you're the left's equivalent of the Koch brothers?

GANGULI: Yeah.

GREEN: You do! Tell me why.

GANGULI: Because we believe in many of those causes.

GREEN: So you think it's good to take advantage of the existing legal structures because ultimately you're going to do good?

GANGULI: We will make sure we are compliant with all of the laws as they are. And should they change, we will make sure we are compliant.

Several things are significant about this interview. First, its timing. It was published in November 2021, a mere two weeks before Arabella's nonprofits had to publicly release their Form 990s for 2020, which would reveal a staggering leap in nonprofit revenue from $740 million the previous year to $1.74 billion in that fateful election year. It's hard to believe Arabella didn't set up the *Atlantic* interview in hopes of having a friendly conversation that would soften the blow of this amazing windfall, which so clearly shows how political an operation Arabella is.

But instead of helping Arabella cover over its politicking, the left-leaning magazine understood all too well the creature it was dealing with. I chuckled over several of the *Atlantic's* questions that seemed to be lifted from criticisms of Arabella I had made the year before in the *Wall Street Journal*.[10] Above all, the magazine relentlessly hammered Arabella's central hypocrisy: Like all good left-wingers, the empire pays lip service to the evils of "dark money" in politics, even as it piles up billions of that money for its own political purposes. As I read the interviewer, over and over, demand to know how Ganguli could live with Arabella's perfidy, I began to feel sorry for the hapless CEO, who was so clearly unprepared to deal with the issue.

Nor was I surprised when, a month or so later, Arabella Advisors announced that Chief Revenue Officer Rick Cruz would "take on day-to-day leadership of the firm effective immediately, as Sampriti Ganguli prepares to step away from her current position as Arabella's CEO on April 15, 2022," so she "can spend more time with family."[11]

While the name Arabella Advisors does not as yet have the same prominence as the Gates Foundation or George Soros's philanthropy, its fame has been growing among those who follow policy debates and electoral politics. Search the largest news database in LexisNexis and you find no instances of "dark money" references to any of Arabella Advisors' groups appearing in 2017. By contrast, search for such references appearing in 2022 and you find 163 articles referencing Arabella's network and "dark money" (not including references on Capital Research Center's own websites). Given that Arabella's nonprofit revenues have reached nearly $2 billion in each of the last two years available (2020 and 2021), these references will continue to grow.

Arabella's Dark Money

Number of times names associated with Arabella were used
within 20 words of "dark money"

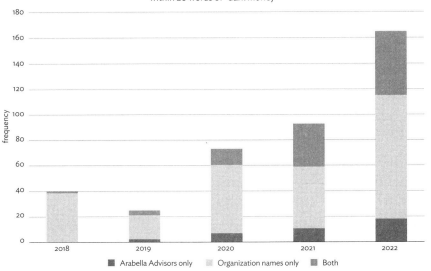

■ Arabella Advisors only   ▨ Organization names only   ■ Both

A Look at Arabella from the Inside

Questions about Arabella and its operations don't just come from the outside. In late October 2022, a Capital Research colleague, Hayden Ludwig, broke the story that Sarah Walker, an employee of both Arabella's New Venture Fund and Secure Democracy (a group not hitherto associated with Arabella), had filed a lawsuit against New Venture, Secure Democracy, and Secure Democracy USA, claiming that the groups provided a hostile work environment, that she was a victim of racial discrimination, and that she was retaliated against because of her complaints over both the racial discrimination and her internal whistleblowing on violations of nonprofit laws.[12] The 112-page complaint and exhibits detail eleven separate causes of action, allege discriminatory practices against additional employees, and expose the internal activities of two "pop-up" groups that operated within the Arabella sphere: Voting Rights Lab, a (c)(3) organization, and Secure Democracy, a (c)(4).[13] (According to Walker's complaint, Secure Democracy was dissolved, and Secure Democracy USA was launched, at the end of 2021, apparently in response to the serious allegations she had made internally about Secure Democracy's improprieties.)

The complaint makes quite interesting reading:

> 10. Due to her position, Ms. Walker discovered that [New Venture Fund; NVF] and [Secure Democracy; SD] were discriminating against numerous employees, particularly female employees of color, by paying them less than their white counterparts, denying them equal opportunity for advancement, and denying them equal access to benefits, among other forms of discrimination. In addition, Ms. Walker discovered that NVF and SD were engaged in numerous violations of the Internal Revenue Code, jeopardizing their tax exempt status. The Defendants' pattern of employment discrimination and intentional tax violations indicate that NVF and SD are simply unconcerned about following the law.
>
> 11. When Ms. Walker spoke up about the workplace injustices and non-compliant tax practices engaged in by NVF and SD, those organizations swiftly retaliated against her. In addition to furthering a hostile work environment that severely compromised her ability to perform her duties for SD and NVF, the organizations terminated her in such a way so as to severely damage her reputation and inflict emotional distress that exacerbated her disability, negatively impacting her physical and mental health. Unsurprisingly, in seeming acknowledgement of the unlawful tax practices Ms. Walker alleged, SD, the 501(c)(4) enmeshed in the misconduct was dissolved less than two months after she reported the improper federal tax practices.

A second shoe dropped in January 2023, when another black woman, Dr. Francesca Weaks, filed a lawsuit against New Venture Fund and its pop-up Local Solutions Support Center (LSSC) for "breach of their written contract and wrongful termination." New Venture hired Weaks, a racial equity consultant, on behalf of their client, LSSC, a hub of organizations that combat legislation introduced at the state level to pre-empt local ordinances. In her complaint, Weaks describes multiple instances of LSSC and New Venture employees subjecting Weaks and other black consultants to "racial harassment."[14] She notes that one white female executive was "often openly hostile to the DEI [Diversity Equity and Inclusion] consultants," and that black-led organizations were repeatedly disparaged on conference calls. Like Walker, Weaks claims discrimination in compensation practices. She felt used:

> as nothing more than a token to be shown to the funders as an example of diversity without paying [Weaks] her worth, despite the fact that all other non-black consultants received their request for pay equity increases. . . . To add insult to injury, the other non-black DEI consultant received the "increased funding" pay increase despite [Weaks] doing the majority of the work. When [Weaks] finally received a . . . pay increase it was still below the other consultants' increases.

When the *Washington Free Beacon* broke the story on the second lawsuit, it described another allegation:

> Weaks alleges in her lawsuit that her New Venture Fund colleagues duped prospective donors by falsely claiming the organization was partnered with the nation's most renowned black advocacy organization, the NAACP. Weaks, who once worked for the NAACP, said she was alarmed to learn in 2021 that a white New Venture Fund consultant was trying to trick donors by falsely claiming the charity struck a partnership with her former employer.[15]

Later, the *Free Beacon* continued its coverage of these expanding scandals with two deep dives into misdeeds revealed by the whistleblowers. I'm proud Capital Research Center assisted this excellent reporting by providing expertise on the complicated nonprofit legal issues raised. The *Free Beacon* also spoke with multiple nonprofit lawyers and with no less than five former Arabella empire employees, who raised "questions about Arabella's commitment to the law." The former employees paint a picture of major deception: they say, and document, that Secure Democracy, a 501(c)(4) nonprofit that was supposedly entirely independent of Arabella, was in fact being controlled by a 501(c)(3) project under Arabella's New Venture Fund.[16]

Great efforts went into this deception, partly to allow Secure Democracy to avoid appearing to serve Democratic Party interests. That camouflage, in turn, helped agents of Secure Democracy as they tried to infiltrate conservative groups working on election integrity and, with the aid of cash, also helped the group to seduce state-level Republicans into cooperating with its agenda. Similarly, Secure Democracy was treated as a non-Democratic effort by the R Street Institute, which invited its participation on an election policy panel.[17] As one former employee put it regarding Secure Democracy's lobbying, "Every lawmaker at the state level was misled."

Legal experts reviewing the evidence were particularly concerned about what Arabella did once Sarah Walker blew the whistle on the supposedly independent 501(c)(4) group being controlled by an Arabella 501(c)(3) project. In response, Arabella allegedly directed one of its internal (c)(4) groups, the North Fund, to have employees alter their past timesheets to make it appear North Fund had subsidized the "independent" nonprofit's work the previous year. "The attempt to retroactively involve a c4 in the spending is an indication that someone realized how risky the political activity is for the charity," one nonprofit attorney told the *Free Beacon*. "While nonprofits regularly file amendments, going back and changing time sheets after the books are closed and nearly 18 months prior is unusual to say the least."[18]

Further efforts to clean up this mess have resulted in the internal Arabella (c)(3) project, the Voting Rights Lab, leaving the New Venture Fund to become part of the independent Secure Democracy group of nonprofits, as the same *Free Beacon* article explains.

Sarah Walker's lawsuit has not been scheduled for a hearing at this writing. The judge in Weaks's lawsuit denied New Venture Fund's motion to dismiss, though New Venture has filed for reconsideration, claiming it did not breach a statement of work or a master service agreement. At press time, parties are scheduled to enter into mediation in January 2024.

Further Troubles for Arabella

In addition to the problems swirling around Arabella's two lawsuits, it saw its 2021 revenues dip from the historic highs of 2020. In the aftermath, it laid off 10 percent of its staff, about thirty employees, in 2023, and it once again saw its top leader step down precipitously, with no successor in sight. The board let CEO Rick Cruz go with "decidedly mixed emotions" less than two weeks after the *Free Beacon*'s embarrassing reports on alleged improprieties at the network.[19]

Another threat to Arabella's finances appeared in 2023 when the chairman of the House Administration Committee, Rep. Bryan Steil (R-WI), introduced legislation that would affect Arabella because of the empire's receipt of hundreds of millions of dollars from foreign donor Hansjörg Wyss over the years. The proposed law forbids "dark money" groups like Arabella's Sixteen Thirty Fund from giving to political action committees if they accept foreign donations.

Still more embarrassments struck Arabella in 2023. The conservative-leaning watchdog group Americans for Public Trust filed an IRS complaint alleging, among other things, that the New Venture and Sixteen Thirty Funds misled the IRS in their applications for tax-exemption. In identical language, when filing their applications for tax-exempt status, both New Venture Fund and Sixteen Thirty informed the IRS "that their administrative support arrangements with Arabella would be of limited duration," ending as soon as they had sufficient revenues to provide for themselves in house the administrative services they originally were purchasing from the for-profit Arabella. Of course, two decades have now elapsed, and the two funds have seen spectacular growth in revenues, yet they continue to pay millions to Eric Kessler's Arabella consultancy.[20]

Arabella suffered yet another embarrassment as Sam Bankman-Fried, Democratic mega-donor and disgraced cryptocurrency entrepreneur, went to trial in 2023. Bankman-Fried's father, who is also accused of wrongdoing in the multibillion-dollar collapse of his son's businesses, was revealed in court filings to serve on an advisory board at New Venture Fund. That's not surprising, given that court filings also claim Bankman-Fried's FTX corporation gave New Venture at least $8 million. New Venture isn't saying how much of the donation it still retains, nor which groups received FTX's money, but it suggests it's willing to return remaining funds once the bankruptcy court figures out where they should go.[21]

An Epilogue on Demand Justice

After being a part of the Sixteen Thirty Fund since its inception at a Democracy Alliance meeting in 2018, Demand Justice received its own independent tax-exempt status from the IRS in December 2021. It's hard not to think this move occurred at least in part because of Capital Research Center's exposure of Demand Justice and the Arabella network. The independent designation came just in time for another Supreme Court nomination debate. This time, Demand Justice almost single-handedly lobbied to promote Ketanji Brown Jackson from a lower court to the nation's highest court in a scant few years—something Arabella Advisors itself is quick to say it had no hand in.[22] An updated version of Arabella's web page trying to brush off reporting by Capital Research claims, "In fact, Arabella Advisors does not work for Demand Justice in any capacity."[23]

That may be true of Arabella the company, but not of its nonprofit network, for several reasons. First, Arabella's Sixteen Thirty Fund pumped $110,000 into Demand Justice's PAC, providing roughly one-third of its contributions in the 2022 cycle and making it the PAC's second-largest contributor after Demand Justice itself.[24] Much of that money was paid to consultancies like Mothership Strategies and Scasey Communications—the latter active in Wisconsin elections—for independent expenditures and digital consulting.[25] Another $50,000 went to the Big Labor–aligned Working Families Party in New York.[26]

The other reasons to laugh at Arabella's attempts to distance itself from Demand Justice include the $2 million that Arabella's Sixteen Thirty Fund gave to Demand Justice in 2021 (the most recent year data are available), and the $2.8 million that Arabella's New Venture Fund gave to Demand Justice Initiative, Demand Justice's (c)(3) affiliate that began as a pop-up group at New Venture. These dollars provide millions of reasons to recognize that Demand Justice remains enmeshed in the Arabella web, even as it has become, technically, legally separate.

My Capital Research Center colleagues and I thank Arabella for adding excitement to our work of tracking its tentacles as it makes ever more embarrassed efforts to camouflage its network. Embarrassing though their efforts at mass deception should be, a group like Arabella is beyond embarrassment. Exposing their hypocrisy and their long reach into Americans' lives, though important and valuable work, will not suffice to solve the problem Arabella presents. What can we do once we are aware of Arabella's attempts to manipulate the public by misleading the public? That is the subject of our concluding chapter.

12

Can the Arabella Problem
Be Solved?

T HIS BOOK is a sobering wake-up call to Americans, few of whom have known about Arabella or its multibillion-dollar operation that is so deeply involved in their lives and their elections. Arabella's successes reveal the Left's stunning advantage in money and sophisticated political machinery. Still, the Left faces a major problem: where its ideas become entrenched—from big cities like San Francisco to prestigious colleges—they produce ugly realities that become a hindrance to the Left's utopian dreams of control. Those dreams, when brought into real life, become nightmares, which helps explain why most Americans of all ethnicities and party registration don't hold left-wing views on so many issues, from crime to race relations to voter ID laws. In fact, as I write, the black mayor of Dallas, a longtime Democrat, has switched parties, explaining that his constituents want the city to be hostile to crime but friendly to families and businesses. The best proof that he's telling the truth: a few months *before* his switch, he received 93 percent support for reelection.[1]

I understand readers may become depressed after learning just how much money from numerous billionaires is pouring into all of these fake Arabella groups aligned against ordinary citizens. But it's wrong to despair: people who support America's founding principles of liberty and equality have been overcoming richer and more powerful foes since some backwoods colonials in the 1700s defeated the grandest empire the world had ever seen.

Countering Arabella through Education

That is not to say Arabella can easily be countered just because we are the righteous underdog, but the first steps are obvious and involve educating the public and government officials. We'll consider other means of countering the Left's project shortly, but the first priority must be to achieve a clear picture of the situation. No one can win a battle without first understanding the forces on the other side—their size, their capacities, their preferred ways of fighting, their foreign allies, how they're configured. This book, and the continuing work of my colleagues at Capital Research Center, provide invaluable intelligence into the many ways that Arabella transforms mega-donors' wishes into victories for a vision of America in which elites control the rest of us through propaganda and an ever-more-powerful centralized government.

So far this educational effort to respond to Arabella has gained some ground. As more than one earlier chapter has explained, in just a few years Arabella has gone from something never mentioned in the media to a recognized colossus of "dark money," not just among conservative news outlets but even among elite left-leaning media like the *Atlantic* and the *New York Times*. Arabella has felt the need to spin out some of its more notorious projects into supposedly "independent" status, even if mega-donor money still often passes through Arabella's branches into entities like Demand Justice.

Worse, from Arabella's perspective, as this book is written, the powerful House Ways and Means Committee—which oversees all tax law including the treatment of tax-exempt nonprofits—has begun to raise the alarm over both "the Arabella Advisors network of organizations" and that network's close relations with Hansjörg Wyss, the Swiss billionaire who admits to past illegal meddling in American politics. The chairman of the full Ways and Means Committee, Rep. Jason Smith (R-MO), as well as the chairman of its Subcommittee on Oversight, Rep. David Schweikert (R-AZ), declare that "Public reporting has raised questions about whether tax-exempt sectors are operating in a manner consistent with the laws and regulations that govern such organizations." As they begin their investigations, citing research from Capital Research Center and other watchdogs, the congressmen do not doubt that "significant amounts of foreign money is flowing through 501(c)(3) and 501(c)(4) organizations to influence elections." In its letter launching these inquiries, the committee explicitly names Wyss and notes that he personally controls both types of nonprofits, which in turn have given millions to Arabella's New Venture and Sixteen Thirty Funds.[2] One hopes the committee will hold hearings in which all these groups' leaders are forced to defend these money flows. Let them try to justify what this tsunami of cash has done to Americans and how it has influenced our elections.

Such hearings, conducted rigorously, would deter at least some bad behavior by Arabella and others, and similar hearings could be held in state legislatures. State attorneys general, who in nearly all states are the main enforcers of laws governing nonprofits, could likewise investigate these kinds of problematic behavior.

Another valuable educational response to Arabella consists of highlighting the astounding hypocrisy that its empire and the rest of the Left display when it comes to so-called campaign finance "reform." In its public pieties, the Left claims to love campaign finance reform, insisting laws are needed to end "dark money" by reducing billionaires' influence and forcing the disclosure of all donors. Arabella sometimes joins in mouthing these pieties and, as we saw in chapters 2 and 8, the Sixteen Thirty Fund and the North Fund have taken fat checks in recent years to lobby for passage of H.R. 1, a Democratic-sponsored bill that would make such changes, and much more, federal law.

Yet when the *Atlantic* interviewed Arabella's then-president Sampri-ti Ganguli and pointed out that its empire is a "dark money" behemoth, powered by billionaires, Ganguli was almost reduced to stuttering about the contradiction. Similarly, when the North Fund—which has taken tens of thousands of dollars to lobby for H.R. 1—was pressed by Montana's attorney general to disclose its donors, the Arabella group fought hard *not* to disclose those donors.[3]

As we saw in the last chapter, even friends of Arabella like *Inside Philanthropy* concede the empire is "channeling unaccountable funds to politically sensitive causes."[4] Ganguli has been even more frank, admitting, as we quoted her in chapter 2, that "platforms" like Arabella "are really solving for an end—I don't want to say an end run—but they're a work-around to the tax regime."[5]

Of course, just because Arabella is a world-class hypocrite in its resistance to disclosing donors, that doesn't make government-coerced donor disclosure a good way to counter Arabella, as I'll explain shortly when we consider possible legislative fixes to these problems. But first, let's return to the question I'm so often asked: What do I think are the motivations that lie behind the billions of dollars of work Arabella carries out for its billionaire patrons?

Of course, I can't know with certainty, and I'm speaking here only for myself, not the Capital Research Center, but sometimes the motivation may be garden-variety greed, as when the rich push policies on, say, environmental issues that will lead to governmental subsidies for manufacturers of batteries and electric vehicles in which they've invested. For example, George Soros has been a major investor in Rivian, an upstart electric vehicle manufacturer that benefits from the enormous government subsidies provided to such vehicles.[6] Other left-wing billionaires, including Bill Gates and Laurene Powell Jobs, are heavily invested in two electric battery companies, Redwood Materials and Ioneer, which have received nearly $3 billion in loans from the Biden administration which those billionaires helped to elect, the *Washington Free Beacon* reports.[7]

But greed alone can't explain the relentless drive to interfere in other people's lives that one sees in that early Arabella fight to harass people riding trails in rural Montana (chapter 1). That seems to require a powerful urge to control others, one that doesn't flow in the opposite direction—that is to say, no one can imagine a backwoods motorcyclist in Montana creating a group that, say, harasses left-wing donors in New York's Upper East Side as they listen to author Jane Mayer bewail right-wing "dark money" at a *New Yorker* cocktail party.

If a yearning to control others helps explain the Left's behavior, it must be connected to some puritanical impulse to force others to stop being impure, but in a secularized way that would baffle the original Puritans. I think approaching the question of motivation in this theological way makes sense. After all, the radical environmentalism that first inspired Arabella founder Eric Kessler as an undergraduate is a kind of religion. As the historian Michael Barone observes, environmentalism has "all the trappings of religion" as it warns of a climate apocalypse:

> Original sin: Mankind is responsible for these prophesied disasters, especially those slobs who live in suburbs and drive their SUVs to strip malls and tacky chain restaurants. The need for atonement and repentance: We must impose a carbon tax or cap-and-trade system, which will raise the cost of everything and stunt economic growth. Ritual, from the annual Earth Day to weekly recycling. Indulgences, like those Martin Luther railed against: private jet-fliers like Al Gore and sitcom heiress Laurie David can buy carbon offsets to compensate for their carbon-emitting sins.

The lust to control others may also be associated with narcissism. One scholarly work on narcissism reports that a classic type of the disorder has a "power orientation" that involves "striving for control and coerciveness."[8] A more popular discussion of narcissism in *Psychology Today* sometimes reads like an analysis of Arabella. For example, it reports that narcissists "use a range of covert and overt tactics to manipulate others," and typically project onto others their own behaviors—something that fits the empire's willingness to support, with lip service, efforts to suppress "dark money." Then there's Arabella's use of fake groups pretending to be grassroots efforts, which resembles the way narcissists "value appearance more than substance" and strive to "convince others rather than be honest." But the strongest correlation between Arabella's operations and its donors, on the one hand, and the typical behavior of narcissists on the other, is the way they all "treat others as possessing lesser intelligence or having fewer rights."[9] When others—from trail riders in Montana to an at-home mom selling kitchen products for a Warren Buffett company (chapter 5)—are demeaned, mega-donors and their minions can feel the glow of superiority.

Although the temptation to narcissism is no doubt present to donors across the political spectrum, let me repeat that the libertarian Koch brothers and their nonprofit network are not exactly equivalent to Arabella's network, though they are the largest such network on the opposite end of American politics. As explained in the introduction, the groups led by Charles and the late David Koch are not as politically engaged as Arabella, nor does Arabella have anything like the Kochs' across-the-aisle project of a think tank co-funded with George Soros. Above all, the Koch operations don't dominate the political Right the way Arabella dominates the Left.

While the Biden administration treats Arabella founder Eric Kessler as if he's the deputy secretary of agriculture, looping him into the actual secretary's emails on major policy decisions (chapter 1), neither Koch brother has enjoyed such treatment under a Republican administration. Nor has any Koch organization ever exercised anything like the power over the federal government's regulatory machinery that Arabella's secret Governing for Impact project—funded entirely by Soros philanthropies—has achieved in the Biden administration (chapter 10).

Above all, the Koch network is not aligned with major factions of the Republican Party and the conservative movement, but rather has disputes with them over Donald Trump's leadership, criminal justice issues, and trade policy. Whatever one's views on those issues, the Koch network contrasts sharply with Arabella, which not only works intimately with the leader of the Democratic Party, and with the party's most famous lawyer, Marc Elias, but is also relied on by mega-donors throughout the Left for fights on nearly every policy battlefield.

In fact, Arabella doesn't resemble the Koch network much at all but it *does* bring to mind an earlier project of mega-donors; namely, the widespread drive at the beginning of the last century for eugenics. That will sound shocking to some, but not to those who know the actual history, like longtime philanthropy critic William Schambra. In his classic essay on "Philanthropy's Original Sin," Schambra explains the involvement in this ugly movement of so many of America's first mega-donors and foundation-builders.[10] They saw themselves as fostering capital "s" Science and ushering in an era of progressivism. These big donors, reports Edwin Black, a historian of the movement, "were all in league with some of America's most respected scientists hailing from such prestigious universities as Stanford, Yale, Harvard, and Princeton."[11]

Eugenics was clearly a bid to control people, and these mega-donors not only sponsored research but also lobbied government for policies in support of the movement and its coercive tactics, including forced sterilization by the government of the allegedly "feebleminded." Schambra notes that this pseudo-scientific philanthropic effort was explicitly in revolt against charity—which the movement's leaders accused of coddling the undeserving poor—and also in revolt against the traditional American way of life, in which families, neighborhoods, churches, and local civic groups, not centralized government run by an elite, are the key to a flourishing society. Schambra reports that Margaret Sanger, a Rockefeller grantee and Planned Parenthood's founder, devoted a chapter in her 1922 book *The Pivot of Civilization* to "The Cruelty of Charity."[12] She insisted America's charitable institutions are the "surest signs that our civilization has bred, is breeding and is perpetuating constantly increasing numbers of defectives, delinquents and dependents."

In later decades, foundations and other megadonors would continue to support such brutal elitism in evolving ways, through figures like Frederick H. Osborn, a longtime board member of the main Carnegie foundation. Osborn also wrote the 1940 book *Preface to Eugenics*, hailed by *Time* magazine as a new "eugenics for democracy" that America, as Schambra puts it, "could pursue without fear of being associated with the abuses then becoming embarrassingly evident in the Third Reich." After the war, Osborn succeeded in "rebranding eugenics as medical genetics and 'population control.'" He was still at it in old age when a Rockefeller Foundation executive in 1967 "invited him to write the chapter on 'population problems' for an authoritative volume on the history of American foundations." There Osborn declared, "we can foresee the time when all over the world the control of births is as much the accepted responsibility of governments as is at present their responsibility for the public health."

Just a few years after Osborn wrote those lines, Arabella's Eric Kessler was born, and two decades further on, Kessler would fall under the influence of radical environmentalist David Brower who, in an echo of the eugenicist Osborn, floated the idea of governments requiring all potential parents "to use contraceptive chemicals, the governments issuing antidotes to citizens chosen for childbearing."[13] That sounds deranged to normal people, but this man had such a spell over Kessler that the collegian hitchhiked across several states in order to volunteer to work for Brower. Nor was Brower a fringe figure in left-wing activism at the time. He served as executive director of the Sierra Club for most of the 1950s and 1960s. He also founded Friends of the Earth, Earth Island Institute, and the League of Conservation Voters, the "dark money" powerhouse where Kessler would go on to work and that still heavily colludes with Arabella groups. Brower was even nominated for the Nobel Peace Prize, though ironically his aggressive political interventions when he led the Sierra Club caused the group to lose its charity status with the IRS.[14]

Again, in these musings on the Left's motivations, I am speaking only for myself. I have no idea if Eric Kessler or anyone else at Arabella knows of, much less agrees with, Brower's demented longing to have the central government control Americans' childbearing. Yet the fact remains that this antihuman guru produced a kind of religious conversion experience in Arabella's founder, launching him on the left-wing activism to which he's devoted his life. Around the same time Kessler had his come-to-Gaia experience, a friend of mine was spending months on end living up in a tree as part of his clandestine infiltration of a radical group. That group—which also supported the idea of "tree spiking," a practice that could kill loggers—hoped to use their treetop occupation to stop logging in the Northwest. My friend informs me that Brower was a top inspiration for his arboreal companions, whose environmental religiosity resembled that of ancient ascetics who lived atop pillars.

Of course, eugenics and its more recent cousin, population control, are not the only ways that left-wing philanthropy sets itself at odds with ordinary citizens. This Arabella-aided philanthropy rests on a cold, technocratic, elitist view, in which billionaire foundations and other mega-donors pride themselves on pushing the central government into engineering society as they see fit. This kind of elitism, Schambra observes, conflicts with the traditional American understanding that all of us have dignity and deserve to participate in governing society. That conflict explains why "transforming" America has been a left-wing byword in recent years, as the Left insists that America is a racist nation, a "colonizing" nation whose history and Constitution deserve only scorn. It also explains why camouflage and propaganda by the likes of Arabella are required to advance an agenda that empowers people like Bill Gates and George Soros at the expense of Montana trail riders and so many others.

The need to empower the public at large to resist the Left's agenda leads naturally to the question of whether legislation or other governmental means are well suited to counter Arabella and the Left.

Countering Arabella through Legislation

When the problem of mega-donors and their enablers like Arabella is raised, many people, and not only those on the Left, leap to the conclusion that forcing all nonprofits to disclose their donors is the solution. Not true. As I've repeatedly testified to the Senate, the Supreme Court has long insisted that Americans have a right to privacy for their donations. In fact, the leading case on the issue, *NAACP v. Alabama*, is a 1958 decision which involved that civil rights organization and its resistance to a bigoted state government run by the likes of Sheriff "Bull" Connor.[15] The Court recognized that "privacy in group association" is often "indispensable" to preserving Americans' right to freedom of association, particularly when they join together to voice unpopular opinions critical of the government.

The importance of this kind of constitutional protection of dissident beliefs explains why to this day, the NAACP opposes government-coerced disclosure of nonprofit donors. It also explains why the NAACP, as well as other left-wing groups like the American Civil Liberties Union and the Human Rights Campaign (the nation's largest LGBT group), made common cause with groups in the Koch network to oppose forced donor disclosure in a 2021 Supreme Court case, *Americans for Prosperity Foundation v. Bonta*.[16] There, too, the court upheld donors' right to privacy.

In addition to the constitutional problem with forced donor disclosure, the idea has moral problems: both Judaism and Christianity hold anonymous gifts to be the highest form of giving. Then there are the practical reasons for opposing disclosure, which arise from the very real threats, felt across the political spectrum, of mob harassment and worse. As I told Senator Sheldon Whitehouse (D-RI), the Senate's loudest advocate for disclosure: just as your friends on the Left have more groups, active for more years, and possessed of far more "dark money" than the Right, "so does your side have more mobs."[17]

At the same Senate hearing, two of the left-wing witnesses Senator Whitehouse invited to testify revealed what's behind the Left's demand for donor disclosure. Lisa Graves of the Center for Media and Democracy asserted that conservatives should support disclosure because conservatives claim to have less "dark money," and Ben Jealous (then of People for the American Way, now leading the Sierra Club) agreed. The only possible logical inference from their argument is that forced donor disclosure harms the citizens and groups forced to disclose; therefore, conservatives, who have less "dark money," should support laws that will harm their richer opponents more than themselves. But none of us should seek to harm the donors and groups with which we disagree. Instead, we should forcefully explain why their *ideas* are wrongheaded. Threatening the *people* who support those ideas is abhorrent.

Another possible governmental avenue for dealing with Arabella would be to demand the IRS police left-wing nonprofits more harshly, but this too is not a wise response. We must recognize that federal regulators like the IRS are extremely unlikely to be fair when they interpret nonprofit rules. This was starkly evident in the scandal surrounding Lois Lerner, who ran the nonprofit division of the IRS until her scandalous suppression of hundreds of conservative groups was revealed. Enhanced policing by the IRS is much more likely to harm Arabella's conservative opponents than Arabella's own groups. Indeed, as free speech advocate Brad Smith and I have testified to Senator Whitehouse, one reason Lois Lerner treated conservative nonprofits unjustly is that Whitehouse and other Democrats had waged a long campaign in which they demanded the IRS go after conservative nonprofits they didn't like.[18] The Lerner scandal erupted just weeks after a 2013 hearing at which Whitehouse repeated these demands and sent Lerner a list of nonprofits to persecute.[19] An embarrassed Whitehouse then had to tell the Senate, "the IRS appears to have targeted organizations for inquiry based on Tea Party affiliation. Obviously, that's wrong."[20]

One more undesirable governmental response to Arabella would be to go further down the road of campaign finance "reform" and place smaller limits on what donors can give to politics. This, too, would play into the hands of the Left, especially its billionaire donors who all seem to share the same last name, *Foundation*. The last major campaign finance law was the McCain-Feingold Act of 2002, and nearly all of the funding that aided its passage came from eight billionaire foundations on the left, led by the Pew Charitable Trusts.

As John Fund reported for the *Wall Street Journal*, those foundations provided $123 million of the $140 million spent to pass the bill, and the Pew program officer running the scam later bragged that nearly half the footnotes in the Supreme Court decision upholding the law cited research that Pew funded. Though these foundations made the minimum legally required reports on their giving for the effort, they stayed entirely under the radar with the help of the left-leaning mainstream media, which never exposed their machinations. The Pew officer admitted, "If Congress thought this was a Pew effort, it'd be worthless," because the donors needed "to convey the impression that this was something coming naturally from beyond the Beltway."[21]

What the billionaires' McCain-Feingold Act accomplished was to squeeze political money out of the normal channel for it, namely, the two parties, and so this law actually helped Arabella and its allies by making them stronger, relative to the political parties. This quickly led to more left-wing victories. In the two years following McCain-Feingold's change in our politics, four mega-donors in Colorado moved the state sharply leftward in the 2004 elections, and by 2008 this once mostly Republican state found nearly all its congressional delegation and statewide officers Democrats. The story is well told in Adam Schrager and Rob Witwer's *The Blueprint*, which explains that "campaign finance reform had completely changed the rules of the game. By limiting the amount of money candidates and political parties could raise and spend, the new law had seriously weakened candidates—and all but killed political parties."[22]

What the law did *not* weaken, but strengthen, were foundations and other mega-donors to nonprofits like Arabella. Nor is it hard to understand why someone like George Soros would be pleased at this great shift of power: the Democratic Party does his bidding most of the time, but a nonprofit like those run by Arabella will do his bidding 100 percent of the time. In addition, no law limits how much can be given to charities and social welfare groups. Indeed, there's not even a ban on donations by foreigners like Arabella's great patron Hansjörg Wyss.

Which brings us to a bit of legislation that *could* help counter Arabella. The House Committee on Administration, which oversees election rules, has introduced a bill that would ban 501(c)(4) social welfare groups from contributing to political committees for four years if they accept donations from foreigners. The legislation, known as the American Confidence in Elections (ACE) Act, is advocated by the committee's chairman, Rep. Bryan Steil (R-WI).[23] His colleagues Rep. Brian Fitzpatrick (R-PA) and Rep. Jared Golden (R-ME) have also introduced the Keeping Foreign Money out of Ballot Measures Act that would bar foreign nationals from giving to state ballot initiatives.[24] These efforts have been spurred in part by invaluable reporting from the watchdog group Americans for Public Trust, which has documented the powerful influence Hansjörg Wyss has had through the Arabella network. As the group's executive director, Caitlin Sutherland, sums up the problem:

> Swiss billionaire Hansjörg Wyss has poured staggering sums of money into groups dedicated to advancing exclusively liberal and progressive politics, all with little to no transparency, public scrutiny, or government oversight. By using his foundations to further his radical policy agenda, Wyss has seemingly skirted federal laws that ban foreign nationals from directly or indirectly influencing American elections. APT urges Congress to safeguard our political system by working to stop any and all foreign meddling in our elections.[25]

Another important reform in the nonprofit sector would be for Congress to forbid private foundations and charities to fund or carry out voter registration activities. As Capital Research Center has documented, hundreds of millions of dollars in recent years have quietly gone into left-wing efforts to influence elections in this manner. Indeed, the better known "Zuck Bucks" operation of 2020, described in chapter 4, grew out of this decades-long left-wing scheming, with the difference that Zuck Bucks were sent, not to left-wing nonprofits, but directly into state and local government election offices. Twenty-seven states have passed restrictions on this kind of private funding of government election offices, and a half dozen more state legislatures have passed such laws only to have them vetoed in every instance by Democratic governors, thus proving the partisan nature of such funding.[26]

Congress should similarly ban voter registration work by private foundations and charities. Technically, existing law and IRS rules forbid these charitable entities from engaging in voter registration and related work unless it is carried out in a strictly "nonpartisan" manner. The IRS even states that charitable groups must not even have the "effect," much less the intention, of helping one political party or candidate.[27] But Capital Research Center has documented how George Soros's main foundation, as well as several other billionaire foundations and Arabella's friends at the Democracy Alliance, have long been active in this field, helping one political party.[28] And in 2023, my colleague Parker Thayer released a shocking report on a massive scheme in which well over $100 million, raised almost entirely from charitable groups, was funneled into dozens of other "charities" to register voters who were highly likely to vote Democratic in a handful of swing states. This campaign focused on the 2020 election but is still active going into 2024, and its own reports on its work plausibly suggest it may have provided the margin of victory to Democrats in battleground states with fifty-three electoral college votes.[29]

Naturally Arabella played a significant role in this secretive project, channeling nearly $13 million into it from the New Venture Fund, plus $7.8 million from the Hopewell Fund.[30] Also mixed up in the scheme was a super PAC run by the mother of then billionaire Sam Bankman-Fried.

This "charitable" voter registration problem is a classic instance where a fuzzy law will never be policed honestly by the IRS, and so Congress should simplify the legal issue by banning such work by charitable groups, so no judgment calls by the likes of Lois Lerner will be necessary.

An even more radical legislative possibility has sometimes been advanced: ending the charitable deduction entirely. On the one hand, I sympathize with anyone who is so disgusted by the way the charitable sector has been politicized and exploited by groups like Arabella that he feels the urge to burn it down. I also fear that if the sector doesn't improve by moving away from these rank abuses of "charity," there may be no way to prevent such a radical step.

Yet I cannot endorse ending the charitable deduction, because that deduction fundamentally marks off this sector that is so vital to the proper understanding of America. Our founders were proud of the Constitution they bequeathed us, because the whole point of constitutionally limiting government, especially the centralized government in Washington, D.C., was to allow Americans to flourish, individually and in independent groups they came together to form. We were to care for our families, friends, and neighbors; to freely form independent churches, charities, and civic associations that would let us live out our freedom with little interference from distant governments—and the rich and powerful who so often manipulate those governments.

This abundance of voluntary associations, created by ordinary citizens, is what set America apart and made it thrive, as wise visitors like Alexis de Tocqueville observed: "Everywhere that, at the head of a new undertaking, you see the government in France and a great lord in England, count on it that you will perceive an association in the United States."[31] Tocqueville far preferred the American vision of a free society to the Arabella vision, where great lords—Warren Buffett, George Soros, Hansjörg Wyss, Eric Kessler—collude with centralized government to fight against associations like Montana's BlueRibbon Coalition of off-road motorcyclists. Tocqueville warned against the lust for control because of where it originates in the soul: "a man's admiration of absolute government is proportionate to the contempt he feels for those around him."[32]

No wonder the Obama administration, which greatly expanded the central government, repeatedly urged limiting the charitable deduction. Resisting this impulse, Joanne Florino of the Philanthropy Roundtable warned that these attacks on the charitable deduction are based on the beliefs that the government knows how to spend money better than private citizens, that the public sector can pick winners and losers in the charitable sector, and that monolithic solutions trump diversity and experimentation. If we choose to go down this rocky and treacherous path, we send a clear message to our country that a strong civil society isn't really that important.[33]

The choice America faces is between these two visions: Arabella's style of Big Philanthropy ganging up with Big Government to force the rest of us to live as our betters think we should, or the original American vision, where government is decentralized and limited so that citizens can govern themselves and help each other through their families, neighborhoods, and local groups. As the philanthropy critic William Schambra observes, our republic can only survive if we reject the rule of people who imagine themselves "ungodly bright" and worthy of ruling the rest of us, in favor of a philanthropy of civic renewal that "tackles social problems individual by individual, neighborhood by neighborhood," and that "relies on and entrusts ordinary, public-spirited citizens, familiar with the communities of which they are a part, to lead the way."[34]

ENDNOTES

INTRODUCTION

1   Hulse, Carl. "After Garland Defeat, New Group Hopes to Draw Democrats to Judicial Battlefield." The *New York Times*, May 3, 2018. https://www.nytimes.com/2018/05/03/us/politics/merrick-garland-judicial-trump.html.

2   Ludwig, Hayden. "Leftists Astroturfing the Supreme Court." Capital Research Center, July 10, 2018. https://capitalresearch.org/article/leftists-astroturf-supreme-court/.

3   Massoglia, Anna and West, Geoff. "Kennedy's resignation sparks millions in conservative, liberal ad campaigns." OpenSecrets, June 28, 2018. https://www.opensecrets.org/news/2018/06/kennedys-resignation-sparks-seven-figure-ad-campaigns-from-conservative-liberal-groups/.

4   Lardner, Richard. "Millions from anonymous donors to influence Kavanaugh fight." *National Post,* July 12, 2018. https://nationalpost.com/pmn/news-pmn/millions-from-anonymous-donors-to-influence-kavanaugh-fight.

5   Roth, Gabe. "The Supreme Court Is Being Hypocritical." The *New York Times*, October 11, 2016. https://www.nytimes.com/2016/10/11/opinion/the-supreme-court-is-being-hypocritical.html?searchResultPosition=4.

6   Thayer, Parker. "Fix the Court May Have Financial Disclosure Problems." Capital Research Center, May 15, 2023. https://capitalresearch.org/article/fix-the-court-may-have-financial-disclosure-problems/.

7   Wolf, Richard. "At Supreme Court, secretiveness attracts snoops." *USA Today*, November 12, 2014. https://www.usatoday.com/story/news/politics/2014/11/12/supreme-court-powerful-accountable-fix/18872209/.

8   Kerr, Andrew. "Meet the Major US Philanthropy Financing an Israeli-Designated Terror Group: The Rockefeller Brothers Fund has given more than $3.4 million to Hamas-friendly groups since 2018." *Free Beacon*, October 23, 2023. https://freebeacon.com/

democrats/meet-the-major-u-s-philanthropy-financing-an-israeli-designated-terror-group/.

9   Kaminsky, Gabe. "Supreme Court 'transparency' group hammered by Judiciary GOP over IRS donor blunder." *Washington Examiner*, May 18, 2023. https://www.washingtonexaminer.com/policy/courts/judiciary-gop-rebukes-fix-the-court-after-leak.

10   Lee, Mike. (@BasedMikeLee). "The 'dark money' group unfairly attacking Justice Thomas just got caught with its pants down" Twitter. May 17, 2023. https://twitter.com/BasedMikeLee/status/1659002990122893312.

11   Green, Emma. "The Massive Progressive Dark-Money Group You've Never Heard Of: Over the past half decade, Democrats have quietly pulled ahead of Republicans in untraceable political spending. One group helped make it happen." *The Atlantic*, November 2, 2021. https://www.theatlantic.com/politics/archive/2021/11/arabella-advisors-money-democrats/620553/.

12   Walter, Scott. "Inside the Left's Web of 'Dark Money': Sheldon Whitehouse won't tell you about the Arabella Advisors empire that skirts disclosure requirements." *Wall Street Journal*, October 22, 2020. https://www.wsj.com/articles/inside-the-lefts-web-of-dark-money-11603408114.

13   Vogel, Kenneth P. and Goldmacher, Shane. "Democrats Decried Dark Money. Then They Won With It in 2020." The *New York Times*, January 29, 2022. https://www.nytimes.com/2022/01/29/us/politics/democrats-dark-money-donors.html.

14   Arnsdorf, Isaac. "Koch network to back alternative to Trump after sitting out recent primaries." *Washington Post*, February 5, 2023. https://www.washingtonpost.com/politics/2023/02/05/koch-trump-2024-gop-presidential-primary/.

15   "Quincy Institute for Responsible Statecraft," InfluenceWatch, https://www.influencewatch.org/non-profit/quincy-institute-for-responsible-statecraft/.

16   Ludwig, Hayden. "Philanthropy's Global War on People." Capital Research Center, June 30, 2020. https://capitalresearch.org/article/philanthropysglobal-war-on-people/.

17   Quoted in Schambra, William. "Philanthropy's Original Sin." *The New Atlantis*, summer 2013. https://www.thenewatlantis.com/publications/philanthropys-original-sin. Schambra's source is Fisher, Donald. "The Role of Philanthropic Foundations in the Reproduction and Production of Hegemony: Rockefeller Foundations and the Social Sciences." *Sociology*, March 1983. https://www.jstor.org/stable/42852563.

Chapter 1

1   Skinner, Dave. "Know Thine Enemies…" Blueribbon Coalition, September 2008. Archived from the original March 5, 2009. https://web.archive.org/web/20090305101113/http://www.sharetrails.org/magazine/article.php?id=1632.

2   Ludwig, Hayden and Thayer, Parker. "Arabella's $1.6 Billion 'Dark Money' Haul in

2021." Capital Research Center, November 16, 2022. https://capitalresearch.org/article/arabellas-1-6-billion-dark-money-haul-in-2021/.

3   Kaufman, Noah. "Republican-Proposed 'Carbon Dividend' Is a Great Sign of Progress." World Resources Institute, February 10, 2017. https://www.wri.org/insights/republican-proposed-carbon-dividend-great-sign-progress.

4   "David Brower." Activist Facts. https://www.activistfacts.com/person/3507-david-brower/. Brower floated the idea of governments requiring all potential parents "to use contraceptive chemicals, the governments issuing antidotes to citizens chosen for childbearing." See Friends of the Earth. Progress As If Survival Mattered. San Francisco, 1977, p. 17.

5   "League of Conservation Voters," InfluenceWatch, https://www.influencewatch.org/non-profit/league-of-conservation-voters/. "Collins v. City of Harker Heights." UMKC School of Law. https://www1.law.umkc.edu/justicepapers/CollinsDocs/CollinsAbbreviations.htm.

6   "Board of Directors and Executive Team." League of Conservation Voters. https://www.lcv.org/board/.

7   "Kyle Herrig," InfluenceWatch, https://www.influencewatch.org/person/kyle-herrig/.

8   Ludwig, Hayden. "Arabella's Long War: Web of 'Pop-Up' Groups." Capital Research Center, November 12, 2021. https://capitalresearch.org/article/arabellas-long-war-part-2/.

9   "Accountable.US," InfluenceWatch, https://www.influencewatch.org/non-profit/accountable-us/. "Restore Public Trust," InfluenceWatch, https://www.influencewatch.org/non-profit/restore-public-trust/. "American Oversight," InfluenceWatch, https://www.influencewatch.org/non-profit/american-oversight/. "Western Values Project," InfluenceWatch, https://www.influencewatch.org/non-profit/western-values-project/. "Home." Meet David Bernhardt. https://www.davidbernhardt.org/.

Chapter 2

1   "Arabella Advisors," InfluenceWatch, https://www.influencewatch.org/for-profit/arabella-advisors/. "Rockefeller Family Fund," InfluenceWatch, https://www.influencewatch.org/non-profit/rockefeller-family-fund/. "Ford Foundation," InfluenceWatch, https://www.influencewatch.org/non-profit/ford-foundation/. "Open Society Foundations," InfluenceWatch, https://www.influencewatch.org/non-profit/open-society-foundations/. "Eric Kessler," InfluenceWatch, https://www.influencewatch.org/person/eric-kessler/.

2   Catenacci, Thomas and Schoffstall, Joe. "Biden admin coordinated with liberal dark money behemoth on 'transforming food system,' emails show." Fox News, May 16, 2023. https://www.foxnews.com/politics/biden-admin-coordinated-liberal-dark-money-behemoth-transforming-food-system-emails-show.

3   Ludwig, Hayden. "What Is Arabella Advisors Holdings? And What Is It Hiding?" Capital Research Center, March 11, 2022. https://capitalresearch.org/article/what-is-arabella-advisors-holdings-and-what-is-it-hiding/.

4   "Jennifer Steans." Federal Election Commission. https://www.fec.gov/data/receipts/individual-contributions/?contributor_name=jennifer steans.

5   "Office of the Illinois Secretary of State: Arabella Advisors," InfluenceWatch, https://www.influencewatch.org/app/uploads/2022/03/arabella-advisors-Illinois-secretary-of-state-screencap-03.10.22.png.

6   "Eric Kessler," InfluenceWatch, https://www.influencewatch.org/person/eric-kessler/.

7   "Bruce Boyd," InfluenceWatch, https://www.influencewatch.org/person/bruce-boyd/.

8   "Sampriti Ganguli," InfluenceWatch, https://www.influencewatch.org/person/sampriti-ganguli/.

9   "Chris Hobbs, Chief Operating Officer," InfluenceWatch, https://www.influencewatch.org/app/uploads/2022/03/chris-hobbs-arabella-nonprofit-management.png.

10   "Sixteen Thirty Fund," InfluenceWatch, https://www.influencewatch.org/non-profit/sixteen-thirty-fund/.

11   Watson, Michael. "New Dark Money Front Targets Pro-Life HHS Appointees." Capital Research Center, January 31, 2019. https://capitalresearch.org/article/new-dark-money-front-targets-pro-life-hhs-appointees/.

12   "Arabella Advisors," InfluenceWatch, https://www.influencewatch.org/for-profit/arabella-advisors/.

13   "Location." CARR Workplaces. https://carrworkplaces.com/locations/dc/dupont/.

14   "Jim Gerstein."GBAO Strategies. Archived from the original March 27, 2023. http://web.archive.org/web/20230327015057/http://www.gbaostrategies.com/jim-gerstein/.

15   "Democracy Corps," InfluenceWatch, https://www.influencewatch.org/non-profit/democracy-corps/.

16   "Cristina Uribe," InfluenceWatch, https://www.influencewatch.org/person/cristina-uribe/. "National Education Association," InfluenceWatch, https://www.influencewatch.org/labor-union/national-education-association-nea/.

17   "Wilderness Society," InfluenceWatch, https://www.influencewatch.org/non-profit/wilderness-society/.

18   "Voting Rights Lab," InfluenceWatch, https://www.influencewatch.org/organization/voting-rights-lab/.

19   "Bill and Melinda Gates Foundation," InfluenceWatch, https://www.influencewatch.org/non-profit/bill-and-melinda-gates-foundation/.

20   "Ford Foundation," InfluenceWatch, https://www.influencewatch.org/non-profit/ford-foundation/.

Endnotes

21 "All Above All," InfluenceWatch, https://www.influencewatch.org/non-profit/all-above-all/.

22 "Medication Abortion Care." All* Above All. https://allaboveall.org/campaign/medication-abortion/.

23 Hartmann, Michael E. "The Ford Foundation, the 1967 Cleveland Mayoral Election, and the 1969 Tax Reform Act." Capital Research Center, February 8, 2021. https://capitalresearch.org/article/the-ford-foundation-the-1967-cleveland-mayoral-election-and-the-1969-tax-reform-act/.

24 "Rockefeller Foundation," InfluenceWatch, https://www.influencewatch.org/non-profit/rockefeller-foundation/.

25 "Susan Thompson Buffett Foundation," InfluenceWatch, https://www.influencewatch.org/non-profit/susan-thompson-buffett-foundation/.

26 "Gordon E. and Betty I. Moore Foundation," InfluenceWatch, https://www.influencewatch.org/non-profit/gordon-e-and-betty-i-moore-foundation/.

27 "William and Flora Hewlett Foundation," InfluenceWatch, https://www.influencewatch.org/non-profit/william-and-flora-hewlett-foundation/.

28 "Trusted Elections Fund," InfluenceWatch, https://www.influencewatch.org/non-profit/trusted-elections-fund/. Ludwig, Hayden. "How Much Damage Did Arabella's Trusted Elections Fund Cause in 2020?" Capital Research Center, November·22, 2021. https://capitalresearch.org/article/how-much-damage-did-arabellas-trusted-elections-fund-cause-in-2020/. Ludwig, Hayden. "Going Postal: How the Left Will Use Vote by Mail to Federalize Elections" Capital Research Center, July 9, 2021. https://capitalresearch.org/article/going-postal-how-the-left-will-use-vote-by-mail-to-federalize-elections/.

29 "David and Lucile Packard Foundation," InfluenceWatch, https://www.influencewatch.org/non-profit/david-and-lucile-packard-foundation/.

30 "W. K. Kellogg Foundation," InfluenceWatch, https://www.influencewatch.org/non-profit/w-k-kellogg-foundation/. "Robert Wood Johnson Foundation," InfluenceWatch, https://www.influencewatch.org/non-profit/robert-wood-johnson-foundation/.

31 "Hansjorg Wyss," InfluenceWatch, https://www.influencewatch.org/person/hansjorg-wyss/. "The Hub Project," InfluenceWatch, https://www.influencewatch.org/non-profit/the-hub-project/.

32 "Molly McUsic," InfluenceWatch, https://www.influencewatch.org/person/molly-mcusic/. "Eric Kessler," InfluenceWatch, https://www.influencewatch.org/person/eric-kessler/.

33 "Kyle Herrig," InfluenceWatch, https://www.influencewatch.org/person/kyle-herrig/.

34 "Silicon Valley Community Foundation," InfluenceWatch, https://www.influencewatch.org/non-profit/silicon-valley-community-foundation/. "Fidelity Investments Charitable Gift Fund," InfluenceWatch, https://www.influencewatch.org/non-profit/fidelity-investments-charitable-gift-fund/.

35 Hartmann, Michael E. "501(c)(4)s and 'Dark Money': Donor-Advised Funds." Capital

Research Center, July 30, 2021. https://capitalresearch.org/article/501c4s-and-dark-money-part-5/.

36 "Omidyar Nexus," InfluenceWatch, https://www.influencewatch.org/non-profit/omidyar-nexus/.

37 "Center for Election Innovation Research," InfluenceWatch, https://www.influencewatch.org/non-profit/center-for-election-innovation-research/.

38 "Center for Secure and Modern Elections Action," InfluenceWatch, https://www.influencewatch.org/non-profit/center-for-secure-and-modern-elections-action-csme-action/. "Center for Tech and Civic Life," InfluenceWatch, https://www.influencewatch.org/non-profit/center-for-tech-and-civic-life/. Ludwig, Hayden. "Louisiana Turns Up the Heat on CTCL and Arabella's New Venture Fund." Capital Research Center, April 5, 2022. https://capitalresearch.org/article/louisiana-turns-up-the-heat-on-ctcl-and-arabellas-new-venture-fund/.

39 "Trusted Elections Fund," InfluenceWatch, https://www.influencewatch.org/non-profit/trusted-elections-fund/. Ludwig, Hayden. "How Much Damage Did Arabella's Trusted Elections Fund Cause in 2020?" Capital Research Center, November 22, 2021. https://capitalresearch.org/article/how-much-damage-did-arabellas-trusted-elections-fund-cause-in-2020/.

40 Ludwig, Hayden. "New Ethics Complaint: Soros-Funded Arabella Front Helped Democrats Break Congressional Ethics Rules." Capital Research Center, January 25, 2022. https://capitalresearch.org/article/new-ethics-complaint-soros-funded-arabella-front-helped-democrats-break-congressional-ethics-rules/.

41 "Grant Areas." Tipping Point Fund on Impact Investing. https://tpfii.org/grant-areas.

42 "Democracy Docket Legal Fund." InfluenceWatch, https://www.influencewatch.org/organization/democracy-docket-legal-fund-ddlf/. "Marc Elias," InfluenceWatch, https://www.influencewatch.org/person/marc-elias/.

43 "Trusted Elections Fund," InfluenceWatch, https://www.influencewatch.org/non-profit/trusted-elections-fund/.

44 "2020 Census Project," InfluenceWatch, https://www.influencewatch.org/non-profit/2020-census-project/.

45 Walter, Scott. "Read CRC's Letter to the Editor in the Washington Post." Capital Research Center, December 4, 2019. https://capitalresearch.org/article/read-crcs-letter-to-the-editor-in-the-washington-post/.

46 New Venture Fund, Return of Organization Exempt from Income Tax (Form 990), 2021, Schedule I, Part II.

47 McArthur, Loren. "Four Promising Practices for Philanthropies to Advance Advocacy and Policy Change." Arabella Advisors. https://www.arabellaadvisors.com/blog/four-promising-practices-for-philanthropies-to-advance-advocacy-and-policy-change/.

48 "Arabella Advisors Leader on Generational Differences in Giving." *Chronicle of*

Philanthropy, March 6, 2020. https://www.philanthropy.com/article/arabella-advisors-leader-on-generational-differences-in-giving-podcast/.

49   "America Votes," InfluenceWatch, https://www.influencewatch.org/non-profit/america-votes/.

50   "Center for Tech and Civic Life," InfluenceWatch, https://www.influencewatch.org/non-profit/center-for-tech-and-civic-life/.

51   Ralston, John. (@RalstonReports). (2022, October 31.) "'Who you vote for is private, but whether you vote is a matter of public record. We will be reviewing public records after the election to determine whether or not you joined your neighbors in voting?' You can't be serious, @AmericaVotes? Is this the progressive way? Damn." *Twitter*. October 31, 2022. https://twitter.com/RalstonReports/status/1587129179593580544.

52   Massoglia, Anna and Evers-Hillstrom, Karl. "'Dark money' topped $1 billion in 2020, largely boosting Democrats" OpenSecrets. March 17, 2021. https://www.opensecrets.org/news/2021/03/one-billion-dark-money-2020-electioncycle/.

53   King, Maya, and Montellaro, Zach. "How the Census Bureau Is Adapting to the Pandemic." *Politico*, July 9, 2020. https://www.politico.com/newsletters/morning-score/2020/07/09/how-the-census-bureau-is-adapting-to-the-pandemic-789053.

54   "Defending Democracy Together," InfluenceWatch, https://www.influencewatch.org/non-profit/defending-democracy-together/.

55   "About the Commission," California Commission on the Status of Women and Girls, https://women.ca.gov/about-us/.

56   "Acronym," InfluenceWatch, https://www.influencewatch.org/non-profit/acronym/.

57   "Salk Institute for Biological Studies," InfluenceWatch, https://www.influencewatch.org/non-profit/salk-institute-for-biological-studies/.

58   "Environmental Defense Fund," InfluenceWatch, https://www.influencewatch.org/non-profit/environmental-defense-fund/.

59   "Sixteen Thirty Fund," InfluenceWatch, https://www.influencewatch.org/non-profit/sixteen-thirty-fund/.

60   "Demand Justice," InfluenceWatch, https://www.influencewatch.org/non-profit/demand-justice/.

61   "Fix the Court," InfluenceWatch, https://www.influencewatch.org/non-profit/fix-the-court/.

62   "Q&A Gabe Roth." C-Span March 1, 2016. https://www.c-span.org/video/?405764-1/qa-gabe-roth.

63   "Demand Justice, Naral: Don't Schedule Hearings For Brett Kavanaugh Until His 1M+ Pages Of Documents Get Turned Over To Senate." Demand Justice, July 16, 2018. Archived from the original November 23, 2019. http://web.archive.org/web/20191123164330/http://www.demandjustice.org/press-release-demand-justice-naral-dont-schedule-hearings-for-brett-kavanaugh-until-his-1m-pages-of-documents-get-turned-over-to-senate/.

64 "Sixteen Thirty Fund," InfluenceWatch, https://www.influencewatch.org/non-profit/sixteen-thirty-fund/.

65 Strassel, Kimberley A. "The Trump 'Ethics' Resistance." The *Wall Street Journal*, December 27, 2018. https://www.wsj.com/articles/the-trump-ethics-resistance-11545955715.

66 "Restore Public Trust," InfluenceWatch, https://www.influencewatch.org/non-profit/restore-public-trust/.

67 "American Oversight," InfluenceWatch, https://www.influencewatch.org/non-profit/american-oversight/.

68 "Democracy Forward," InfluenceWatch, https://www.influencewatch.org/non-profit/democracy-forward/. "Marc Elias," InfluenceWatch, https://www.influencewatch.org/person/marc-elias/.

69 "Citizens for Responsibility and Ethics in Washington," InfluenceWatch, https://www.influencewatch.org/non-profit/citizens-for-responsibility-and-ethics-in-washington/. "NARAL Pro-Choice America," InfluenceWatch, https://www.influencewatch.org/non-profit/naral-pro-choice-america/.

70 "2021 Impact Report." New Venture Fund. https://newventurefund.org/wp-content/uploads/2022/11/NVF-2021-Impact-Report-FINAL2-hi-res.pdf.

71 "Civic Engagement Fund," InfluenceWatch, https://www.influencewatch.org/non-profit/civic-engagement-fund/.

72 "About." Campaign for Accountability. https://campaignforaccountability.org/about/.

73 Klein, Joseph. "Inside a Google Summit on Diversity and Inclusion." Capital Research Center, December 12, 2018. https://capitalresearch.org/article/inside-a-google-summit-on-diversity-and-inclusion/.

74 "American Oversight," InfluenceWatch, https://www.influencewatch.org/non-profit/american-oversight/.

75 "Citizens for Responsibility and Ethics in Washington," InfluenceWatch, https://www.influencewatch.org/non-profit/citizens-for-responsibility-and-ethics-in-washington/.

76 "Accountable US," InfluenceWatch, https://www.influencewatch.org/non-profit/accountable-us/.

77 Roberts, Jeff John. "Oracle Is Funding a New Anti-Google Group." *Fortune*, August 19, 2016. http://fortune.com/2016/08/19/google-transparency-project-2/.

78 Roberts, Jeff John. "Oracle Is Funding a New Anti-Google Group." *Fortune*, August 19, 2016. http://fortune.com/2016/08/19/google-transparency-project-2/.

79 "Democracy Alliance," InfluenceWatch, https://www.influencewatch.org/organization/democracy-alliance-da/.

80 Walter, Scott. "A Saintly Conspiracy to Save Democracy?" Capital Research Center, May 11, 2021. https://capitalresearch.org/article/a-saintly-conspiracy-to-save-democracy/.

81   "Arabella Advisors Leader on Generational Differences in Giving (Podcast)." *The Chronicle of Philanthropy*, March 6, 2020. https://www.philanthropy.com/article/arabella-advisors-leader-on-generational-differences-in-giving-podcast/.

82   "Arabella Advisors Responds on 'Dark Money' Donations." The *Wall Street Journal*, September 29, 2022. https://www.wsj.com/articles/arabella-advisors-dark-money-left-wing-nonprofit-donations-11664392305?mod=article_inline.

83   Ludwig, Hayden. "'Dark Money' on the Left." Capital Research Center, October 24, 2022. https://capitalresearch.org/article/dark-money-on-the-left/.

84   "Arabella Gov Docs." Climate Litigation Watch. https://climatelitigationwatch.org/wp-content/uploads/2019/09/Arabella-Govs-docs.pdf. Ludwig, Hayden. "Is the Arabella Network Telling the Truth About Itself? Part 1." Capital Research Center, October 12, 2022. https://capitalresearch.org/article/is-the-arabella-network-telling-the-truth-about-itself-part-1/.

85   "The Arabella Difference." Arabella Advisors. https://www.arabellaadvisors.com/the-arabella-difference/.

86   "Our Story." Arabella Advisors. Archived from the original August 19, 2020. https://web.archive.org/web/20200819215554/https://www.arabellaadvisors.com/company/our-story/.

87   "About New Venture Fund." New Venture Fund. Archived from the original June 15, 2020. https://web.archive.org/web/20200615045855/https:/newventurefund.org/about-nvf/.

88   "The Arabella Difference." Arabella Advisors. https://www.arabellaadvisors.com/the-arabella-difference/.

89   "About New Venture Fund." New Venture Fund. Archived from the original June 15, 2020. https://web.archive.org/web/20200615045855/https:/newventurefund.org/about-nvf/.

90   Barrett, Wililam P. "America's Top 100 Charities." *Forbes*, December 13, 2022. https://www.forbes.com/lists/top-charities/?sh=42ff19c5f501.

91   "A Note on Our Work." Arabella Advisors. https://www.arabellaadvisors.com/company/arabella-basic-facts/.

CHAPTER 3

1   "History." Health Care for America NOW. https://www.healthcareforamericanow.org/about/history/.

2   "Affordable Care Act," InfluenceWatch, https://www.influencewatch.org/legislation/affordable-care-act/.

3   Williams, Clarence. "Police arrest 155 health care protesters at U.S. Capitol." The *Washington Post*, July 19, 2017. https://www.washingtonpost.com/local/public-safety/

police-arrest-155-health-care-protesters-at-us-capitol/2017/07/19/c6a04286-6cd4-11e7-96ab-5f38140b38cc_story.html?utm_term=.861580c05058.

4   "National Health Spending Explorer." PETERSON-KFF Health System Tracker. https://www.healthsystemtracker.org/health-spending-explorer/?output-Type=%24pop&serviceType%5B0%5D=allTypes&sourceOfFunds%5B0%5D=all-Sources&tab=0&yearCompare%5B0%5D=%2A&yearCompare%5B1%5D=%2A&yearRange%5B0%5D=%2A&yearRange%5B1%5D=%2A&yearS-ingle=%2A&yearType=range.

5   "Medicare Enrollment Charts." Chronic Conditions Data Warehouse. https://www2.ccwdata.org/web/guest/medicare-charts/medicare-enrollment-charts.

6   "Fiscal 50: State Trends and Analysis." Pew Charitable Trusts. https://www.pewtrusts.org/en/research-and-analysis/data-visualizations/2014/fiscal-50#ind7.

7   "Medicare-For-All," InfluenceWatch, https://www.influencewatch.org/movement/medicare-for-all/.

8   "The McCain Health Care Plan: More Power to Families." The Heritage Foundation, October 15, 2008. https://www.heritage.org/health-care-reform/report/the-mccain-health-care-plan-more-power-families.

9   "Brookings Institute," InfluenceWatch, https://www.influencewatch.org/non-profit/brookings-institution/. Haseltine, William A. "Affordable Excellence: The Singapore Healthcare Story." Brookings Institution, 2013. https://www.brookings.edu/wp-content/uploads/2016/07/AffordableExcellencePDF.pdf.

10   "Singapore - Country Commercial Guide." International Trade Administration, August 11, 2022. https://www.trade.gov/country-commercial-guides/singapore-healthcare.

11   "National Health Spending Explorer." PETERSON-KFF Health System Tracker. https://www.healthsystemtracker.org/health-spending-explorer/?outputType=%gdp&serviceType%5B0%5D=allTypes&sourceOfFunds%5B0%5D=allSources&tab=0&yearCompare%5B0%5D=%2A&yearCompare%5B1%5D=%2A&year-Range%5B0%5D=%2A&yearRange%5B1%5D=%2A&yearSingle=%2A&yearType=range.

12   "Healthcare for America Now," InfluenceWatch, https://www.influencewatch.org/non-profit/healthcare-for-america-now/.

13   "Safety Net Defense Fund," InfluenceWatch, https://www.influencewatch.org/non-profit/safety-net-defense-fund/.

14   "The Safety Net Defense Fund Project." New Venture Fund, June 2017. https://democracyalliance.org/wp-content/uploads/2017/07/SNDF-C3-Overview.New-Venture-Fund.June-2017_DA2.pdf.

15   "The Safety Net Defense Action Fund Project." Sixteen Thirty Fund, June 2017. http://democracyalliance.org/wp-content/uploads/2017/07/SNDAF-C4-Overview.1630-Fund.June2017_DA2.pdf.

16 Vogel, Kenneth P. and Robertson, Katie. "Top Bidder for Tribune Newspapers Is an Influential Liberal Donor." The *New York Times*, April 13, 2021. https://www.nytimes. com/2021/04/13/business/media/wyss-tribune-company-buyer.html.

17 "Home." Health Care Voter. https://healthcarevoter.org/. "Health Care Voter," InfluenceWatch, https://www.influencewatch.org/non-profit/health-care-voter/.

18 "Home." Health Care Facts.. https://www.healthcarefacts.info/. "Health Care Voter," InfluenceWatch, https://www.influencewatch.org/non-profit/health-care-voter/.

19 "Fidelity Investments Charitable Gift Fund," InfluenceWatch, https://www.influence-watch.org/non-profit/fidelity-investments-charitable-gift-fund/. "Silicon Valley Community Foundation," InfluenceWatch, https://www.influencewatch.org/non-profit/silicon-valley-community-foundation/.

20 "Lower Drug Prices Now," InfluenceWatch, https://www.influencewatch.org/non-profit/lower-drug-prices-now/. "Our Campaign." Lower Drug Prices Now. https://www.lowerdrugpricesnow.org/about-us/#our_campaign.

21 "Donate Now." Lower Drug Prices Now. https://secure.donationpay.org/lowerdrugpricesnow/index.php.

22 "Small Business for America's Future," InfluenceWatch, https://www.influencewatch.org/non-profit/small-business-for-americas-future/.

23 "Policy Agenda." Small Business for America's Future. https://www.smallbusinessforamericasfuture.org/policy-agenda.

24 "Home." Small Business for America's Future. https://www.smallbusinessforamericasfuture.org/. "Home." Sixteen Thirty Fund. https://www.sixteenthirtyfund.org/.

25 DC.gov. "Sixteen Thirty Fund—Initial File Number: 29051." Archived at https://www.influencewatch.org/app/uploads/2023/10/Sixteen-Thirty-Trade-Names.pdf.

26 "Sixteen Thirty Fund: Lobbying for H.R. 1," InfluenceWatch, https://www.influence-watch.org/non-profit/sixteen-thirty-fund/#lobbying-for-h-r-1-2019-2020.

27 Bland, Scott. "Liberal secret-money network hammers House GOP." *Politico*, July 29, 2018. https://www.politico.com/story/2018/07/29/democrats-dark-money-mid-terms-house-745145.

28 Wyland, Michael. "Darker-than-Dark Money Targeting GOP House Candidates." *Nonprofit Quarterly*, July 30, 2018. https://nonprofitquarterly.org/darker-than-dark-money-targeting-gop-house-candidates/.

29 "Arizonans United for Health Care," InfluenceWatch, https://www.influencewatch.org/non-profit/arizonans-united-for-health-care/. "Colorado United for Families," InfluenceWatch, https://www.influencewatch.org/non-profit/colorado-united-for-families/. "Floridians for a Fair Shake," InfluenceWatch, https://www.influencewatch.org/non-profit/floridians-for-a-fair-shake/. "Health Care Voters of Colorado," InfluenceWatch, https://www.influencewatch.org/non-profit/health-care-voters-of-nevada/. "Keep Iowa Healthy," InfluenceWatch, https://www.influencewatch.org/non-profit/

keep-iowa-healthy/. "Mainers Against Health Care Cuts," InfluenceWatch, https://www.influencewatch.org/non-profit/mainers-against-health-care-cuts/. "Michigan Families for Economic Prosperity," InfluenceWatch, https://www.influencewatch.org/non-profit/michigan-families-for-economic-prosperity/. "North Carolinians for a Fair Economy," InfluenceWatch, https://www.influencewatch.org/non-profit/north-caro-linians-for-a-fair-economy/. "Ohioans for Economic Opportunity," InfluenceWatch, https://www.influencewatch.org/non-profit/ohioans-for-economic-opportunity/. InfluenceWatch, "SoCal Healthcare Coalition," https://www.influencewatch.org/non-profit/socal-healthcare-coalition/. "Speak Out Central New York," InfluenceWatch, https://www.influencewatch.org/non-profit/speak-out-central-new-york/.

30   Sixteen Thirty Fund, Return of Organization Exempt from Income Tax (Form 990), 2018, Schedule O. "New Jersey for a Better Future," InfluenceWatch, https://www.influencewatch.org/non-profit/new-jersey-for-a-better-future/. "For Our Families," InfluenceWatch, https://www.influencewatch.org/non-profit/for-our-families/.

31   Burns, Alexander. "With $30 Million, Obscure Democratic Group Floods the Zone in House Races." The *New York Times*, October 31, 2018. https://www.nytimes.com/2018/10/31/us/politics/democrats-dark-money-midterms.html.

32   "Home." Ohioans for Economic Opportunity. Archived from the original January 28, 2023. http://web.archive.org/web/20230128134225/https://www.oheconomicopportunity.org/.

33   "Protect Our Care," InfluenceWatch, https://www.influencewatch.org/non-profit/protect-our-care/. "Save My Care," InfluenceWatch, https://www.influencewatch.org/non-profit/save-my-care/. Sixteen Thirty Fund, Return of Organization Exempt from Income Tax (Form 990), 2018, Schedule O.

34   King, Robert. "Obamacare allies plot campaign to punish advocates of repeal." *Washington Examiner*, February 20, 2018. https://www.washingtonexaminer.com/obamacare-allies-plot-campaign-to-punish-advocates-of-repeal.

35   West, Geoff and Maguire, Robert. "TV ads in midterms up nearly 90 percent fueled by non-disclosing groups." *OpenSecrets*, May 7, 2018. https://www.opensecrets.org/news/2018/05/tv-ads-in-midterms-up-nearly-90-percent-fueled-by-nondisclosing-groups/.

36   Burns, Alexander. "With $30 Million, Obscure Democratic Group Floods the Zone in House Races." The *New York Times*, October 31, 2018. https://www.nytimes.com/2018/10/31/us/politics/democrats-dark-money-midterms.html.

37   "Arabella Advisors," InfluenceWatch, https://www.influencewatch.org/for-profit/arabella-advisors/.

CHAPTER 4

1   "Center for Technology and Civic Life (CTCL)." Capital Research Center. https://capitalresearch.org/tag/ctcl/. "Center for Tech and Civic Life," InfluenceWatch, https://

www.influencewatch.org/non-profit/center-for-tech-and-civic-life/.

2 Ludwig, Hayden. "New York Times Op-Ed Admits Zuck Bucks Boosted Democrats in 2020." Capital Research Center, February 22, 2022. https://capitalresearch.org/article/new-york-times-admits-zuck-bucks-boosted-democrats-in-2020/.

3 Ludwig, Hayden. "The Origins of 'Zuck Bucks': Center for Tech and Civic Life." Capital Research Center, January 26, 2023. https://capitalresearch.org/article/the-origins-of-zuck-bucks-part-4/.

4 "New Venture Fund," InfluenceWatch, https://www.influencewatch.org/non-profit/new-venture-fund/. Vogel, Kenneth P. and Robertson, Katie. "Top Bidder for Tribune Newspapers Is an Influential Liberal Donor." The New York Times, April 13, 2021. https://www.nytimes.com/2021/04/13/business/media/wyss-tribune-company-buyer.html.

5 "Center for Secure and Modern Elections," InfluenceWatch, https://www.influencewatch.org/non-profit/center-for-secure-and-modern-elections/. "Controversial Texas voting bill likely dead this year after failing to be set for debate." McGaughy, Lauren. The Dallas Morning News, May 20, 2019. https://www.dallasnews.com/news/politics/2019/05/20/controversial-texas-voting-bill-likely-dead-this-year-after-failing-to-be-set-for-debate/. "New Campaign Launches to Seek Federal Funding For Secure Election Infrastructure in Congressional Infrastructure Bill." Election Infrastructure Initiative, May 6, 2021. https://www.modernizeourelections.org/updates/newcampaign. "The Carter-Baker Commission, 16 Years Later: Voting by Mail." Rice University's Baker Institute for Public Policy. https://www.bakerinstitute.org/event/carter-baker-commission-16-years-later-voting-mail.

6 Liptak, Adam. "Error and Fraud at Issue as Absentee Voting Rises." The New York Times, October 6, 2012. https://www.nytimes.com/2012/10/07/us/politics/as-more-vote-by-mail-faulty-ballots-could-impact-elections.html.

7 "Prominent Republican speaks out against Texas bill to punish voter registration errors." The Fulcrum, May 9, 2019. https://thefulcrum.us/criminalizing-texas-voter-registration.

8 "Center for Tech and Civic Life: Unlawful Private Funding of Elections Lawsuit (2020-2021)," InfluenceWatch, https://www.influencewatch.org/non-profit/center-for-tech-and-civic-life/#unlawful-private-funding-of-elections-lawsuit-2020.

9 "State of Louisiana versus Center for Tech and Civic Life and New Venture Fund," InfluenceWatch, https://www.influencewatch.org/app/uploads/2021/05/Louisiana-v-CTCL-New-Venture-Fund.-10.02.2020.pdf.

10 "The 2016 Elections + Nonpartisan Grantmaking." Funders' Committee for Civic Participation, January 11, 2016. https://funderscommittee.org/2016-annual-report-table-of-contents/2016-virtual-discussions/the-2016-elections-nonpartisan-grantmaking/. "Funders Committee for Civic Participation," InfluenceWatch, https://www.influencewatch.org/non-profit/the-funders-committee-for-civic-participation-fccp/.

11 "NEO Philanthropy," InfluenceWatch, https://www.influencewatch.org/non-profit/

neo-philanthropy-formerly-public-interest-projects/.

12 "Funders Committee for Civic Participation," InfluenceWatch, https://www.influencewatch.org/non-profit/the-funders-committee-for-civic-participation-fccp/.

13 "Center for Secure and Modern Elections: Funding," InfluenceWatch, https://www.influencewatch.org/non-profit/center-for-secure-and-modern-elections/#funding.

14 "New Venture Fund," InfluenceWatch, https://www.influencewatch.org/non-profit/new-venture-fund/. "Sixteen Thirty Fund," InfluenceWatch, https://www.influencewatch.org/non-profit/sixteen-thirty-fund/.

15 "Bauman Family Foundation," InfluenceWatch, https://www.influencewatch.org/non-profit/bauman-family-foundation/. "Democracy Fund," InfluenceWatch, https://www.influencewatch.org/non-profit/democracy-fund/. "Democracy Fund Voice," InfluenceWatch, https://www.influencewatch.org/non-profit/democracy-fund-voice/. "Center for Secure and Modern Elections." Blaustein Philanthropic Group. Archived from the original April 11, 2023. http://web.archive.org/web/20230411013325/https://blaufund.org/center-for-secure-and-modern-elections/. "Wellspring Philanthropic Fund," InfluenceWatch, https://www.influencewatch.org/non-profit/wellspring-philanthropic-fund/#:~:text=The%20Wellspring%20Philanthropic%20Fund%2C%20formerly,Frederick%20Taylor. "Joyce Foundation," InfluenceWatch, https://www.influencewatch.org/non-profit/joyce-foundation/.

16 "The Joyce Foundation Grants Database: New Venture Fund." Capital Research Center. https://capitalresearch.org/app/uploads/joyce-foundation-new-venture-fund-csme-grant-2020.pdf.

17 "Center for Tech and Civic Life," InfluenceWatch, https://www.influencewatch.org/non-profit/center-for-tech-and-civic-life/.

18 "Center for Tech and Civic Life: Financial Overview," InfluenceWatch, https://www.influencewatch.org/non-profit/center-for-tech-and-civic-life/#financial-overview.

19 Scheck, Tom, Hing, Geoff, Robinson, Sabby, and Stockton, Gracie. "How Private Money From Facebook's CEO Saved The 2020 Election." NPR, December 8, 2020. https://www.npr.org/2020/12/08/943242106/how-private-money-from-facebooks-ceo-saved-the-2020-election.

20 Ludwig, Hayden. "The States Are Dialing 'Zuck Bucks' out of Elections for Good." Capital Research Center, March 14, 2022. https://capitalresearch.org/article/the-states-are-dialing-zuck-bucks-out-of-elections-for-good/.

21 "State Tracking for Digital Resource on Elections and COVID-19." We the Action, March 25, 2020. https://wetheaction.org/projects/510-state-tracking-for-digital-resource-on-elections-and-covid-19.

22 Ferrechio, Susan. "Election report finds Facebook mogul's 'Zuck Bucks' broke law, swayed election outcome in Wisconsin." The *Washington Times*, March 1, 2022. https://www.washingtontimes.com/news/2022/mar/1/election-report-finds-facebook-moguls-zuck-bucks-b/.

Endnotes

23   "Ashish S." LinkedIn. https://www.linkedin.com/in/ashishsinha/. "Center for Tech and Civic Life Green Bay Safe Voting Plan Emails," InfluenceWatch, https://www. influencewatch.org/app/uploads/2021/11/green-bay-ctcl-csme-2020-election-emails. pdf. "National Vote at Home Institute," InfluenceWatch, https://www.influencewatch. org/non-profit/national-vote-at-home-institute/.

24   Ludwig, Hayden. "Going Postal: How the Left Will Use Vote by Mail to Federalize Elections." Capital Research Center, July 9, 2021. https://capitalresearch.org/article/ going-postal-how-the-left-will-use-vote-by-mail-to-federalize-elections/.

25   Ludwig, Hayden. "CTCL's 'Zuck Bucks' Invade Michigan and Wisconsin." Capital Research Center, February 3, 2021. https://capitalresearch.org/article/ctcls-zuck-bucks-invade-michigan-and-wisconsin/.

26   Miller, Shannon. "In quest to automatically register voters at DMV, permits that allow undocumented residents to drive prove a hang-up." The *Nevada Independent*, October 31, 2019. https://thenevadaindependent.com/article/in-quest-to-automatically-register-voters-at-dmv-permits-that-allow-undocumented-residents-to-drive-prove-a-hang-up. "New Organizing Institute," InfluenceWatch, https://www.influencewatch.org/non-profit/new-organizing-institute/.

27   Ludwig, Hayden. "The New New Organizing Institute." Capital Research Center, January 14, 2021. https://capitalresearch.org/article/the-new-new-organizing-institute/.

28   Shepherd, Todd. "Broad + Liberty investigative reporter Todd Shepherd testifies in Harrisburg on CTCL 'Zuckbucks.' Broad + Liberty, April 8, 2022. https:// broadandliberty.com/2022/04/08/broad-liberty-investigative-reporter-todd-shepherd-testifies-in-harrisburg-on-ctcl-zuckbucks/.

29   Ludwig, Hayden. "The Origins of 'Zuck Bucks': Center for Tech and Civic Life." Capital Research Center, January 26, 2023. https://capitalresearch.org/article/the-origins-of-zuck-bucks-part-4/.

30   "Automatic Voter Registration," InfluenceWatch, https://www.influencewatch.org/app/ uploads/2021/11/csme-automatic-voter-registration.pdf.

31   "Support for SB 24 Email," InfluenceWatch, https://www.influencewatch.org/ app/uploads/2021/11/csme-testimony-connecticut.pdf. "Oregon Should Expand Automatic Voter Registration to Additional Agencies." Oregon Legislature. https:// olis.oregonlegislature.gov/liz/2021R1/Downloads/PublicTestimonyDocument/23943. "Mainers for Modern Elections." League of Women Voters of Maine. https://www. lwvme.org/MME. "The Center for Secure and Modern Elections: SB831 – Favorable With Amendments." Maryland General Assembly. https://mgaleg.maryland.gov/cmte_ testimony/2021/ehe/1BZrG-VljNdgdhK8v8bKSD-8wLaNJ-lvT.pdf.

32   "New Venture Fund Statement of Work," InfluenceWatch, https://www.influencewatch. org/app/uploads/2021/11/new-venture-fund-csme-statement-of-work-2020.pdf.

33   "Governor Cuomo Signs Automatic Voter Registration into Law in New York."

Brennan Center for Justice, December 21, 2020. https://www.brennancenter.org/our-work/analysis-opinion/governor-cuomo-signs-automatic-voter-registration-law-new-york.

34   Shepherd, Todd. "Democratic-Leaning Counties Selectively Invited to Apply for Election Grants." *Front Page Magazine*, October 18, 2021. https://www.frontpagemag.com/fpm/2021/10/democratic-leaning-counties-selectively-invited-todd-shepherd/. "Marc Solomon, Partner." Civitas Public Affairs Group. https://civitaspublicaffairs.com/team/marc-solomon/. "Our Clients." Civitas Public Affairs Group. https://civitaspublicaffairs.com/#our-clients.

35   "Freedom to Marry," InfluenceWatch, https://www.influencewatch.org/non-profit/freedom-to-marry/.

36   Ludwig, Hayden. "Gay Marriage Activists Push Carbon Taxes on the GOP." Capital Research Center, April 24, 2019. https://capitalresearch.org/article/gay-marriage-activists-push-carbon-taxes-on-the-gop/.

37   Ludwig, Hayden. "Lawsuit Exposes Arabella Advisors and Zuckerberg Meddling in Louisiana's Elections." Capital Research Center, June 7, 2021. https://capitalresearch.org/article/lawsuit-exposes-arabella-advisors-and-zuckerberg-meddling-in-louisianas-elections/. "Center for Tech and Civic Life," InfluenceWatch, https://www.influencewatch.org/non-profit/center-for-tech-and-civic-life/. "New Venture Fund," InfluenceWatch, https://www.influencewatch.org/non-profit/new-venture-fund/.

38   Thayer, Parker and Ludwig, Hayden. "Which States Did CTCL Flood with 'Zuck Bucks'?" Capital Research Center, January 21, 2022. https://capitalresearch.org/article/which-states-did-ctcl-flood-with-zuck-bucks/. Thayer, Parker and Ludwig, Hayden. "UPDATED: Shining a Light on Zuck Bucks in the 2020 Battleground States." Capital Research Center, January 18, 2022. https://capitalresearch.org/article/shining-a-light-on-zuck-bucks-in-key-states/.

39   Lee, Sarah and Ludwig, Hayden. "States Banning or Restricting 'Zuck Bucks.'" Capital Research Center, May 25, 2023. https://capitalresearch.org/article/states-banning-zuck-bucks/.

40   "State of Louisiana versus Center for Tech and Civic Life, et al.," InfluenceWatch, https://www.influencewatch.org/app/uploads/2022/04/louisiana-lawsuit-reversal-ctcl-and-new-venture-fund-2022.pdf.

41   "State of Louisiana versus Center for Tech and Civic Life, et al.," InfluenceWatch, https://www.influencewatch.org/app/uploads/2022/04/louisiana-lawsuit-reversal-ctcl-and-new-venture-fund-2022.pdf.

42   "State of Louisiana versus Center for Tech and Civic Life, et al.," InfluenceWatch, https://www.influencewatch.org/app/uploads/2022/04/louisiana-lawsuit-reversal-ctcl-and-new-venture-fund-2022.pdf.

43   "Center for Secure and Modern Elections (CSME) Action." Democracy Fund Voice, March 27, 2020. https://democracyfundvoice.org/center-for-secure-and-modern-

elections-csme-action/.

44   "U.S. Alliance for Election Excellence," InfluenceWatch, https://www.influencewatch.org/non-profit/u-s-alliance-for-election-excellence/. See also "Zuck Bucks 2.0: The U.S. Alliance for Election Excellence." Honest Elections Project. https://www.honestelections.org/wp-content/uploads/2023/04/HEP_Alliance-for-Election_v5.pdf.

45   "FAQs." U.S. Alliance for Election Excellence. https://www.electionexcellence.org/faq.

46   "U.S. Alliance for Election Excellence Announces Finalists for 2023 Program." U.S. Alliance for Election Excellence. https://www.electionexcellence.org/updates/us-alliance-for-election-excellence-announces-finalists-for-2023-program.

47   "The Elections Group," InfluenceWatch, https://www.influencewatch.org/for-profit/the-elections-group/.

48   "Center for Civic Design," InfluenceWatch, https://www.influencewatch.org/non-profit/center-for-civic-design/. "National Vote at Home Institute," InfluenceWatch, https://www.influencewatch.org/non-profit/national-vote-at-home-institute/.

49   "Democracy Fund," InfluenceWatch, https://www.influencewatch.org/non-profit/democracy-fund/.

50   "Hasso Plattner Institute of Design (d.school)." Stanford University. https://engineering.stanford.edu/get-involved/give/hasso-plattner-institute-design. "Home." Prototyping Systems Lab. https://prototypingsystems.org/. "U.S. Digital Response," InfluenceWatch, https://www.influencewatch.org/non-profit/u-s-digital-response/. "Building an Election Website." Center for Tech and Civic Life. https://www.techandciviclife.org/course/building-an-election-website/.

51   "State Abortion Laws." Law Atlas. https://lawatlas.org/datasets/abortion-laws.

52   "Sam Oliker-Friedland." LinkedIn. https://www.linkedin.com/in/sam-oliker-friedland-6b557b153/.

53   "Final Frontier: After Our Election Systems are Bought, They'll Never Look the Same Again." Public Interest Legal Foundation, August 2022. https://publicinterestlegal.org/wp-content/uploads/2022/08/Report-Montana-Final_Frontier-Web.pdf.

54   Sugar, Rebecca. "'Zuckerbucks'-Type Offer of Funding for Election Office Divides One of the Richest Towns in America." The *New York Sun*, March 11, 2023. https://www.nysun.com/article/zuckerbucks-type-offer-of-funding-for-election-office-divides-one-of-the-richest-towns-in-america. Flanagan, Brenna. "'If it's not broke, don't fix it': Brunswick BOE reject commissioners private money condemnation." *Port City Daily*, April 22, 2023. https://portcitydaily.com/latest-news/2023/04/22/if-its-not-broke-dont-fix-it-brunswick-boe-reject-commissioners-private-money-condemnation/.

55   Leach, Sarah. "Ottawa County clerk declines $1.5M grant opportunity, cites private funding concerns." The *Holland Sentinel*, January 31, 2023. https://

www.hollandsentinel.com/story/news/politics/elections/county/2023/01/31/
ottawa-county-clerk-declines-1-5m-grant-opportunity-cites-private-funding-
concerns/69859404007/.

CHAPTER 5

1   LaFranco, Rob and Peterson-Withorn, Chase. "The Richest in 2023." *Forbes*. https://
     www.forbes.com/billionaires/#1eddaf7c251c.

2   Soliven, Ernesto. "Warren Buffett Net Worth: Berkshire Hathaway CEO Is Super
     Frugal, Still Lives In 1958 Home." *International Business Times*, March 17, 2020.
     https://www.ibtimes.com/warren-buffett-net-worth-berkshire-hathaway-ceo-super-
     frugal-still-lives-1958-home-2941776.

3   Wilkie, Christina. "The Giving Pledge: Bill Gates, Warren Buffett Visit Obama."
     HuffPost, July 18, 2011. https://www.huffpost.com/entry/obama-to-host-warren-
     buff_n_901472.

4   Frank, Robert. "Warren Buffett is the most charitable billionaire." CNBC, September
     21, 2017. https://www.cnbc.com/2017/09/21/warren-buffet-is-the-most-charitable-
     billionaire.html.

5   "Planned Parenthood Federation of America," InfluenceWatch, https://www.
     influencewatch.org/non-profit/planned-parenthood-federation-of-america/. "MSI
     Reproductive Choices (Marie Stopes International)," InfluenceWatch, https://www.
     influencewatch.org/non-profit/marie-stopes-international-msi/. "Guttmacher Institute,"
     InfluenceWatch, https://www.influencewatch.org/non-profit/guttmacher-institute/.

6   "Medicaid Coverage of Abortion." Guttmacher Institute, February 2021. Archived from
     the original July 28, 2022. http://web.archive.org/web/20220728070504/https://www.
     guttmacher.org/evidence-you-can-use/medicaid-coverage-abortion#.

7   "US States - Ranked by Population 2023." *World Population Review*. https://
     worldpopulationreview.com/states.

8   Callahan, David. "Who's Who At The Secretive Susan Thompson Buffett Foundation?"
     Inside Philanthropy, February 4, 2014 https://www.insidephilanthropy.com/
     home/2014/2/4/whos-who-at-the-secretive-susan-thompson-buffett-foundation.
     html. Perry, Suzanne. "A Family Foundation Is About to Become One of the Nation's
     Wealthiest." The *Chronicle of Philanthropy*, July 20, 2006. https://www.philanthropy.
     com/article/A-Family-Foundation-Is-About/171541.

9   Callahan, David. "Who's Who At The Secretive Susan Thompson Buffett Foundation?"
     Inside Philanthropy, February 4, 2014. https://www.insidephilanthropy.com/
     home/2014/2/4/whos-who-at-the-secretive-susan-thompson-buffett-foundation.html.

10   "DKT International," InfluenceWatch, https://www.influencewatch.org/non-profit/dkt-
     international/. "Pathfinder International," InfluenceWatch, https://www.influencewatch.
     org/non-profit/pathfinder-international/.

11   Ludwig, Hayden. "The Big Money Behind Abortion Activism." Capital Research

Center, January 21, 2022. https://capitalresearch.org/article/the-big-money-behind-abortion-activism/.

12 "Guttmacher Institute," InfluenceWatch, https://www.influencewatch.org/non-profit/guttmacher-institute/.

13 "EngenderHealth," InfluenceWatch, https://www.influencewatch.org/non-profit/engenderhealth/.

14 "Society of Family Planning Research Fund," InfluenceWatch, https://www.influencewatch.org/non-profit/society-of-family-planning-research-fund/.

15 "Center for Reproductive Rights," InfluenceWatch, https://www.influencewatch.org/non-profit/center-for-reproductive-rights/.

16 "Population Council," InfluenceWatch, https://www.influencewatch.org/non-profit/population-council/.

17 "NARAL Pro-Choice America," InfluenceWatch, https://www.influencewatch.org/non-profit/naral-pro-choice-america/.

18 "Gynuity Health Projects," InfluenceWatch, https://www.influencewatch.org/non-profit/gynuity-health-projects/. Ludwig, Hayden. "Gynuity's Abortion Experiments in Africa Funded by Philanthropy and 'Dark Money.'" Capital Research Center, March 4, 2020. https://capitalresearch.org/article/gynuitys-abortion-experiments-in-africa-funded-by-philanthropy-and-dark-money/.

19 "Catholics for Choice," InfluenceWatch, https://www.influencewatch.org/non-profit/catholics-for-choice/.

20 "National Network of Abortion Funds," InfluenceWatch, https://www.influencewatch.org/non-profit/national-network-of-abortion-funds/.

21 Paquette, Danielle. "Have an IUD? Thank Warren Buffett." The *Washington Post*, July 31, 2015. https://www.washingtonpost.com/news/wonk/wp/2015/07/31/warren-buffetts-family-secretly-funded-a-birth-control-revolution/.

22 Rovner, Julie. "More Buffett Money Likely Headed to Pro-Choice Groups." NPR, June 27, 2006. https://www.npr.org/templates/story/story.php?storyId=5514406.

23 Lowe, Janet. *Damn Right: Behind the Scenes with Berkshire Hathaway Billionaire Charlie Munger*. Hoboken, New Jersey: Wiley, 2003, 138.

24 Lowe, Janet. *Damn Right: Behind the Scenes with Berkshire Hathaway Billionaire Charlie Munger*. Hoboken, New Jersey: Wiley, 2003.. Hardin, Garrett. "Biology: Its Human Implications." Internet Archive. https://archive.org/details/in.ernet.dli.2015.84777/page/n611/mode/2up?view=theater&q=downward/.

25 Weintraub, Pam. "The miracle of the commons." *Aeon*. https://aeon.co/essays/the-tragedy-of-the-commons-is-a-false-and-dangerous-myth.

26 "Susan A. Buffett," InfluenceWatch, https://www.influencewatch.org/person/susan-a-buffett/. D'Agostino, J. "Gates-Buffett Marriage Designed Not to Bear Fruit." *Human*

Events, July 10, 2006. Archived from the original August 11, 2021. http://web.archive.org/web/20210811174018/https://humanevents.com/2006/07/10/gatesbuffett-marriage-designed-not-to-bear-fruit/.

27   "Allen Greenberg," InfluenceWatch, https://www.influencewatch.org/person/allen-greenberg/. "Public Citizen," InfluenceWatch, https://www.influencewatch.org/non-profit/public-citizen/.

28   "Philanthropy Awards, 2019." *Inside Philanthropy*, December 31, 2019. https://www.insidephilanthropy.com/home/2019/philanthropy-awards.

29   Townsend, Liz. "Massive Buffett Donations Will Fund Pro-Abortion Agenda around the World." *National Right to Life News*, July 2006. https://www.nrlc.org/archive/news/2006/NRL07/BuffettDonation.html.

30   Statt, Nick. "Bill Gates says Trump's anti-abortion 'gag rule' endangers millions of women and children." *The Verge*, February 14, 2017. https://www.theverge.com/2017/2/14/14613860/bill-and-melinda-gates-foundation-trump-anti-abortion-gag-rule. Rovner, Julie. "More Buffett Money Likely Headed to Pro-Choice Groups." NPR, June 27, 2006. https://www.npr.org/templates/story/story.php?storyId=5514406.

31   Zimmerman, Rachel. "Abortion-Pill Venture Keeps To Shadows Awaiting Approval." The *Wall Street Journal*, September 5, 2000. https://www.wsj.com/articles/SB968103355754057093.

32   Hemingway, Mark. "An American Later-Term Abortion Trial on Women in Impoverished Africa." *RealClearInvestigations*, December 26, 2019. https://www.realclearinvestigations.com/articles/2019/12/22/us_abortion_trial_in_impoverished_burkina_faso_121725.html.

33   Rovner, Julie. "More Buffett Money Likely Headed to Pro-Choice Groups." NPR, June 27, 2006. https://www.npr.org/templates/story/story.php?storyId=5514406.

34   Hadro, Matt. "Pro-lifers condemn testing of 'chemical coat hanger' on African women." *Catholic News Agency*, September 20, 2019. https://www.catholicnewsagency.com/news/pro-lifers-condemn-testing-of-chemical-coat-hanger-on-african-women-76555.

35   "Board." Gynuity. https://gynuity.org/board-of-directors.

36   Ludwig, Hayden. "Gynuity's Abortion Experiments in Africa Funded by Philanthropy and 'Dark Money.'" Capital Research Center, March 4, 2020. https://capitalresearch.org/article/gynuitys-abortion-experiments-in-africa-funded-by-philanthropy-and-dark-money/.

37   "Study Record: Mifepristone and Misoprostol for 2nd Trimester Termination of Pregnancy in Burkina Faso." ClinicalTrials.gov, May 30, 2019. https://clinicaltrials.gov/ct2/show/study/NCT03269279.

38   "Donors." Gynuity.. https://gynuity.org/donors.

39   "Award Profile Grant Summary; Project Grant FAIN R01FD003107." USASpending.gov. https://www.usaspending.gov/award/ASST_NON_R01FD003107_7524. The

grant was awarded to GHP Solutions, LLC; in the recipient profile on USASpending. gov, GHP Solutions, LLC, is also known by one other name, Gynuity Health Projects. See https://www.usaspending.gov/recipient/72ad5f21-b786-1de3-e7d3-9ab3c99f7d5d-R/latest.

40 "Hopewell Fund," InfluenceWatch, https://www.influencewatch.org/non-profit/hopewell-fund/.

41 Ludwig, Hayden. "Wellspring Philanthropic: An Ocean of 'Dark Money' on the Left." Capital Reseach Center, December 12, 2019. https://capitalresearch.org/article/wellspring-part-1/.

42 "Grants to Gynuity Health Projects LLC (2003-2017)," InfluenceWatch, https://www.influencewatch.org/app/uploads/2020/02/Gynuity-Grantors-with-Grant-Descriptions.xlsx.

43 "Hopewell Fund," InfluenceWatch, https://www.influencewatch.org/non-profit/hopewell-fund/.

44 "New Venture Fund," InfluenceWatch, https://www.influencewatch.org/non-profit/new-venture-fund/.

45 "Hopewell Fund," InfluenceWatch, https://www.influencewatch.org/non-profit/hopewell-fund/.

46 "Resources for Abortion Delivery," InfluenceWatch, https://www.influencewatch.org/non-profit/resources-for-abortion-delivery/.

47 "Resources for Abortion Delivery." Capital Research Center. https://capitalresearch.org/app/uploads/resources-for-abortion-delivery-homepage-screencap.png.

48 "Resources for Abortion Delivery." Tara Health Foundation. Archived from the original May 15, 2021. http://web.archive.org/web/20210515150330/https://tarahealthfoundation.org/resources-for-abortion-delivery-rad/.

49 "Resources for Abortion Delivery Job Listing." Capital Research Center. https://capitalresearch.org/app/uploads/resources-for-abortion-delivery-job-listing-02.2020.pdf.

50 "Guttmacher Institute," InfluenceWatch, https://www.influencewatch.org/non-profit/guttmacher-institute/.

51 "Media." Abortion Care Training Incubator for Outstanding Nurse Scholars. https://actions.ucsf.edu/media.

52 "Home." Equity Forward. https://equityfwd.org/. "HHS Watch." Equity Forward. https://equityfwd.org/hhs-watch.

53 "Arabella Advisors," InfluenceWatch, https://www.influencewatch.org/for-profit/arabella-advisors/. "Hopewell Fund," InfluenceWatch, https://www.influencewatch.org/non-profit/hopewell-fund/. "Equity Forward Hopewell Fund." Idealist. Archived from the original October 3, 2019. http://web.archive.org/web/20191003115041/https://www.idealist.org/en/nonprofit/a8721230f2c34cc28a0f2ddc15e1c16c-equity-forward-hopewell-fund-new-york.

54   "Southern Poverty Law Center," InfluenceWatch, https://www.influencewatch.org/non-profit/southern-poverty-law-center-splc/.

55   "Mary Alice Carter." Equity Forward. Archived from the original January 22, 2020. http://web.archive.org/web/20200122173143/https://equityfwd.org/mary-alice-carter.

56   "Planned Parenthood Federation of America." InfluenceWatch, https://www.influencewatch.org/non-profit/planned-parenthood-federation-of-america/. "Physicians For Reproductive Health," InfluenceWatch, https://www.influencewatch.org/non-profit/physicians-for-reproductive-health/. "National Institute for Reproductive Health," InfluenceWatch, https://www.influencewatch.org/non-profit/national-institute-for-reproductive-health/. "NARAL Pro-Choice America," InfluenceWatch, https://www.influencewatch.org/non-profit/naral-pro-choice-america/.

57   "Abortion Access Front," InfluenceWatch, https://www.influencewatch.org/non-profit/abortion-access-front/.

58   Smittle, Staphanie. "On the 'Vagical Mystery Tour.'" *Arkansas Times*, June 8, 2017. https://arktimes.com/entertainment/ae-feature/2017/06/08/on-the-vagical-mystery-tour.

59   "We Changed Our Name... We're Abortion Access Front Now!" Abortion Access Front. https://www.aafront.org/lady-parts-justice-league-name-change/?fbclid=IwAR02kdBXlHY-XGhg5i6NO-_8WpLiGTfv3NbZUYxQT2CbzHVZPEq-i5dBsF8.

60   Logan, Elizabeth. "Talking Comedy and Reproductive Rights with 'Daily Show' Co-Creator Lizz Winstead." Glamour, September 28, 2016. https://www.glamour.com/story/golden-probes-lady-parts-justice-lizz-winstead.

61   "NEO Philanthropy," InfluenceWatch, https://www.influencewatch.org/non-profit/neo-philanthropy-formerly-public-interest-projects/. Ludwig, Hayden. "The Left's 'Dark Money' Coordinator: Just Passing Through." Capital Research Center, July 10, 2019. https://capitalresearch.org/article/the-lefts-dark-money-coordinator-part-2/.

62   "Tides Foundation," InfluenceWatch, https://www.influencewatch.org/non-profit/tides-foundation/.

63   Menta, Anna. "'The Daily Show' Co-Creator Lizz Winstead is on to Her Next Legacy: Lady Parts Justice League." *Newsweek*, June 16, 2018. https://www.newsweek.com/daily-show-creator-lizz-winstead-lady-parts-justice-league-974421.

64   "Lady Parts Justice," InfluenceWatch, https://www.influencewatch.org/non-profit/lady-parts-justice/.

65   Kazenoff, Harry. "Creative Majority's Creative Deception." Capital Research Center, January 25, 2019. https://capitalresearch.org/article/creative-majoritys-creative-deception/. "Sixteen Thirty Fund," InfluenceWatch, https://www.influencewatch.org/non-profit/sixteen-thirty-fund/. "Arabella Advisors," InfluenceWatch, https://www.influencewatch.org/for-profit/arabella-advisors/.

66   "Warren Buffett Ends Support for Population Control Programs." Population Research

Institute, July 1, 2003. https://www.pop.org/warren-buffett-ends-support-for-population-control-programs-2/.

CHAPTER 6

1   Watson, Michael. "Yes, America, There Is a War on Cars." Capital Research Center, June 16, 2023. https://capitalresearch.org/article/yes-america-there-is-a-war-on-cars/.

2   "Blog of the Interior." U.S. Department of the Interior. https://www.doi.gov/blog/how-interior-increasing-access-public-lands#:~:text=Across%20the%20more%20than%20450,advocate%20for%20America's%20great%20outdoors..

3   "Federal land ownership by state." *Ballotpedia*. https://ballotpedia.org/Federal_land_ownership_by_state.

4   "Accomplishments Under President Donald J. Trump January 2017 – January 2021." U.S. Department of the Interior. https://www.doi.gov/sites/doi.gov/files/asiia-accomplishments-2017-to-2020_0.pdf.

5   "Center for Biological Diversity," InfluenceWatch, https://www.influencewatch.org/non-profit/center-for-biological-diversity/. "Merkley Introduces Major New Legislation to Stop New Fossil Fuel Leases on Federal Lands." Jeff Merkley, November 4, 2015. https://www.merkley.senate.gov/news/press-releases/merkley-introduces-major-new-legislation-to-stop-new-fossil-fuel-leases-on-federal-lands.

6   "350.org," InfluenceWatch, https://www.influencewatch.org/non-profit/350-org/. "New Bill Would Keep Fossil Fuel Reserves on Public Lands in the Ground." Jeff Merkley, November 4, 2015. https://www.merkley.senate.gov/news/in-the-news/new-bill-would-keep-fossil-fuel-reserves-on-public-lands-in-the-ground.

7   "President Obama cancels 2016 and 2017 oil lease sales in the Chukchi and Beaufort seas." World Wildlife Fund, October 19, 2015. https://www.worldwildlife.org/stories/president-obama-cancels-2016-and-2017-oil-lease-sales-in-the-chukchi-and-beaufort-seas. "2016 Democratic Party Platform." Democratic Platform Committee, July 8-9, 2016. https://democrats.org/wp-content/uploads/2018/10/2016_DNC_Platform.pdf.

8   "Clinton Calls Ban on Future Extraction on Public Lands a 'Done Deal.'" 350 Action, February 5, 2016. https://350action.org/clinton-calls-ban-on-future-extraction-on-public-lands-a-done-deal/.

9   Cain, Andrew. "Tim Kaine says he now opposes offshore drilling, citing Defense Department concerns." *Richmond Times Dispatch*, August 15, 2016. https://richmond.com/news/local/government-politics/tim-kaine-says-he-now-opposes-offshore-drilling-citing-defense-department-concerns/article_8db256c8-ea45-5b4c-bbb1-c7cc54219259.html.

10 Richards, Heather and Cama, Timothy. "Dems want to kill oil and gas leasing. Here's why it matters." *PoliticoPro*, August 6, 2019. https://www.eenews.net/stories/1060860731.

11   Alexander, Kurtis. "Biden halts new oil drilling on federal lands. Here's what major climate move means for California." *San Francisco Chronicle*, January 27, 2021. https://www.sfchronicle.com/environment/article/Biden-to-halt-new-oil-drilling-in-major-climate-15901950.php.

12   "What If...Energy Production Was Banned on Federal Lands and Waters?" Institute for 21st Century Energy, 2016. https://www.globalenergyinstitute.org/sites/default/files/2019-07/er-offlimits-16.pdf.

13   "Revenues and Disbursements from Oil and Natural Gas Production on Federal Lands." Congressional Research Service, September 22, 2020. https://fas.org/sgp/crs/misc/R46537.pdf.

14   "What If...Energy Production Was Banned on Federal Lands and Waters?" Institute for 21st Century Energy, 2016. https://www.globalenergyinstitute.org/sites/default/files/2019-07/er-offlimits-16.pdf.

15   "Western Values Project," InfluenceWatch, https://www.influencewatch.org/non-profit/western-values-project/. "Western Values Project Action," InfluenceWatch, https://www.influencewatch.org/non-profit/western-values-project-action/.

16   "Sixteen Thirty Fund: Key Staff," InfluenceWatch, https://www.influencewatch.org/non-profit/sixteen-thirty-fund/#key-staff.

17   "About Us." Western Values Project. Archived from the original October 4, 2019. https://web.archive.org/web/20191004111231/https:/westernvaluesproject.org/about-us/. "End Citizens United," InfluenceWatch, https://www.influencewatch.org/political-party/end-citizens-united-ecu/.

18   "About Us." Western Values Project. Archived from the original October 4, 2019. https://web.archive.org/web/20191004111231/https:/westernvaluesproject.org/about-us/.

19   "Progressnow Colorado," InfluenceWatch, https://www.influencewatch.org/non-profit/progressnow-colorado/.

20   "National Wildlife Federation," InfluenceWatch, https://www.influencewatch.org/non-profit/national-wildlife-federation/.

21   "Caroline Ciccone," InfluenceWatch, https://www.influencewatch.org/person/caroline-ciccone/. "Restore Public Trust," InfluenceWatch, https://www.influencewatch.org/non-profit/restore-public-trust/.

22   "Americans United for Change," InfluenceWatch, https://www.influencewatch.org/non-profit/americans-united-for-change/. "Robert Creamer: 2016 Presidential Campaign Controversy," InfluenceWatch, https://www.influencewatch.org/person/robert-creamer/#2016-presidential-campaign-controversy.

23   "Kyle Herrig," InfluenceWatch, https://www.influencewatch.org/person/kyle-herrig/. "American Oversight," InfluenceWatch, https://www.influencewatch.org/non-profit/american-oversight/. "Allied Progress," InfluenceWatch, https://www.influencewatch.

org/non-profit/allied-progress/.

24   "Accountable.US," InfluenceWatch, https://www.influencewatch.org/non-profit/
     accountable-us/.

25   "Sixteen Thirty Fund: 2018 Form 990," InfluenceWatch, http://www.influencewatch.
     org/app/uploads/2019/11/Sixteen-Thirty-Fund-2018-Form-990.pdf.

26   "Home." Western Values Project. Archived from the original October 9, 2018. https://
     web.archive.org/web/20181009144947/https:/westernvaluesproject.org/.

27   "David Bernhardt." Department of Influence. Archived from the original September 19,
     2017. https://web.archive.org/web/20170919092100/https:/departmentofinfluence.
     org/person/david-bernhardt/.

28   Cama, Timothy and Green, Miranda. "Interior chief Zinke to leave administration." The
     Hill, December 15, 2018. https://thehill.com/policy/energy-environment/415988-
     interior-secretary-ryan-zinke-steps-down.

29   "The FOIA Project: Western Values Project v. U.S. Department of the Interior,"
     InfluenceWatch, https://www.influencewatch.org/app/uploads/2021/02/FOIA-
     Project.-Western-Values-Project-FOIA-2017-2019.pdf.

30   Skinner, Dave. "More Big Bucks." Flathead Beacon, September 6, 2017. https://
     flatheadbeacon.com/2017/09/06/more-big-bucks/.

31   "Western Values Project v. Department of the Interior." The FOIA Project, September
     28, 2017. http://foiaproject.org/dc_view/?id=4063478-DC-1-2017cv02001-
     complaint.

32   "American Oversight," InfluenceWatch, https://www.influencewatch.org/non-profit/
     american-oversight/.

33   "Western Values Project and American Oversight v. U.S. Department of the Interior."
     The FOIA Project, October 10, 2018. http://foiaproject.org/dc_view/?id=5005093-
     DC-1-2018cv02336-complaint.

34   "Western Values Project v. Department of the Interior." The FOIA Project, October 23,
     2017. http://foiaproject.org/dc_view/?id=4117476-DC-1-2017cv02190-complaint.

35   "Western Values Project v. U.S. Department of the Interior." The FOIA Project, October
     5, 2017. http://foiaproject.org/dc_view/?id=4081461-DC-1-2017cv02070-complaint.

36   "Western Values Project v. U.S. Department of the Interior." The FOIA Project,
     August 31, 2017. http://foiaproject.org/dc_view/?id=3985460-DC-1-2017cv01779-
     complaint.

37   "Western Values Project v. U.S. Department of the Interior." The FOIA Project, April 25,
     2017. http://foiaproject.org/dc_view/?id=3680511-DC-1-2017cv00757-complaint.

38   Eilperin, Juliet, Rein, Lisa, and Dawsey, Josh. "Interior Secretary Zinke's approach
     to wife's travels raised red flags, report finds." The Washington Post, October 18,
     2018. https://www.washingtonpost.com/politics/trump-administration-does-

about-face-on-its-own-announcement-that-top-aide-at-hud-would-be-interiors-watchdog/2018/10/18/d90bbf7a-d2fb-11e8-8c22-fa2ef74bd6d6_story.html.

39 "Western Values Project Statement on Zinke Probe Referred to DOJ." Western Values Project. Archived from the original January 25, 2019. https://web.archive.org/web/20190125004826/https:/westernvaluesproject.org/western-values-project-statement-on-zinke-probe-referred-to-doj/. "Western Values Project Calls for Secretary Zinke's Resignation." Western Values Project, November 1, 2018. Archived from the original May 2, 2019. https://web.archive.org/web/20190502052858/https:/westernvaluesproject.org/western-values-project-calls-for-secretary-zinkes-resignation/.

40 "Home." Has Ryan Zinke been fired yet? Archived from the original February 2, 2019. https://web.archive.org/web/20190202231315/http:/www.hasryanzinkebeenfiredyet.com/.

41 "Western Values Project Zinke Attack Ad," InfluenceWatch, https://www.influencewatch.org/app/uploads/2021/02/Western-Values-Project-Zinke-Attack-Ad-Press-Release-2019.pdf. "Western Values Project Zinke Attack Ad," InfluenceWatch, https://www.influencewatch.org/app/uploads/2021/02/Western-Values-Project-Zinke-Attack-Ad-2019.pdf.

42 "Center for Western Priorities," InfluenceWatch, https://www.influencewatch.org/non-profit/center-for-western-priorities/. "Resources Legacy Fund," InfluenceWatch, https://www.influencewatch.org/non-profit/resources-legacy-fund/. Ludwig, Hayden. "Environmentalists Spent a Record $2.4 Billion Pushing Global Warming Ideology." Capital Research Center, February 22, 2021. https://capitalresearch.org/article/environmentalists-spent-a-record-2-4-billion-pushing-global-warming-ideology/.

43 "Ryan Zinke to resign as Interior Secretary, leaving behind a legacy of corruption." Center for Western Priorities, December 15, 2018. https://westernpriorities.org/2018/12/15/ryan-zinke-to-resign-as-interior-secretary-leaving-behind-a-legacy-of-corruption/.

44 "Winners and losers from Ryan Zinke's tenure at the Interior Department." Center for Western Priorities, January 2, 2019. https://westernpriorities.org/2019/01/02/winners-and-losers-from-ryan-zinkes-tenure-at-the-interior-department/.

45 "Bernhardt Nomination." GovInfo, May 18, 2017. https://www.govinfo.gov/content/pkg/CHRG-115shrg26073/html/CHRG-115shrg26073.htm.

46 Davenport, Coral and Fandos, Nicholas. "As Interior Secretary Swaggers Through Parks, His Staff Rolls Back Regulations." The New York Times, July 25, 2017. https://www.nytimes.com/2017/07/25/us/politics/interior-secretary-zinke-staff-conservation-regulations.html.

47 Brekke, Dan. "Trump Appoints Valley Water District's Lobbyist to Interior Department Post." KQED, April 28, 2017.. https://ww2.kqed.org/news/2017/04/28/trump-appoints-valley-water-districts-lobbyist-to-interior-department-post/.

48 Prentice-Dunn, Jesse. "Walking conflict of interest." *Medium*, December 17, 2018. https://medium.com/westwise/walking-conflict-of-interest-fffe8593feaa.

49 "Home." Meet David Bernhardt. Archived from the original December 17, 2018. https://web.archive.org/web/20181217174459/https://www.davidbernhardt.org/.

50 Prentice-Dunn, Jesse. "Memo: Background on Acting Interior Secretary David Bernhardt's ties to the oil and gas industry and conflicts of interests." Center for Western Priorities, March 26, 2019. https://westernpriorities.org/2019/03/26/memo-background-on-acting-interior-secretary-david-bernhardts-ties-to-the-oil-and-gas-industry-and-conflicts-of-interests/. O'Neill, Jayson. "Bernhardt's Interior Ignores Own Representations to Court Over Public Records Deadline." Western Values Project, February 25, 2019. https://westernvaluesproject.org/bernhardts-interior-ignores-own-representations-to-court-over-public-records-deadline/. "Democracy Forward," InfluenceWatch, https://www.influencewatch.org/non-profit/democracy-forward/. "Perkins Coie," InfluenceWatch, https://www.influencewatch.org/for-profit/perkins-coie/.

51 "Campaign for Accountability," InfluenceWatch, https://www.influencewatch.org/non-profit/campaign-for-accountability/. "Correction: Funding for Nonprofit's Google 'Transparency' Campaign." The *Chronicle of Philanthropy*, July 21, 2019. https://www.philanthropy.com/article/correction-funding-for-nonprofits-google-transparency-campaign/, "Campaign for Accountability David Bernhardt Investigation Petition," InfluenceWatch, https://www.influencewatch.org/app/uploads/2021/02/campaign-for-accountability-david-bernhardt-investigation-petition.pdf. "Statement on the Nomination of David Bernhardt for Secretary of the Department of the Interior." Campaign for Accountability, February 4, 2019. https://campaignforaccountability.org/statement-on-the-appointment-of-david-bernhardt-as-the-acting-secretary-of-the-department-of-the-interior/.

52 "Citizens for Responsibility and Ethics in Washington," InfluenceWatch, https://www.influencewatch.org/non-profit/citizens-for-responsibility-and-ethics-in-washington/. "American Oversight," InfluenceWatch, https://www.influencewatch.org/non-profit/american-oversight/.

53 Rehmann, Marc. "David Bernhardt Is President Trump's Most Conflicted Cabinet Nominee." Center for American Progress, March 15, 2019. https://www.americanprogress.org/issues/green/news/2019/03/15/467373/david-bernhardt-president-trumps-conflicted-cabinet-nominee/.

54 "Interior Inspector General Urged to Investigate David Bernhardt." Greenpeace, December 20, 2018. https://www.greenpeace.org/usa/news/interior-inspector-general-urged-to-investigate-david-bernhardt/.

55 Brown, Gabby. "Fossil Fuel Lobbyist David Bernhardt Proves He Can't Be Trusted at Interior." Sierra Club, March 28, 2019. https://www.sierraclub.org/press-releases/2019/03/fossil-fuel-lobbyist-david-bernhardt-proves-he-can-t-be-trusted-interior. "Parks Group Rejects Nomination of David Bernhardt for Interior Secretary." National Parks Conservation Association, February 4, 2019. https://www.npca.org/

articles/2106-parks-group-rejects-nomination-of-david-bernhardt-for-interior-secretary. "Urge your senators to say NO to David Bernhardt." NRDC Action Fund. Archived from the original July 10, 2022. http://web.archive.org/web/20220710110256/https://act. nrdc.org/letter/af-bernhardt-190315.

56   "Western Values Project Action 2019 Buy Bernhardt Ad," InfluenceWatch, https://www. influencewatch.org/app/uploads/2021/02/western-values-project-action-2019-ad-buy-bernhardt.pdf.

57   "Western Values Project v. U.S. Department of the Interior." The FOIA Project, August 21, 2019. http://foiaproject.org/dc_view/?id=6350796-DC-1-2019cv02527-complaint. Siler, Wes. "The David Bernhardt Scandal Tracker." Outside, April 19, 2019. https://www.outsideonline.com/2390596/david-bernhardt-scandal-tracker.

58   O'Neill, Jayson. "Yes, Trump Really is Coming to Take Your Public Lands." Western Values Project, August 20, 2019. https://westernvaluesproject.org/yes-trump-really-is-coming-to-take-your-public-lands/.

59   Evans, Brandon. "US drilling on federal and Indian lands surges in 2019." S&P Global, October 28, 2019. https://www.spglobal.com/platts/en/market-insights/latest-news/natural-gas/102819-us-drilling-on-federal-and-indian-lands-surges-in-2019.

60   "Weekly Retail Gasoline and Diesel Prices." U.S. Energy Information Administration. https://www.eia.gov/dnav/pet/pet_pri_gnd_dcus_nus_a.htm.

61   "The United States Was Energy Independent in 2019 for the First Time Since 1957." Institute for Energy Research, May 11, 2020. https://www.instituteforenergyresearch. org/fossil-fuels/gas-and-oil/the-united-states-was-energy-independent-in-2019-for-the-first-time-since-1957/.

62   "The United States Was Energy Independent in 2019 for the First Time Since 1957." Institute for Energy Research, May 11, 2020. https://www.instituteforenergyresearch. org/fossil-fuels/gas-and-oil/the-united-states-was-energy-independent-in-2019-for-the-first-time-since-1957/.

63   Prentice-Dunn, Jesse. "Inside Interior Secretary David Bernhardt's Wildly Destructive Track Record." *Medium*, December 3, 2020. https://medium.com/westwise/inside-interior-secretary-david-bernhardts-wildly-destructive-track-record-e57f7ddb7298.

64   Rott, Nathan. "Deb Haaland Confirmed As 1st Native American Interior Secretary." NPR, March 15, 2021. https://www.npr.org/2021/03/15/977558590/deb-haaland-confirmed-as-first-native-american-interior-secretary.

65   Oven, Sarah. "Despite criticism, confirmation of Interior Secretary Deb Haaland makes history." NonDoc, March 18, 2021. https://nondoc.com/2021/03/18/confirmation-of-interior-secretary-deb-haaland/. "Representative Debra Haaland (D)." League of Conservation Voters. https://scorecard.lcv.org/moc/debra-haaland.

66   "Deb Haaland's Ratings and Endorsements." Vote Smart. https://justfacts.votesmart. org/candidate/evaluations/149368/deb-haaland.

67   Rott, Nathan. "Interior Nominee Deb Haaland Faces Tough Questions On Climate Goals." NPR, February 23, 2021. https://www.npr.org/2021/02/23/970242295/interior-nominee-deb-haaland-faces-tough-questions-on-climate-goals. "Deb Haaland: Climate and Energy," InfluenceWatch, https://www.influencewatch.org/app/uploads/2021/02/debra-haaland-2018-campaign-site-energy.pdf.

68   "President Biden's Fiscal Year 2022 Budget Makes Significant Investments in Interior Department." U.S. Department of the Interior, May 28, 2021. https://www.doi.gov/pressreleases/president-bidens-fiscal-year-2022-budget-makes-significant-investments-interior.

69   Middleton, Arthur. "Here's how Biden can help conserve 30 percent of U.S. land by 2030." *Berkeley News*, January 25, 2021. https://blogs.berkeley.edu/2021/01/25/heres-how-biden-can-help-conserve-30-percent-of-u-s-land-by-2030/#:~:text=The%20plan%20is%20known%20as,carbon%20in%20plants%20and%20soil.

70   "Science Moms Privacy Policy." Capital Research Center. https://capitalresearch.org/app/uploads/science-moms-privacy-policy.pdf. "Potential Energy Coalition," InfluenceWatch," https://www.influencewatch.org/non-profit/potential-energy-coalition/.

71   Schrag, Daniel P. "Confronting Climate Change Over the Next Three Decades." Harvard Business School. https://www.alumni.hbs.edu/Documents/events/Dan_Schragg_Slides_3.4.20.pdf.

72   "Grants: Windward Fund For The Potential Energy Coalition." William and Flora Hewlett Foundation. https://hewlett.org/grants/windward-fund-for-the-potential-energy-coalition/. "Windward Foundation," InfluenceWatch, https://www.influencewatch.org/non-profit/windward-fund/. "Arabella Advisors," InfluenceWatch, https://www.influencewatch.org/for-profit/arabella-advisors/.

73   "William and Flora Hewlett Foundation," InfluenceWatch, https://www.influencewatch.org/non-profit/william-and-flora-hewlett-foundation/. "McKnight Foundation," InfluenceWatch, https://www.influencewatch.org/non-profit/mcknight-foundation/.

74   "KR Foundation List of grants 2019." Capital Research Center. https://capitalresearch.org/app/uploads/kr-foundation-2019-grant-list.pdf.

75   "Potential Energy Coalition Job Listing." Capital Research Center. https://capitalresearch.org/app/uploads/potential-energy-coalition-job-listing-windward-fund.pdf.

76   Potential Energy Coalition Inc, Return of Organization Exempt from Income Tax (Form 990), 2020, Schedule O.

77   "Privacy Policy." Potential Energy Coalition, September 21, 2021. https://potentialenergycoalition.org/wp-content/uploads/PotentialEnergyCoalition_PrivacyPolicy.pdf.

78   "Windward Fund," InfluenceWatch, https://www.influencewatch.org/non-profit/blueprint-nc/.

79   "League of Conservation Voters," InfluenceWatch, https://www.influencewatch.org/non-profit/league-of-conservation-voters/.

80   "Blueprint North Carolina," InfluenceWatch, https://www.influencewatch.org/non-profit/democracy-north-carolina/.

81   "Home." Carbon Mapper. https://carbonmapper.org/.

82   "Potential Energy Coalition," InfluenceWatch, https://www.influencewatch.org/non-profit/potential-energy-coalition/. Ludwig, Hayden. "The Global Warming Guys—and 'Dark Money'—Behind 'Science Moms.'" Capital Research Center, August 18, 2022. https://capitalresearch.org/article/the-global-warming-guys-and-dark-money-behind-science-moms/.

83   Mamula, Ned. "Gold Into Dross: The Importance of Pebble." Capital Research Center, January 23, 2018. https://capitalresearch.org/article/one-gold-into-dross/.

84   "Copper Drives Electric Vehicles." Copper Development Association. https://www.copper.org/publications/pub_list/pdf/A6191-ElectricVehicles-Factsheet.pdf.

85   "Wind Energy Basics." Copper Development Association. https://www.copper.org/environment/green/casestudies/wind_energy/wind_energy.html.

86   Greenfield, Nicole and Turrentine, Jeff. "Crushing Alaska's Pebble Mine." NRDC, February 13, 2023. https://www.nrdc.org/stop-pebble-mine-save-bristol-bay.

87   "Join the Fight to Protect Bristol Bay from Dangerous Open-Pit Mining!" League of Conservation Voters. Archived from the original October 27, 2021. http://web.archive.org/web/20211027011434/http://p2a.co/gmb3Z6S?resetcookie=1.

88   "Trout Unlimited," InfluenceWatch, https://www.influencewatch.org/non-profit/trout-unlimited/.

89   "Roadless Area Conservation National Advisory Committee." Forest Service, December 23, 2008. https://www.fs.usda.gov/Internet/FSE_DOCUMENTS/stelprdb5050457.pdf.

90   "Nature Conservancy," InfluenceWatch, https://www.influencewatch.org/non-profit/nature-conservancy/. "Bill and Melinda Gates Foundation," InfluenceWatch, https://www.influencewatch.org/non-profit/bill-and-melinda-gates-foundation/. "William and Flora Hewlett Foundation," InfluenceWatch, https://www.influencewatch.org/non-profit/william-and-flora-hewlett-foundation/. "Wyss Foundation," InfluenceWatch, https://www.influencewatch.org/non-profit/wyss-foundation/.

91   "New Venture Fund," InfluenceWatch, https://www.influencewatch.org/non-profit/new-venture-fund/.

92   "Donate." SalmonState. Archived from the original January 5, 2020. https://web.archive.org/web/20200105132126/https://secure.donationpay.org/salmonstate/.

93   "Stop Pebble Mine." The Alaska Center. https://akcenter.org/salmon-clean-water/stop-pebble-mine/.

94 "Elections." The Alaska Center. Archived from the original October 2, 2019. https://
    web.archive.org/web/20191002182826/https:/akcenter.org/elections/.

95 "Leg With Louie: Alaska Legislature and 415 Parts Per Million." The Alaska Center.
    https://akcenter.org/2019/05/17/leg-with-louie-alaska-legislature-and-415-parts-per-
    million/.

96 Parliamentary Budget Officer. "PBO releases updated analysis of the impact of the
    federal fuel charge on households." Office of the Parliamentary Budget Officer, March
    30, 2023. https://www.pbo-dpb.ca/en/news-releases--communiques-de-presse/pbo-
    releases-updated-analysis-of-the-impact-of-the-federal-fuel-charge-on-households-
    le-dpb-publie-une-analyse-actualisee-de-lincidence-de-la-redevance-federale-sur-les-
    combustibles-sur-les-menages.

97 Bohrer, Becky and Whittle, Patrick. "Alaska gold, copper mine blocked over
    environmental worries." AP News, January 31, 2023. https://apnews.com/
    article/politics-us-environmental-protection-agency-alaska-business-fish-
    139ceb6e697c006737d09f984456b0e1.

98 "Rewiring America," InfluenceWatch, https://www.influencewatch.org/non-profit/
    rewiring-america/. "Windward Fund," InfluenceWatch, https://www.influencewatch.
    org/non-profit/windward-fund/.

99 "Rockefeller Brothers Grant to Rewiring America," InfluenceWatch, https://www.
    influencewatch.org/app/uploads/2021/03/Rockefeller-Brothers-grant-to-Rewiring-
    America.-03.21.pdf. "Rockefeller Brothers Fund," InfluenceWatch, https://www.
    influencewatch.org/non-profit/rockefeller-brothers-fund/. "Policy Hub." Rewiring
    America. https://www.rewiringamerica.org/policy.

100 "The BUILD GREEN Infrastructure and Jobs Act." Elizabeth Warren for
     Massachusetts. https://www.warren.senate.gov/imo/media/doc/BUILD_GREEN_Act
     Summary.pdf.

101 Lehman, Mattias. "The Climate Justice Movement Must Oppose White Supremacy
     Everywhere—By Supporting M4BL." Sunrise Movement, May 29, 2020. https://www.
     sunrisemovement.org/movement-updates/the-climate-justice-movement-must-oppose-
     white-supremacy-everywhere-by-supporting-m4bl-4e338cf91b19/.

102 "9 Key Elements of Joe Biden's Plan for a Clean Energy Revolution." JoeBiden.
     com. Archived from the original March 24, 2023. http://web.archive.org/
     web/20230324214055/https://joebiden.com/9-key-elements-of-joe-bidens-plan-for-a-
     clean-energy-revolution/#.

103 "Democrats Unveil 'Build Green' Infrastructure and Jobs Act." *EcoWatch,* March 20,
     2021. https://www.ecowatch.com/build-green-act-2651149717.html. "Home." 350.org.
     https://350.org/.

104 "Lobbying Registration: AJW, Inc." U.S. Senate Lobbying Disclosure, January 5, 2021.
     https://lda.senate.gov/filings/public/filing/7ef95281-b6f6-4b6a-9ebb-7d980a208dee/
     print/.

105 Ludwig, Hayden. "UN Report: U.S. Doesn't Need the Paris Agreement to 'Save' the World." Capital Research Center, February 5, 2021. https://capitalresearch.org/article/un-report-u-s-doesnt-need-the-paris-agreement-to-save-the-world/.

106 Natter, Ari. "US Safety Agency to Consider Ban on Gas Stoves Amid Health Fears." Bloomberg, January 9, 2023. https://www.bloomberg.com/news/articles/2023-01-09/us-safety-agency-to-consider-ban-on-gas-stoves-amid-health-fears#xj4y7vzkg. "Rocky Mountain Institute," InfluenceWatch, https://www.influencewatch.org/non-profit/rocky-mountain-institute/.

107 Bloch, Elizabeth. "Calm down, the government isn't coming for your gas stove." The *Philadelphia Inquirer*, January 12, 2023. https://www.inquirer.com/news/gas-stove-ban-biden-safety-20230112.html.

108 McCann Ramirez, Nikki. "No, The Government Is Not Seizing Your Gas Stove." *Rolling Stone*, January 11, 2023. https://www.rollingstone.com/politics/politics-news/gas-stoves-subject-gop-latest-culture-war-ronny-jackson-1234659387/.

CHAPTER 7

1 "Wyss Foundation: Financial Overview," InfluenceWatch, https://www.influencewatch.org/non-profit/wyss-foundation/#financial-overview. "Wyss Foundation: Financial Overview," InfluenceWatch, https://www.influencewatch.org/non-profit/wyss-foundation/#financial-overview. "HSUS Gets Nearly $1 Million from the New George Soros." Humane Watch, March 22, 2019. https://humanewatch.org/hsus-gets-nearly-1-million-from-the-new-george-soros/.

2 "Democracy Alliance," InfluenceWatch, https://www.influencewatch.org/organization/democracy-alliance-da/.

3 "Center for American Progress," InfluenceWatch, https://www.influencewatch.org/non-profit/center-for-american-progress-cap/. "Center for American Progress," InfluenceWatch, https://www.influencewatch.org/non-profit/center-for-american-progress-cap/.

4 Vogel, Kenneth P. and Robertson, Katie. "Top Bidder for Tribune Newspapers Is an Influential Liberal Donor." The *New York Times*, April 13, 2021. https://www.nytimes.com/2021/04/13/business/media/wyss-tribune-company-buyer.html. Thayer, Parker. "A 'Dark Money' Assault on U.S. Elections: Meet the Team." Capital Research Center, October 9, 2020. https://capitalresearch.org/article/a-dark-money-assault-on-u-s-elections-part-2/.

5 "Wilderness Society," InfluenceWatch, https://www.influencewatch.org/non-profit/wilderness-society/.

6 "Sierra Club Foundation," InfluenceWatch, https://www.influencewatch.org/non-profit/sierra-club-foundation/. "Defenders of Wildlife," InfluenceWatch, https://www.influencewatch.org/non-profit/defenders-of-wildlife/. "Trout Unlimited,"

InfluenceWatch, https://www.influencewatch.org/non-profit/trout-unlimited/. "National Religious Partnership for the Environment," InfluenceWatch, https://www. influencewatch.org/non-profit/national-religious-partnersip-for-the-environment/. "Natural Resources Defense Council," InfluenceWatch, https://www.influencewatch. org/non-profit/natural-resources-defense-council-nrdc/.

7   "LCV Education Fund," InfluenceWatch, https://www.influencewatch.org/non-profit/lcv-education-fund/. "Environment America Research and Policy Center," InfluenceWatch, https://www.influencewatch.org/non-profit/environment-america-research-and-policy-center/. "Project Vote," InfluenceWatch, https://www. influencewatch.org/non-profit/project-vote/.

8   Vogel, Kenneth P. and Robertson, Katie. "Top Bidder for Tribune Newspapers Is an Influential Liberal Donor." The *New York Times*, April 13, 2021. https://www.nytimes. com/2021/04/13/business/media/wyss-tribune-company-buyer.html.

9   Pollock, Richard. "EXCLUSIVE: Foreign Clinton Donor Made Donations to US Campaigns." *Daily Caller*, February 28, 2016. https://dailycaller.com/2016/02/28/exclusive-clintons-swiss-ally-gave-big-bucks-to-u-s-campaigns/.

10   Massoglia, Anna. "'Dark money' networks hide political agendas behind fake news sites." *OpenSecrets*, May 22, 2020. https://www.opensecrets.org/news/2020/05/dark-money-networks-fake-news-sites/. "The Newsroom," InfluenceWatch, https://www. influencewatch.org/non-profit/the-newsroom/.

11   Vogel, Kenneth P. and Robertson, Katie. "Top Bidder for Tribune Newspapers Is an Influential Liberal Donor." The *New York Times*, April 13, 2021. https://www.nytimes. com/2021/04/13/business/media/wyss-tribune-company-buyer.html.

12   Smith, Gary. "Tribune Journalists Are Close To an Improbable Win in Quest for New Owners." Currently, April 6, 2021. Archived from the original April 29, 2021. http://web.archive.org/web/20210429141953/https://currently.att.yahoo.com/att/tribune-journalists-close-improbable-win-224913332.html.

13   Chozick, Amy. "Conservative Koch Brothers Turning Focus to Newspapers." The *New York Times*, April 20, 2013. https://www.nytimes.com/2013/04/21/business/media/koch-brothers-making-play-for-tribunes-newspapers.html. Farhi, Paul. "Billionaire Koch brothers use Web to take on media reports they dispute." The *Washington Post*, July 14, 2013. https://www.washingtonpost.com/lifestyle/style/billionaire-koch-brothers-use-web-to-take-on-media-reports-they-dispute/2013/07/14/6a0953a0-e5b5-11e2-a11e-c2ea876a8f30_story.html. Folenflik, David. "Koch Brothers' Newspaper Takeover Could Spark 'Culture Clash.'" NPR, April 26, 2013. https://www.npr. org/2013/04/26/179179653/billionaire-koch-brothers-increase-their-role-in-u-s-politics.

14   Robertson, Katie. "Hansjorg Wyss is said to end his bid for Tribune Publishing." The *Chicago Tribune*, April 17, 2021. https://www.chicagotribune.com/business/ct-aud-biz-nyt-tribune-publishing-hansjorg-wyss-20210417-gofh7t2wgzdwzgxu5zbegyduca-story. html.

15 Butler, Rhett A. "One man's quest to save the world's wildest places: Hansjörg Wyss." Mongabay, October 18, 2017. https://news.mongabay.com/2017/10/one-mans-quest-to-save-the-worlds-wildest-places/.

16 Chaidez, Alexandra A. and Ryan, Aidan F. "Wyss Donates $131 Million Gift Toward Namesake Institute." The Harvard Crimson, June 7, 2019. https://www.thecrimson.com/article/2019/6/7/wyss-131-million-donation/.

17 "Hansjoerg Wyss." Bloomberg. https://www.bloomberg.com/billionaires/profiles/hansjoerg-wyss/.

18 Kimes, Mina. "Bad to the bone: A medical horror story." Fortune, September 18, 2012. https://fortune.com/2012/09/18/bad-to-the-bone-a-medical-horror-story/.

19 Pollock, Richard. "EXCLUSIVE: NJ Township Re-opens Sexual Assault Investigation on Democrat Mega-Donor Tied to Hillary and John Podesta." Daily Caller, January 29, 2018. https://dailycaller.com/2018/01/29/wyss-sexual-assault-investigation/.

20 "Civitas Public Affairs Group," InfluenceWatch, https://www.influencewatch.org/for-profit/civitas-public-affairs-group/. "Brady Campaign to Prevent Gun Violence," InfluenceWatch, https://www.influencewatch.org/non-profit/brady-campaign-to-prevent-gun-violence/. "Voter Participation Center," InfluenceWatch, https://www.influencewatch.org/non-profit/voter-participation-center/.

21 "Pew Charitable Trusts," InfluenceWatch, https://www.influencewatch.org/non-profit/pew-charitable-trusts/. "Media Matters for America," InfluenceWatch, https://www.influencewatch.org/non-profit/media-matters-for-america/. "Center for American Progress," InfluenceWatch, https://www.influencewatch.org/non-profit/center-for-american-progress-cap/. "American Civil Liberties Union," InfluenceWatch, https://www.influencewatch.org/non-profit/american-civil-liberties-union-aclu/. "NARAL Pro-Choice America," InfluenceWatch, https://www.influencewatch.org/non-profit/naral-pro-choice-america/. "William J. Brennan Center for Justice," InfluenceWatch, https://www.influencewatch.org/non-profit/william-j-brennan-center-for-justice/. "Center for Popular Democracy," InfluenceWatch, https://www.influencewatch.org/non-profit/center-for-popular-democracy/.

22 "The Restriction of Political Campaign Intervention by Section 501(c)(3) Tax-Exempt Organizations." The Internal Revenue Service. https://www.irs.gov/charities-non-profits/charitable-organizations/the-restriction-of-political-campaign-intervention-by-section-501c3-tax-exempt-organizations.

23 "Influencing Elections and Carrying on Voter Registration Drives." The Internal Revenue Service. https://www.irs.gov/charities-non-profits/private-foundations/influencing-elections-and-carrying-on-voter-registration-drives.

24 "Arabella Advisors: Network Financial Overview," InfluenceWatch, https://www.influencewatch.org/for-profit/arabella-advisors/#network-financial-overview.

25 Vogel, Kenneth P. and Robertson, Katie. "Top Bidder for Tribune Newspapers Is an Influential Liberal Donor." The New York Times, April 13, 2021. https://www.nytimes.

com/2021/04/13/business/media/wyss-tribune-company-buyer.html. "New Venture Fund," InfluenceWatch, https://www.influencewatch.org/non-profit/new-venture-fund/.

26 Gaudiano, Nicole. "Progressive campaigns nationwide get a silent partner." *USA Today*, January 1, 2017. https://www.usatoday.com/story/news/politics/2017/01/01/progressive-campaigns-nationwide-get-a-silent-partner/96004224/. "The Hub Project," InfluenceWatch, https://www.influencewatch.org/non-profit/the-hub-project/.

27 "The Hub Project," InfluenceWatch, https://www.influencewatch.org/non-profit/the-hub-project/. "Sixteen Thirty Fund," InfluenceWatch, https://www.influencewatch.org/non-profit/sixteen-thirty-fund/. "Hub Education and Engagement Fund," InfluenceWatch, https://www.influencewatch.org/non-profit/hub-education-and-engagement-fund/. "New Venture Fund," InfluenceWatch, https://www.influencewatch.org/non-profit/new-venture-fund/.

28 Vogel, Kenneth P. and Robertson, Katie. "Top Bidder for Tribune Newspapers Is an Influential Liberal Donor." The *New York Times*, April 13, 2021. https://www.nytimes.com/2021/04/13/business/media/wyss-tribune-company-buyer.html.

29 Bland, Scott and Severns, Maggie. "Documents reveal massive 'dark-money' group boosted Democrats in 2018." *Politico*, November 19, 2019.https://www.politico.com/news/2019/11/19/dark-money-democrats-midterm-071725.

30 Graham, David A. "An Experiment in Wisconsin Changed Voters' Minds About Trump." The *Atlantic*, September 17, 2020. https://www.theatlantic.com/ideas/archive/2020/09/experiment-wisconsin-might-reveal-key-defeating-trump/616367/.

31 Lizza, Ryan, Okun, Eli and Ross, Garrett. "POLITICO Playbook PM: Top takeaways from our Ron Klain interview." *Politico*, April 1, 2020. https://www.politico.com/newsletters/playbook-pm/2021/04/01/top-takeaways-from-our-ron-klain-interview-492326.

32 "Arizonans United for Health Care," InfluenceWatch, https://www.influencewatch.org/non-profit/arizonans-united-for-health-care/. "Floridians for a Fair Shake," InfluenceWatch, https://www.influencewatch.org/non-profit/floridians-for-a-fair-shake/. "Keep Iowa Healthy," InfluenceWatch, https://www.influencewatch.org/non-profit/keep-iowa-healthy/. "New Jersey for a Better Future," InfluenceWatch, https://www.influencewatch.org/non-profit/new-jersey-for-a-better-future/. "North Carolinians for a Fair Economy," InfluenceWatch, https://www.influencewatch.org/non-profit/north-carolinians-for-a-fair-economy/.

33 "Arkadi Gerney," InfluenceWatch, https://www.influencewatch.org/person/arkadi-gerney/. Everytown for Gun Safety," InfluenceWatch, https://www.influencewatch.org/non-profit/everytown-for-gun-safety/. "Center for American Progress," InfluenceWatch, https://www.influencewatch.org/non-profit/center-for-american-progress-cap/.

34 "Berger Action Fund," InfluenceWatch, https://www.influencewatch.org/non-profit/berger-action-fund/.

35 "Berger Action Fund: Donors to Berger Action Fund," InfluenceWatch, https://www. influencewatch.org/non-profit/berger-action-fund/#donors-to-berger-action-fund.

36 "League of Conservation Voters," InfluenceWatch, https://www.influencewatch.org/ non-profit/league-of-conservation-voters/. Beckel, Michael. "League of Conservation Voters becoming 'dark money' heavyweight." Center for Public Integrity, November 22, 2013. https://publicintegrity.org/federal-politics/league-of-conservation-voters-becoming-dark-money-heavyweight/. "Planned Parenthood Action Fund," InfluenceWatch, https://www.influencewatch.org/non-profit/planned-parenthood-action-fund/. "Center for Popular Democracy Action Fund," InfluenceWatch, https:// www.influencewatch.org/non-profit/center-for-popular-democracy-action-fundaction-for-the-common-good/. "Democracy Alliance," InfluenceWatch, https://www. influencewatch.org/organization/democracy-alliance-da/.

37 "Molly McUsic," InfluenceWatch, https://www.influencewatch.org/person/molly-mcusic/. "Eric Kessler," InfluenceWatch, https://www.influencewatch.org/person/eric-kessler/.

38 "League of Conservation Voters," InfluenceWatch, https://www.influencewatch.org/ non-profit/league-of-conservation-voters/.

39 "Molly McUsic," InfluenceWatch, https://www.influencewatch.org/person/molly-mcusic/.

40 "Board of Directors and Executive Team." League of Conservation Voters. https://www. lcv.org/board/.

41 "National Resources Defense Council," InfluenceWatch, https://www.influencewatch. org/non-profit/natural-resources-defense-council-nrdc/. "John Leshy." UC Hastings. Archived from the original April 23, 2023. http://web.archive.org/ web/20230423063456/https://www.uchastings.edu/people/john-leshy/.

42 "Kyle Herrig," InfluenceWatch, https://www.influencewatch.org/person/kyle-herrig/.

43 "Accountable.US," InfluenceWatch, https://www.influencewatch.org/non-profit/ accountable-us/. "Restore Public Trust," InfluenceWatch, https://www.influencewatch. org/non-profit/restore-public-trust/. American Oversight," InfluenceWatch, https:// www.influencewatch.org/non-profit/american-oversight/. "Western Values Project," InfluenceWatch, https://www.influencewatch.org/non-profit/western-values-project/. "Home." Meet David Bernhardt. https://www.davidbernhardt.org/.

44 Ludwig, Hayden. "Former Arabella 'Pop-Up' Caught Blacklisting Trump Administration Officials." Capital Research Center, March 23, 2021. https:// capitalresearch.org/article/former-arabella-pop-up-caught-blacklisting-trump-administration-officials/.

45 "Congress Letter to American Oversight, February 22, 2021," InfluenceWatch, https:// www.influencewatch.org/app/uploads/2021/02/Congress-Letter-to-American-Oversight.-02.22.21.pdf.

46 "Home." Americans for Public Trust. https://americansforpublictrust.org/. Klein, Melissa. "Watchdog calls for probe into Swiss billionaire's US political spending." *New*

York Post, May 15, 2021. https://nypost.com/2021/05/15/watchdog-calls-for-probe-into-swiss-billionaires-political-spending/.

47   "APT v. FEC Complaint." Americans for Public Trust, April 25, 2022. Archived from the original May 20, 2022. http://web.archive.org/web/20220520161328/https://americansforpublictrust.org/document/apt-v-fec-complaint/. "Americans for Public Trust Reveals Swiss Billionaire, Who's Donated Millions to Democratic and Liberal Campaigns and Causes, is Not a U.S. Citizen." Americans for Public Trust, April 26, 2022. Archived from the original May 18, 2022. http://web.archive.org/web/20220518112506/https://americansforpublictrust.org/news/americans-for-public-trust-reveals-swiss-billionaire-whos-donated-millions-to-democratic-and-liberal-campaigns-and-causes-is-not-a-u-s-citizen%EF%BF%BC/. "Individual Contributions: Hansjorg Wyss and Hansjoerg Wyss." Federal Election Commission. https://www.fec.gov/data/receipts/individual-contributions/?contributor_name=Wyss%2C+Hansjoerg&contributor_name=Wyss%2C+Hansjorg.

48   Imfeld, Nicholas. "Billionaire and philanthropist Hansjörg Wyss (86) is considering buying the Champions League winner from oligarch Abramovich." *Blick*, March 1, 2022. https://www.blick.ch/wirtschaft/milliardaer-und-philanthrop-hansjoerg-wyss-86-prueft-kauf-des-champions-league-gewinners-von-oligarch-abramowitsch-ich-kann-mir-den-einstieg-bei-chelsea-gut-vorstellen-id17281885.html. "Americans for Public Trust Reveals Swiss Billionaire, Who's Donated Millions to Democratic and Liberal Campaigns and Causes, is Not a U.S. Citizen." Americans for Public Trust, April 26, 2022. Archived from the original July 1, 2022. https://web.archive.org/web/20220701083040/https://americansforpublictrust.org/news/americans-for-public-trust-reveals-swiss-billionaire-whos-donated-millions-to-democratic-and-liberal-campaigns-and-causes-is-not-a-u-s-citizen%EF%BF%BC/.

49   "Foreign nationals." Federal Election Commission. https://www.fec.gov/help-candidates-and-committees/foreign-nationals/.

50   Vogel, Kenneth P. and Robertson, Katie. "Top Bidder for Tribune Newspapers Is an Influential Liberal Donor." The *New York Times*, April 13, 2021. https://www.nytimes.com/2021/04/13/business/media/wyss-tribune-company-buyer.html.

51   Vogel, Kenneth P. "Swiss Billionaire Quietly Becomes Influential Force Among Democrats." The *New York Times*, May 3, 2021. https://www.nytimes.com/2021/05/03/us/politics/hansjorg-wyss-money-democrats.html.

Chapter 8

1   "Pair of measures would legalize marijuana in Montana." *Explore Big Sky*, October 22, 2020. https://www.explorebigsky.com/pair-of-measures-would-legalize-marijuana-in-montana/36437.

2   "North Fund," InfluenceWatch, https://www.influencewatch.org/non-profit/north-fund/.

3   Ludwig, Hayden. "What Is the North Fund, Anyway?" Capital Research Center, November 11, 2022. https://capitalresearch.org/article/what-is-the-north-fund-anyway/.

4   "North Fund," InfluenceWatch, https://www.influencewatch.org/non-profit/north-fund/.

5   "North Fund Public Disclosure 2020," InfluenceWatch, https://www.influencewatch.org/app/uploads/2021/11/North_Fund_2020_Public_Disclosure_Copy-002.pdf.

6   "Sixteen Thirty Fund," InfluenceWatch, https://www.influencewatch.org/non-profit/sixteen-thirty-fund/. "New Venture Fund," InfluenceWatch, https://www.influencewatch.org/non-profit/new-venture-fund/.

7   "North Fund Public Disclosure 2020," InfluenceWatch, https://www.influencewatch.org/app/uploads/2021/11/North_Fund_2020_Public_Disclosure_Copy-002.pdf.

8   "Future Forward USA Action," InfluenceWatch, https://www.influencewatch.org/non-profit/future-forward-usa-action/. "Future Forward PAC," InfluenceWatch, https://www.influencewatch.org/political-party/future-forward-pac/.

9   "North Fund: 2020 Spending," InfluenceWatch, https://www.influencewatch.org/non-profit/north-fund/#2020-spending. "Future Forward USA Independent Expenditures." *OpenSecrets*. https://www.opensecrets.org/political-action-committees-pacs/future-forward-usa/C00669259/independent-expenditures/2020.

10   "Future Forward USA PAC Donors." OpenSecrets. https://www.opensecrets.org/political-action-committees-pacs/future-forward-usa/C00669259/donors/2020?start=1&page_length=25.

11   "Home." 50 State. https://50-state.com/.

12   "Home." Yes on National Popular Vote. https://www.yesonnationalpopularvote.com/.

13   "Living United for Change in Arizona," InfluenceWatch, https://www.influencewatch.org/non-profit/living-united-for-change-in-arizona-lucha/. Luchetta, Julie. "Activists ambush Sen. Kyrsten Sinema at ASU over immigration, Build Back Better Act." *AZ Central*, October 3, 2021. https://www.azcentral.com/story/news/politics/arizona/2021/10/04/activists-ambush-sen-kyrsten-sinema-asu-build-back-better-act/5985790001/.

14   "Colorado Proposition 115, 22-Week Abortion Ban Initiative (2020)." *Ballotpedia*. https://ballotpedia.org/Colorado_Proposition_115,_22-Week_Abortion_Ban_Initiative_(2020).

15   "Colorado Proposition 118, Paid Medical and Family Leave Initiative (2020)." *Ballotpedia*. https://ballotpedia.org/Colorado_Proposition_118,_Paid_Medical_and_Family_Leave_Initiative_(2020).

16   "2007 Campaign Finance Forms." Missouri Ethics Commission. https://www.mec.mo.gov/CampaignFinanceReports/Generator.aspx?Keys=B2G41dEVPKgI8cDcdGFsgJsm99XwPL2GHPZObUuOQdVGtr5bzON4Hsvf6TpIwrb0pw%2fS59cB9OtD-vStbnmEG03L33u%2buRBgg.

17   "Ohio Minimum Wage Increase Initiative (2020)." *Ballotpedia*. https://ballotpedia.org/

Ohio_Minimum_Wage_Increase_Initiative_(2020).

18 "North Fund." Virginia Public Access Project. https://www.vpap.org/lobbying/client/364951-north-fund/.

19 Kurzius, Rachel. "This New Campaign Plans To Spend 'Seven Figures' Pushing For D.C. Statehood. But It Won't Disclose Its Funders." *DCist*, May 3, 2019. https://dcist.com/story/19/05/23/this-new-campaign-plans-to-spend-seven-figures-pushing-for-d-c-statehood-but-it-wont-disclose-its-funders/.

20 "North Fund Contributions." Capital Research Center. https://capitalresearch.org/app/uploads/north-fund-contributions-montana-marijuana-campaign-2020.pdf. "Montana I-190, Marijuana Legalization Initiative (2020)." *Ballotpedia*. https://ballotpedia.org/Montana_I-190,_Marijuana_Legalization_Initiative_(2020). Ambarian, Jonathon. "Group that backed marijuana legalization ordered to reveal donors." KTVH, December 29, 2020. https://www.ktvh.com/news/group-that-backed-marijuana-legalization-ordered-to-reveal-donors.

21 "North Fund 2020 financial records." Document Cloud. https://www.documentcloud.org/documents/20987863-north-fund-records.

22 "H.R.1 - For the People Act of 2021." U.S. Congress. https://www.congress.gov/bill/117th-congress/house-bill/1/text. For North Fund's lobbying, see "Lobbying by North Fund." *ProPublica*. https://projects.propublica.org/represent/lobbying/r/301025518.

23 "Common Cause," InfluenceWatch, https://www.influencewatch.org/non-profit/common-cause/.

24 "NARAL Pro-Choice America," InfluenceWatch, https://www.influencewatch.org/non-profit/naral-pro-choice-america/.

25 "Home," Our Voice, Our Vote. https://www.ourvoiceourvote.us/.

26 "Run for Something," InfluenceWatch, https://www.influencewatch.org/political-party/run-for-something/.

27 "Secure Democracy," InfluenceWatch, https://www.influencewatch.org/non-profit/secure-democracy/. Ludwig, Hayden. "BREAKING: Arabella-Aligned Groups Sued for Racial Discrimination, Violating Civil Rights Laws." Capital Research Center, November 3, 2022. https://capitalresearch.org/article/breaking-arabella-aligned-groups-sued-for-racial-discrimination-violating-civil-rights-laws/.

28 "Jim Gerstein." GBAO Strategies. Archived from the original March 27, 2023. http://web.archive.org/web/20230327015057/http://www.gbaostrategies.com/jim-gerstein/.

29 "Democracy Corps," InfluenceWatch, https://www.influencewatch.org/non-profit/democracy-corps/.

30 "Cristina Uribe," InfluenceWatch, https://www.influencewatch.org/person/cristina-uribe/. "National Education Association," InfluenceWatch, https://www.influencewatch.org/labor-union/national-education-association-nea/.

31   "Wilderness Society," InfluenceWatch, https://www.influencewatch.org/non-profit/wilderness-society/.

32   "Perkins Coie," InfluenceWatch, https://www.influencewatch.org/for-profit/perkins-coie/. "Elias Law Group," InfluenceWatch, https://www.influencewatch.org/for-profit/elias-law-group/. "Marc Elias," InfluenceWatch, https://www.influencewatch.org/person/marc-elias/.

33   "Arabella Advisors cease and desist letter." Document Cloud, February 3, 2022. https://www.documentcloud.org/documents/21198861-arabella-advisors-cease-and-desist-letter.

34   Elias, Marc E. [@marceelias]. (2022, July 24). *Too many law firms feel the need to see "both-sides." @EliasLawGroup's mission is clear: Help Democrats win. Citizens vote.* [Tweet]. Twitter. http://web.archive.org/web/20221017012113/https://mobile.twitter.com/marceelias/status/1551003433167212549?s=21&t=RYdTk1cYpoqFgppwn8VTmw.

35   Kerr, Andrew. "Former Employees Slap The Left's Favorite Dark Money Group With Racial Discrimination Lawsuits." The *Washington Free Beacon*, February 9, 2023. https://freebeacon.com/democrats/former-employees-slap-the-lefts-favorite-dark-money-group-slapped-with-racial-discrimination-lawsuits/.

36   Vogel, Kenneth P. and Goldmacher, Shane. "Democrats Decried Dark Money. Then They Won With It in 2020." The *New York Times*, January 29, 2022. https://www.nytimes.com/2022/01/29/us/politics/democrats-dark-money-donors.html.

37   Ludwig, Hayden. "What's the North Fund and How Did It Muck Up the 2020 Election?" Capital Research Center, December 17, 2021. https://capitalresearch.org/article/whats-the-north-fund-and-how-did-it-muck-up-the-2020-election/.

38   "Home." The North Fund. http://www.NorthFund.org.

CHAPTER 9

1   Vadum, Matthew and Dellinger, James. "Billionaires for Big Government: What's Next for George Soros's Democracy Alliance?" Capital Research Center, January 2008. https://capitalresearch.org/app/uploads/FW0108.pdf.

2   "Democracy Alliance Conferences," InfluenceWatch, https://www.influencewatch.org/organization/democracy-alliance-conferences/.

3   Markay, Lachlan. "Live from the George Soros Secret Donor Retreat." The *Washington Free Beacon*, April 14, 2015. https://freebeacon.com/politics/live-from-the-george-soros-secret-donor-retreat/. "Democracy Alliance Conferences," InfluenceWatch, https://www.influencewatch.org/organization/democracy-alliance-conferences/.

4   "Democracy Alliance: 2020 Investment Portfolio Report," InfluenceWatch, https://www.influencewatch.org/app/uploads/2019/04/Democracy-Alliance-2020-Investment-Portfolio-Report.pdf.

Endnotes

5   Democracy Alliance, "2020 Investment Portfolio Progress & Updates," Fall 2016, p. 28. Archived at "Democracy Alliance: 2020 Investment Portfolio Report," InfluenceWatch, https://www.influencewatch.org/app/uploads/2019/04/Democracy-Alliance-2020-Investment-Portfolio-Report.pdf.

6   Ludwig, Hayden and Mooney, Kevin. "Plans to Flip Pennsylvania: One Pennsylvania." Capital Research Center, March 23, 2020. https://capitalresearch.org/article/plans-to-flip-pennsylvania-part-5/.

7   "Daaiyah Bilal Threats," InfluenceWatch, https://www.influencewatch.org/person/daaiyah-bilal-threats/.

8   Roberts, Joel. "Democrats Show Rare Unity." CBS News, May 28, 2004. https://www.cbsnews.com/news/democrats-show-rare-unity/.

9   "America Votes: Donors to America Votes," InfluenceWatch, https://www.influencewatch.org/non-profit/america-votes/#donors-to-america-votes.

10   "America Votes," InfluenceWatch, https://www.influencewatch.org/non-profit/america-votes/.

11   "ACRONYM," InfluenceWatch, https://www.influencewatch.org/non-profit/acronym/. Walter, Scott. "WALTER: Nonprofit Behind Faulty Iowa Caucus App Has Ties To Hillary Clinton, Obama." The *Daily Caller*, February 4, 2020. https://dailycaller.com/2020/02/04/walter-hypocrisy-in-the-iowa-debacle/.

12   "Worse Than We Thought." N.C. Values Coalition. Archived from the original October 2, 2022. http://web.archive.org/web/20221002184644/https://www.ncvalues.org/worse_than_we_thought.

13   Helmlinger, Connie. "J. Adam Abram Appointed Chair of North Carolina Housing Finance Agency Board of Directors." North Carolina Housing Finance Agency, November 12, 2019. https://www.nchfa.com/news/j-adam-abram-appointed-chair-north-carolina-housing-finance-agency-board-directors.

14   "North Carolina Citizens for Progress: Top Contributors." *Open Secrets*. https://www.opensecrets.org/527s/527cmtedetail_contribs.php?ein=453626206&cycle=2018.

15   "The Restriction of Political Campaign Intervention by Section 501(c)(3) Tax-Exempt Organizations." The Internal Revenue Service. https://www.irs.gov/charities-non-profits/charitable-organizations/the-restriction-of-political-campaign-intervention-by-section-501c3-tax-exempt-organizations.

16   "Democracy Alliance: 2020 Investment Portfolio Report," InfluenceWatch, http://www.influencewatch.org/app/uploads/2019/04/Democracy-Alliance-2020-Investment-Portfolio-Report.pdf.

17   "Faith In Action (PICO National Network)," InfluenceWatch, https://www.influencewatch.org/non-profit/pacific-institute-for-community-organizations-pico-national-network/.

18   "National Employment Law Project," InfluenceWatch, https://www.influencewatch.org/non-profit/national-employment-law-project/.

19   "William J. Brennan Center for Justice," InfluenceWatch, https://www.influencewatch.
      org/non-profit/william-j-brennan-center-for-justice/.

20   "America Votes," InfluenceWatch, https://www.influencewatch.org/non-profit/america-
      votes/. "ProgressNow," InfluenceWatch, https://www.influencewatch.org/non-profit/
      progressnow/. "Wellstone Action," InfluenceWatch, https://www.influencewatch.
      org/non-profit/wellstone-action/. "Working America," InfluenceWatch, https://www.
      influencewatch.org/labor-union/working-america/.

21   "Color of Change," InfluenceWatch, https://www.influencewatch.org/non-profit/color-
      of-change/.

22   "Center for Popular Democracy," InfluenceWatch, https://www.influencewatch.org/
      non-profit/center-for-popular-democracy/.

Chapter 10

1   Schoffstall, Joe. "Secretive Soros-funded group works behind the scenes with Biden
      admin on policy, documents show." Fox News, April 26, 2022. https://www.foxnews.
      com/politics/secretive-soros-funded-group-works-behind-scenes-biden-admin-policy-
      documents. "Governing for Impact," InfluenceWatch, https://www.influencewatch.org/
      non-profit/governing-for-impact/.

2   "Awarded Grants: Governing for Impact." Open Society Foundations. https://www.
      opensocietyfoundations.org/grants/past?filter_keyword=governing+for+impact.

3   Bettelheim, Adriel. "Axios-Ipsos poll: Americans back work requirements for federal
      aid." Axios, May 18, 2023. https://www.axios.com/2023/05/18/axios-ipsos-poll-work-
      requirements-medicaid-snap.

4   "HHS Announces Proposed Rule to Strengthen Nondiscrimination in Health
      Care." U.S. Department of Health and Human Services, July 25, 2022. https://www.
      hhs.gov/about/news/2022/07/25/hhs-announces-proposed-rule-to-strengthen-
      nondiscrimination-in-health-care.html.

5   Peirce, Hester, Stratmann, Thomas and Robinson, Ian. "How Are Small Banks Faring
      under Dodd-Frank?" Mercatus Center, February 27, 2014. https://www.mercatus.org/
      students/research/working-papers/how-are-small-banks-faring-under-dodd-frank.

6   Schoffstall, Joe. "Biden's Title IX proposal mirrors action memo from Soros-funded group
      pushing gender identity into rules." Fox News, June 28, 2022. https://www.foxnews.com/
      politics/bidens-title-ix-proposal-mirrors-soros-funded-group-gender-identity-rules.

7   Schoffstall, Joe. "Biden's Title IX proposal mirrors action memo from Soros-funded group
      pushing gender identity into rules." Fox News, June 28, 2022. https://www.foxnews.com/
      politics/bidens-title-ix-proposal-mirrors-soros-funded-group-gender-identity-rules.

8   Meckler, Laura. "New Title IX rules set to assert rights of transgender students."
      The Washington Post, May 30, 2022. https://www.washingtonpost.com/

education/2022/03/30/transgender-discrimination-title-ix-rule-students/.

9   "Protecting the Rights of LGBTQ+ Students Under Title IX of the Education
     Amendments of 1972." Governing for Impact, November 2020. https://govforimpact.
     wpengine.com/wp-content/uploads/2021/07/04_Protecting-the-Rights-of-LGBTQ-
     Students-under-Title-IX.pdf.

10   "Our Work." Governing for Impact. https://governingforimpact.org/our-work/.

11   "Addressing Sexual Violence Under Title IX of the Education Amendments of 1972."
     Governing for Impact, November 2020. https://govforimpact.wpengine.com/wp-
     content/uploads/2021/07/01_Addressing-Sexual-Violence-Under-Title-IX.pdf.

12   "Robert David (KC) Johnson." Brooklyn College. https://www.brooklyn.cuny.edu/
     web/academics/faculty/faculty_profile.jsp?faculty=25. Johnson, KC. "Expect the Title
     IX Inquisition." *Tablet*, June 28, 2022. https://www.tabletmag.com/sections/news/
     articles/expect-the-title-ix-inquisition.

13   "State of New York v United States Department of Education." *Court Listener*, August 9,
     2020. https://storage.courtlistener.com/recap/gov.uscourts.nysd.538098/gov.uscourts.
     nysd.538098.81.0.pdf. "Know Your IX v. Devos." ACLU. https://www.aclu.org/know-
     your-ix-v-devos.

14   Powell, Michael. "Trump Overhaul of Campus Sex Assault Rules Wins Surprising
     Support." *The New York Times*, June 25, 2020. https://www.nytimes.com/2020/06/25/
     us/college-sex-assault-rules.html.

15   "Protecting the Rights of LGBTQ+ Students Under Title IX of the Education
     Amendments of 1972." Governing for Impact, November 2020. https://govforimpact.
     wpengine.com/wp-content/uploads/2021/07/04_Protecting-the-Rights-of-LGBTQ-
     Students-under-Title-IX.pdf.

16   "Nondiscrimination on the Basis of Sex in Education Programs or Activities Receiving
     Federal Financial Assistance." Defense of Freedom Institute. https://dfipolicy.
     org/wp-content/uploads/2022/09/DFI-Public-Submission-on-Title-IX-NPRM-
     website-9-12-22.pdf.

17   "The Attack on Title IX." Defense of Freedom Institute. https://dfipolicy.org/titleix/.

18   Eitel, Robert S. "Biden Revives the Title IX Menace." *National Review*, July 19, 2022.
     https://www.nationalreview.com/2022/07/biden-revives-the-title-ix-menace/.

19   Parshall Perry, Sarah and Kassal, Abby. "Lia Thomas Was Just the Beginning. Biden
     Administration Wants to Eliminate Women's Sports." Heritage Foundation, April
     11, 2022. https://www.heritage.org/gender/commentary/lia-thomas-was-just-the-
     beginning-biden-administration-wants-eliminate-womens.

20   Jones, Jeffrey M. "More Say Birth Gender Should Dictate Sports Participation." Gallup,
     June 12, 2023. https://news.gallup.com/poll/507023/say-birth-gender-dictate-sports-
     participation.aspx.

21   "National Student Legal Defense Network," InfluenceWatch, https://www.

influencewatch.org/non-profit/national-student-legal-defense-network/.

22 "Automating the Discharge of Federal Student Loan Debt for Individuals Who are Totally and Permanently Disabled." Governing for Impact, November 2020. https://govforimpact.wpengine.com/wp-content/uploads/2021/07/05_Automating-the-Discharge-of-Federal-Student-Loan-Debt-for-Individuals-Who-are-Totally-and-Permanently-Disabled.pdf. Cowley, Stacy. "$10 Billion in Student Debt Erased Under Biden, but Calls Grow for More." The *New York Times*, September 10, 2021. https://www.nytimes.com/2021/09/10/business/student-loan-forgiveness-biden.html.

23 "American Federation of Teachers," InfluenceWatch, https://www.influencewatch.org/labor-union/american-federation-of-teachers/.

24 "National Education Association," InfluenceWatch, https://www.influencewatch.org/labor-union/national-education-association-nea/.

25 "AFT's Randi Weingarten on Department of Education's Title IX Rule Changes." American Federation of Teachers, May 6, 2020. https://www.aft.org/press-release/afts-randi-weingarten-department-educations-title-ix-rule-changes.

26 Flannery, Mary Ellen. "With Title IX changes, Betsy DeVos puts more students at risk of violence." National Education Association, May 12, 2020. https://www.nea.org/advocating-for-change/new-from-nea/title-ix-changes-put-students-at-risk.

27 "Support of the Rights of Transgender Persons—AFT Stands in Unity Against Discrimination in North Carolina and Mississippi." American Federation of Teachers. https://www.aft.org/resolution/support-rights-transgender-persons-aft-stands-unity-against-discrimination. "Student Debt Support." National Education Association. https://www.nea.org/student-debt-support.

28 "AG Slatery Leads 22 States Against Biden Administration for Threatening to Withhold Nutrition Assistance for Schools; Programs that Don't Adhere to 'Gender Identity', 'Sexual Orientation' Policy." Attorney General and Reporter, July 26, 2022. https://www.tn.gov/attorneygeneral/news/2022/7/26/pr22-24.html.

29 Jiminez, Kayla. "Biden administration will release new Title IX rules in May. What to expect." *USA Today*, February 8, 2023. https://www.usatoday.com/story/news/education/2023/02/08/biden-administration-release-new-title-ix-rules-may/11163003002/.

30 Ferrechio, Susan. "Teachers unions worked with CDC to keep schools closed for Covid, GOP report says." *The Washington Times*, March 30, 2022. https://www.washingtontimes.com/news/2022/mar/30/republican-report-shows-teachers-unions-helped-cdc/.

Chapter 11

1 Ludwig, Hayden R. "Big Money in Dark Shadows." Capital Research Center, April 25, 2019. https://capitalresearch.org/publication/big-money-in-dark-shadows/.

Endnotes

2   Bland, Scott and Severns, Maggie. "Documents reveal massive 'dark-money' group boosted Democrats in 2018." *Politico*, November 19, 2019. https://www.politico.com/news/2019/11/19/dark-money-democrats-midterm-071725.

3   Bland, Scott. "Liberal secret-money network hammers House GOP." *Politico*, July 29, 2018. https://www.politico.com/story/2018/07/29/democrats-dark-money-midterms-house-745145.

4   Roje, Philip. "Big Builds: A Look Inside Arabella Advisors." *Inside Philanthropy*, January 14, 2020. https://www.insidephilanthropy.com/home/2019/1/14/big-builds-a-look-inside-arabella-advisors.

5   "A Note on Our Work." Arabella Advisors. Archived from the original August 19, 2020. https://web.archive.org/web/20200819215404/https://www.arabellaadvisors.com/company/arabella-basic-facts/.

6   Walter, Scott. "A Saintly Conspiracy to Save Democracy?" Capital Research Center, May 11, 2021. https://capitalresearch.org/article/a-saintly-conspiracy-to-save-democracy/. Ludwig, Hayden. "Ketanji Brown Jackson, Demand Justice's Nominee for the Supreme Court." Capital Research Center, March 2, 2022. https://capitalresearch.org/article/ketanji-brown-jackson-demand-justices-nominee-for-the-supreme-court/.

7   Vogel, Kenneth P. and Robertson, Katie. "Top Bidder for Tribune Newspapers Is an Influential Liberal Donor." The *New York Times*, April 13, 2021. https://www.nytimes.com/2021/04/13/business/media/wyss-tribune-company-buyer.html.

8   Shaw, Donald. "Gates Foundation Was Major Donor to Pro-Biden 'Dark Money' Network." *Sludge*, September 14, 2021. https://readsludge.com/2021/09/14/gates-foundation-was-major-donor-to-pro-biden-dark-money-network/.

9   Green, Emma. "The Massive Progressive Dark-Money Group You've Never Heard Of." *The Atlantic*, November 2, 2021. https://www.theatlantic.com/politics/archive/2021/11/arabella-advisors-money-democrats/620553/.

10   Walter, Scott. "Inside the Left's Web of 'Dark Money.'" The *Wall Street Journal*, October 22, 2020. https://www.wsj.com/articles/inside-the-lefts-web-of-dark-money-11603408114.

11   "Arabella Advisors Appoints Rick Cruz as President, Announces Transition of Sampriti Ganguli." Arabella Advisors. https://www.arabellaadvisors.com/blog/arabella-advisors-appoints-rick-cruz-as-president-announces-transition-of-sampriti-ganguli/.

12   Ludwig, Hayden. "BREAKING: Arabella-Aligned Groups Sued for Racial Discrimination, Violating Civil Rights Laws." Capital Research Center, November 3, 2022. https://capitalresearch.org/article/breaking-arabella-aligned-groups-sued-for-racial-discrimination-violating-civil-rights-laws/.

13   "Sarah Walker v New Venture Fund, Secure Democracy, and Secure Democracy USA."

The *Washington Free Beacon*, October 28, 2020. https://freebeacon.com/wp-content/uploads/2023/02/Sarah-Walker-Complaint-and-Exhibits.pdf. In previous research produced by Capital Research Center, we observed that Arabella appeared to align its management of pop-up groups based on the project's 501(c) status. In other words, a (c)(3) project would be managed by Arabella's New Venture, Hopewell, or Windward Funds, which are 501(c)(3)s, while a (c)(4) project would be managed by the Sixteen Thirty Fund or the North Fund, which are 501(c)(4)s. Walker's lawsuit demonstrates that Secure Democracy, a (c)(4), was effectively (though secretly) managed by New Venture Fund, a (c)(3).

14   "Francesca Weaks v Local Solutions Support and New Venture Fund." *The Washington Free Beacon*, January 1, 2023. https://freebeacon.com/wp-content/uploads/2023/02/Francesca-Weaks-Complaint.pdf.

15   Kerr, Andrew. "Former Employees Slap The Left's Favorite Dark Money Group With Racial Discrimination Lawsuits." *The Washington Free Beacon*, February 9, 2023. https://freebeacon.com/democrats/former-employees-slap-the-lefts-favorite-dark-money-group-slapped-with-racial-discrimination-lawsuits/.

16   Kerr, Andrew, and Simonson, Joseph. "Top Democratic Operatives Were Quietly Pulling the Strings at a Voting Rights Group. Lawyers Say They May Have Broken the Law: The shady scheme implicates the Left's largest dark money network, Arabella Advisors." The *Washington Free Beacon*, July 10, 2023. https://freebeacon.com/democrats/top-democratic-operatives-were-quietly-pulling-the-strings-at-a-voting-rights-group-lawyers-say-they-may-have-broken-the-law/.

17   R Street Institute. "Loser's Consent: How do we stabilize our democracy?" https://www.rstreet.org/events/losers-consent-how-do-we-stabilize-our-democracy/.

18   Kerr, Andrew, and Simonson, Joseph. "Top Democratic Operatives Were Quietly Pulling the Strings at a Voting Rights Group. Lawyers Say They May Have Broken the Law: The shady scheme implicates the Left's largest dark money network, Arabella Advisors." The *Washington Free Beacon*, July 10, 2023. https://freebeacon.com/democrats/top-democratic-operatives-were-quietly-pulling-the-strings-at-a-voting-rights-group-lawyers-say-they-may-have-broken-the-law/.

19   Kerr, Andrew, and Simonson, Joseph. "Arabella Advisors Fires CEO Amid Financial and Political Setbacks." The *Washington Free Beacon*, July 21, 2023. https://freebeacon.com/democrats/arabella-advisors-fires-ceo-amid-financial-and-political-setbacks/.

20   Americans for Public Trust. "Complaint Against Several Tax-Exempt Organizations Paying Excessive Compensation, Directly or Indirectly, to Eric Kessler." https://assets.bwbx.io/documents/users/iqjWHBFdfxIU/rLho51zULTIY/v0.

21   Kerr, Andrew. "Lawsuit Unearths Link Between Dem Megadonor SBF, Parents, and Democratic Dark Money Behemoth Arabella Advisors." The *Washington Free Beacon*,

September 20, 2023. https://freebeacon.com/democrats/sam-bankman-frieds-dad-secretly-advised-democratic-dark-money-kingpin-arabella-advisors/.

22   Ludwig, Hayden. "Ketanji Brown Jackson, Demand Justice's Nominee for the Supreme Court." Capital Research Center, March 2, 2022. https://capitalresearch.org/article/ketanji-brown-jackson-demand-justices-nominee-for-the-supreme-court/.

23   "A Note on Our Work." Arabella Advisors. https://www.arabellaadvisors.com/company/arabella-basic-facts/.

24   "Demand Justice PAC," InfluenceWatch, https://www.influencewatch.org/political-party/demand-justice-pac/. "Demand Justice PAC." Federal Election Commission. https://www.fec.gov/data/committee/C00760827/.

25   "Mothership Strategies," InfluenceWatch, https://www.influencewatch.org/for-profit/mothership-strategies/. "Scasey Communications Payments." Transparency USA. https://www.transparencyusa.org/wi/payee/scasey-communications/payments.

26   "Working Families Party," InfluenceWatch, https://www.influencewatch.org/political-party/working-families-party/.

CHAPTER 12

1   Blaff, Ari. "Democratic Mayor of Dallas Switches Parties." *National Review*, September 22, 2023. https://www.nationalreview.com/news/american-cities-need-republicans-democratic-mayor-of-dallas-switches-parties/.

2   U.S. House Ways and Means Committee, "Ways & Means Seeks Public Input on Tax-Exempt Organizations: Potential Violations of Rules on Political Activities, Inappropriate Use of Charitable Funds, & Rise in Foreign Sources of Funding." August 14, 2023. https://waysandmeans.house.gov/ways-means-seeks-public-input-on-tax-exempt-organizations-potential-violations-of-rules-on-political-activities-inappropriate-use-of-charitable-funds-rise-in-foreign-sources-of-funding/

3   Ambarian, Jonathon. "Group that backed marijuana legalization ordered to reveal donors." KTVH, December 29, 2020. https://www.ktvh.com/news/group-that-backed-marijuana-legalization-ordered-to-reveal-donors. For North Fund's lobbying, see "Lobbying by North Fund." *ProPublica*. https://projects.propublica.org/represent/lobbying/r/301025518.

4   Roje, Philip. "Big Builds: A Look Inside Arabella Advisors." *Inside Philanthropy*, January 14, 2020. https://www.insidephilanthropy.com/home/2019/1/14/big-builds-a-look-inside-arabella-advisors.

5   "Arabella Advisors Leader on Generational Differences in Giving." *Chronicle of Philanthropy*, March 6, 2020. https://www.philanthropy.com/article/arabella-advisors-leader-on-generational-differences-in-giving-podcast/.

6   Olinga, Luc. "Rivian Burns Billionaire George Soros." *The Street*, May 13, 2023. https://www.thestreet.com/technology/rivian-burns-billionaire-george-soros.

7   Anderson, Collin. "How Biden's 'Green Energy Economy' is Benefiting Left-Wing Billionaires: Dem megadonors Bill Gates and Laurene Powell Jobs see green energy investments flooded with taxpayer cash." The *Washington Free Beacon*, February 23, 2023. https://freebeacon.com/energy/the-winners-of-bidens-clean-energy-economy-emerge-liberal-billionaires/.

8   Miller, W. Keith, and Joshua D. Miller, eds. *The Handbook of Narcissism and Narcissistic Personality Disorder: Theoretical Approaches, Empirical Findings, and Treatments.* Hoboken, N.J.: John Wiley & Sons, 2011, p. 52.

9   Neuharth, Dan, Ph.D. "8 Insidious Ways Narcissists Try to Control You: How to sidestep narcissistic manipulation and gaslighting." *Psychology Today*, March 9, 2021. https://www.psychologytoday.com/us/blog/narcissism-demystified/202103/8-insidious-ways-narcissists-try-control-you.

10   Schambra, William A. "Philanthropy's Original Sin: On U.S. foundations' legacy of support for eugenics, and the charitable alternative to scientific progressivism." *The New Atlantis*, summer 2013. https://www.thenewatlantis.com/publications/philanthropys-original-sin.

11   Black, Edwin. "The Horrifying American Roots of Nazi Eugenics." History News Network, September 2003. http://hnn.us/articles/1796.html.

12   Sanger, Margaret. *The Pivot of Civilization*. New York: Brentano's, 1922. https://archive.org/details/pivotofcivilizat00sang/page/104/mode/2up?view=theater.

13   Friends of the Earth. Progress As If Survival Mattered. San Francisco, 1977, p. 17.

14   "David Brower." Sierra Club, undated. https://www.sierraclub.org/library/david-brower.

15   New York Times Editorial Board. "NAACP v. Alabama." *New York Times*, June 6, 1964. https://timesmachine.nytimes.com/timesmachine/1964/06/06/issue.html.

16   For the left-wing groups' amicus brief, see https://www.aclu.org/cases/americans-prosperity-foundation-v-xavier-becerra-attorney-general-california.

17   Walter, Scott. "Highlights from Scott Walter's Answers to Questions for the Record from Sen. Whitehouse." Capital Research Center, April 15, 2021. https://capitalresearch.org/article/highlights-from-scott-walters-answers-to-questions-for-the-record-from-sen-whitehouse/.

18   Brad Smith and I testified at a hearing held by the Senate Finance Subcommittee on Taxation and IRS Oversight. My testimony is available at https://capitalresearch.org/article/scott-walter-testifies-to-a-senate-finance-subcommittee-on-the-political-activities-of-tax-exempt-entities/. The full hearing is available at https://www.finance.senate.gov/hearings/laws-and-enforcement-governing-the-political-activities-of-tax-exempt-entities?blm_aid=0.

19   The full 2013 hearing is available at https://www.judiciary.senate.gov/committee-activity/hearings/current-issues-in-campaign-finance-law-enforcement.

20   Whitehouse, Sheldon. "The Two Scandals at the IRS: As Prepared for Delivery on the Senate Floor." Whitehouse.Senate.gov, May 15, 2013. https://www.whitehouse.senate.gov/news/press-releases/the-two-scandals-at-the-irs. After this brief concession, the senator went on at much greater length about the "other scandal," i.e., "allowing big shadowy forces to meddle in elections anonymously." And by the time I was testifying to him in 2022, the senator was denying Lois Lerner had done anything wrong.

21   Fund, John. "Astroturf Politics: How liberal foundations fooled Congress into passing McCain-Feingold." *Wall Street Journal*, March 22, 2005. https://www.wsj.com/articles/SB122512338741472357.

22   Witwer, Rob, and Adam Schrager. *The Blueprint: How the Democrats Won Colorado (and Why Republicans Everywhere Should Care)*. Colorado: Fulcrum Publishing, 2010, 72. See also Wallison, Peter and Gara, Joel. *Better Parties, Better Government: A Realistic Program for Campaign Finance Reform*. Washington: AEI Press, 2009. Available at https://www.aei.org/wp-content/uploads/2013/12/-better-parties-better-government-book_105440591173.pdf?x91208, and Walter, Scott. "Dam political speech." *Philanthropy Daily*, April 21, 2011. https://philanthropydaily.com/dam-political-speech/.

23   Nichols, Hans, and Kight, Stef W. "Scoop: GOP plan targets foreign dark money for 2024." *Axios*, July 10, 2023. https://www.axios.com/2023/07/10/gop-targets-foreign-dark-money-2024-election.

24   Their announcement is available at https://fitzpatrick.house.gov/2023/7/fitzpatrick-golden-introduce-bipartisan-legislation-to-protect-american-elections-from-foreign-money.

25   Americans for Public Trust's report is available at https://americansforpublictrust.org/news/report-left-wing-swiss-billionaire-exploiting-the-foreign-influence-loophole/.

26   Lee, Sarah, and Ludwig, Hayden. "States Banning or Restricting Zuck Bucks." Capital Research Center, May 25, 2023. https://capitalresearch.org/article/states-banning-zuck-bucks/.

27   Current IRS guidance is available at https://www.irs.gov/charities-non-profits/charitable-organizations/the-restriction-of-political-campaign-intervention-by-section-501c3-tax-exempt-organizations, which states, "voter education or registration activities with evidence of bias that (a) would favor one candidate over another; (b) oppose a candidate in some manner; or (c) have the effect of favoring a candidate or group of candidates, will constitute prohibited participation or intervention."

28   Braun, Ken. "Big Left Foundations Fund Biased Barely-Legal Voter Programs: Tax-exempt organizations legally obligated to be non-partisan show clear signs of coordination with Democratic megadonors." Capital Research Center, June 3, 2021. https://capitalresearch.org/article/big-left-foundations-fund-biased-barely-legal-voter-programs/.

29   Thayer, Parker. "REPORT: How Charities Secretly Help Win Elections." Capital Research Center, August 15, 2023. https://capitalresearch.org/article/report-how-charities-secretly-help-win-elections/.

30   See ibid., Appendix 4: Grants to the VRP Network.

31   de Tocqueville, Alexis. *Democracy in America.* Chicago: University of Chicago Press, 2000, 489.

32   de Tocqueville, Alexis. *The Old Regime and the French Revolution.* New York: Doubleday, 1955, xv.

33   Quoted in Walter, Scott. "Less charity and more taxes, please." *Philanthropy Daily*, March 6, 2012. https://philanthropydaily.com/less-charity-and-more-taxes-please/.

34   Schambra, William A. "The Ungodly Bright: Should They Lead Philanthropy into the Future." In Kass, Amy, ed., *Giving Well, Doing Good.* Bloomington: Indiana University Press, 2008, 477. Amusingly, the phrase "ungodly bright" comes from Warren Buffett, describing Bill and Melinda Gates and justifying his intention to turn over most of his fortune to them in his will.

INDEX

Index

Index

Index

Index